MW00813401

The Call of Human Nature

The Call of Human Nature

The Role of Scatology

in Modern German Literature

Dieter and Jacqueline Rollfinke

The University of Massachusetts Press

Amherst

1986

Copyright © 1986 by The University of Massachusetts Press
All rights reserved
Printed in the United States of America
Set in Linotron Aster and Franklin Gothic at G&S Typesetters Inc.

Library of Congress Cataloging-in-Publication Data

Rollfinke, Dieter, 1942–
    The call of human nature.

    Bibliography: p.
    Includes index.
    1. German literature—20th century—History and
criticism.   2. Scatology in literature.   I. Rollfinke,
Jacqueline, 1940–   .   II. Title.
    PT405.R58   1986   830'.9'353   86–1490
    ISBN 0–87023–536–2 (alk. paper)

Grateful acknowledgment is made for permission to quote from material under copyright:
    To Twayne Publishers for a lengthy extract from *Georg Büchner* by Ronald Hauser, copyright 1974, reprinted with the permission of Twayne Publishers, a division of G. K. Hall & Co., Boston.
    To Grove Press for excerpts from *Baal* by Bertolt Brecht, copyright © 1962 by Eric Bentley and Martin Esslin. Reprinted by permission of Grove Press, Inc.

"Unsere Dichter sind die mutigsten Kloreiniger gewesen."

("Our poets never flinched from cleaning out a john.")

Leni, in Heinrich Böll, *Gruppenbild mit Dame*

Contents

List of Illustrations

Acknowledgments

There are many persons whom one would like to thank for their help and support when one completes a long-term project such as this, but a few who were particularly significant must be singled out for special mention. This study owed its foundation to the wise guidance of William McClain and Lieselotte Kurth, and it might never have reached the point of publication without the advice and kindness of William Keating and the encouragement and flexibility of Richard Martin, editor at the University of Massachusetts Press.

Since the project's beginning, numerous colleagues, friends, and students readily supplied us with suggestions and pertinent materials and bolstered our enthusiasm; especially indispensable in this regard were Beverley and Truman Eddy.

Both of us are extremely grateful to Dickinson College for grants to Dieter Rollfinke from the Research and Development Committee, which made the completion of the book possible.

Warm thanks go to Eduard Ascher and Frank Hartman for providing useful background information in the field of psychology. The photographic expertise of Marjorie Akin was invaluable in producing the illustrations for this volume, and our appreciation is extended to her as well as to Stephanie Keifer for her skillful typing.

Many times during the writing of this book we reflected with gratitude upon the professors who first introduced us to the field of literary criticism, Hans Freund and Karl Patten.

Without the patience and understanding of family members, especially our children, Brian and Lee, and parents Friedrich and Erna Rollfinke, the manuscript never would have been completed. It creates a difficult situation for children when both Mom and Dad are absorbed in a scholarly project—and *such* a project! (We'll never know how they explained it to their friends.)

The idea for this book grew from a course on "The Grotesque in German Art and Literature," which Dieter Rollfinke team-taught with Joseph Hoffman and in which Jacqueline Rollfinke participated. It was Professor Hoffman's perceptive, open-minded treatment of scatology in German art and literature that enabled us to remove our blinders and attempt a frank examination of the imagery so often overlooked by the critics. Joseph Hoffman is a scholar/teacher whose approach to his subject matter, his colleagues, and his students is truly *menschlich;* to him, with deepest gratitude and respect, this book is dedicated.

Remarks on the Translations

The attempt to compile in English translation a study of scatology in modern German literature has been a challenge, to say the least. It probably is not surprising that many of the works discussed have never found translators, given their ostensibly disagreeable subject matter, imagery, or language. Producing our own English versions was often perplexing because of the lack of precise equivalents for some of the German excremental terms. Even more maddening was the impossibility of using an existing translation such as A. W. Wheen's English rendition of *All Quiet on the Western Front* because of its deletion of key scatological passages. By and large, however, the existing translations proved faithful, and only occasionally was it necessary for us to call the reader's attention to the exact meaning of the original German.

It is a curious phenomenon that, faced with a scatological expression, a translator who ordinarily proceeds with clockwork precision suddenly may decide that it is time for a "loose" translation. Why do translators substitute nonexcremental words for scatological ones? It is more than likely that some, such as Wheen, find such language offensive and want to keep it in the closet (no pun intended). But why do other translators, who normally stick very closely to the original and do not hesitate to translate scatological terms with courageous accuracy, occasionally feel free to substitute a word with different or milder connotations? Sometimes, of course, it is not possible to preserve the scatological implications of the original. Why, however, does Ralph Manheim translate *Scheißkerl* as "swine" rather than "shithead," when he does not hesitate to use the word *shit* at other points in his translation of "Soul of Wood"? Furthermore, was it only the need of a rhyme that inspired him to convert *Mückenschwein* to *Mückenprick?* Or why, in *And Where Were You, Adam?* does the brilliant Leila Vennewitz, who most deservedly won the Society of Authors award for her translating skills, render *Mistbande* ("bunch of manure") as "rabble"?

The answer, it seems to us, is that the literary world does not recognize the significance of scatological motifs and is unaware of their specialized, distinctive imagery. The fact that little is known of the important role played by scatological themes in the history of German literature creates pitfalls for both critics and translators. In choosing an equivalent for a "bad word," the translators often conclude that any other malediction will do, and whether its connotations are sexual or scatological is irrelevant. We hope this study will prove that they are wrong.

The Call of Human Nature

1

Introduction

In today's world of relaxed moral standards and explicit language, the waste products and secretions of our bodies—urine and feces, perspiration and mucus—represent the last real taboo. For readers and theatergoers, the bedroom is chic, but the bathroom is still in dubious taste. It is curious that a number of German writers and artists have long ignored this taboo, and their readers and critics, in turn, have chosen to overlook their imprudence. As long as a head-in-the-sand attitude continues, our understanding of the techniques and intentions of these German writers and artists, particularly those of the modern period, will be incomplete. It is time to unlock the bathroom door.

Scatological elements have been found in the works of some writers and artists for centuries. The basic fact that excrement is part of human beings and the world they inhabit has generally been ignored or suppressed by those artists with a tendency to idealize, but many realistically inclined artists have acknowledged the existence of excrement and have incorporated it into their works.[1] The use of scatological elements in literature serves a surprisingly large range of artistic intentions. Sometimes scatology provides light humor; very often it is part of the author's gentle or biting satire; at times we shall even see the excremental employed in a reversal of the standard societal values. In the latter case, the writer clearly demonstrates that those elements condemned by society as excremental really represent the nobility of life, whereas those parts of human life that society considers valuable often should be discarded and despised. Then there are writers who have an ambiguous view of excrement. They acknowledge it as part of nature and the life cycle and see some good in it, but they

3

never manage to free themselves totally from a certain revulsion. Finally, there are those extreme pessimists who see this world as a mountain of excrement and agree with Martin Luther's low opinion of our corporeal existence; Luther compared the human body to a *Laugensack* or bucking cloth, a washing utensil consisting of a porous cheeseclothlike sack filled with lye (which could be made not only from vegetable ashes but also from stale urine or cow manure) "through which flows nothing but nasty sweat, urine, spit, and more effluences than it has members."[2]

Although such renowned writers as Aristophanes, Dante, Swift, Rabelais, Chaucer, Thoreau, and Brecht have at times used scatological references or scatological imagery for various rhetorical or poetic purposes, critics and scholars have given this subject a surprisingly cursory treatment. Very few books and scholarly articles are concerned primarily with an examination of scatology in literature.[3] Occasionally, anal or excremental elements are discussed in connection with another topic,[4] but most often, when the subject does arise, it is limited either to a brief tribute to the author's courage in shocking his readers through the use of scatology or to an angry outcry against such "obscenity" or "pornography." Obviously, the attacks against scatology usually come from morally and politically conservative persons, who are generally offended and angry, as the following example shows: "*Dog Years*, the new novel by Günter Grass, is the product of an imagination that ardently fishes around in the obscene and the excremental. . . . It is an obscene, unfair, and, furthermore, a blasphemous book."[5]

In view of the long tradition of scatology in art and literature, and considering the great increase in the use of scatological elements in twentieth-century literature, it is unfortunate that scholars have shied away from detailed and unemotional analyses of this topic. Although many critics will not hesitate to comment on literary examples of sadistic and masochistic practices of a sexual and nonsexual nature, almost no one wants to deal with a given author's treatment of the fact that all human beings have digestive systems and produce waste matter. One of the very few scholars to have broken the silence on the use of scatology in literature is Paul Englisch, who in 1928 treated this subject in his book *Das skatologische Element in Literatur, Kunst, und Volksleben.*[6] Englisch has focused much of his attention on such marginal areas as a history of the toilet and the chamber pot, graffiti, and scatological proverbs. The literary examples cited by Englisch are usually totally unknown and often belong to the genre of pornography; he does, however, present scatological material from such important writers as Abraham a Santa Clara, Johann Michael Moscherosch,

Hans Sachs, and Jörg Wickram. Besides pointing out that writers dating from medieval times through the seventeenth century felt relatively at ease when using scatological expressions, Englisch does little in the way of analysis of the examples he presents. Instead, he merely seems to enjoy retelling or quoting scatological passages.

Also important, if for no other reason than that it finally approached this forbidden subject in some detail, is Jae Num Lee's *Swift and Scatological Satire*, which appeared in 1971. In his study, Lee does not get involved in any discussion of the aesthetic merits or demerits of scatology (probably an unsolvable question, because it involves each individual's highly subjective and often very emotional attitude toward this subject). It is Lee's contention that an objective analysis of scatology must presuppose the following assumption: "Scatology as such does not make a work 'bad' or 'good' in a thematic, moral, or rhetorical sense. The author's skill and thematic purposes in handling scatology determine whether a work is 'bad' or 'good.' Once we agree to adopt a neutral attitude towards scatology, we are able to examine its literary functions in a given work and divorce them from such extraneous considerations as the author's psychology or biography."[7] Such neutrality is essential for an unbiased examination of scatology as a literary technique, and we have adopted it as a necessary presupposition for our own analysis of scatology in modern German literature.

Lee devotes the first third of his book to a survey of scatology in English as well as Continental literature prior to the time of Swift. He presents examples from such writers as Aristophanes, Martial, Juvenal, Dante, Rabelais, Chaucer, and Pope and refers to English jests, but nowhere does he mention an example of scatology in German literature. Similarly, in an even more recent article on scatology by John R. Clark, a reference to Günter Grass's *Cat and Mouse* is the only example given from German literature, even though most of the works cited stem from the twentieth century, a time of abundant usage of scatological elements by German writers. Even the one recent book on scatology by a German scholar, Jost Hermand, forgoes an analysis of scatological elements in the works of the well-known German writers in favor of a discussion of emotionally determined excremental outbursts and accusations by both the clean-minded conservative Right and the antiestablishment artistic underground or political Left. What Hermand has done, in fact, is to examine the psychological and sociological bases of these extremist scatological writings rather than to explore scatology as a literary device. As Hermand himself states, literary concerns are secondary in most of the cases he discusses: "Indeed, the creation of literature is the farthest thing from these persons' minds. What they want is something direct and spontaneous, which stinks right off the bat and as a result shocks all 'good citizens.' Mere 'shit' will hardly fulfill such a function, however, even if it is employed on a massive scale."[8]

The fact that scholars are just beginning to approach the subject of scatology with any kind of objectivity and seriousness, coupled with the current tendency to explore the psychological rather than the literary reasons behind the most extreme usages of excrement, makes additional research into the subject of scatology in literature desirable.[9] Even those studies that deal with scatology on a purely literary basis generally do little more than to quote scatological passages from the works of different authors. The various quotations are sometimes grouped together thematically or by literary period, but there is a general lack of comparative analysis of how various authors differ in their presentation of scatological material. The cited scatological passages are then linked by scholarly observations that are often quite informative, but most of these comments are too general and discuss only the obvious.

Another shortcoming of the available scholarly work on scatology is the almost unanimous opinion that the only real literary value of scatology lies in its use as a shocking and powerful satirical weapon. If scatology in nonsatirical forms is discussed at all, it is usually described as useless dirty humor of a subliterary nature. Thus Jae Num Lee feels it necessary to make the following distinction: "If non-satirical uses of scatology need apology, satirical uses do not. We have noted in the preceding chapter their prominent function in serious literary works in continental literature."[10] Although it is certainly true that scatology often is employed as a satirical tool, this satire is by no means always of the most shocking variety; it can range from the relatively gentle to the most contemptuous kind. Furthermore, German writers have also included scatology in nonsatirical writings, with both humorous and serious intentions. In fact, the excremental at times plays a very important role in the *Weltanschauung* of some German authors.

To judge from the several books and articles on scatology that have been published, it appears that, at least until very recently, the number of English and American writers who have included scatological elements in their works is quite small; in fact, writers making extensive use of scatology are a rarity, the two most prominent names mentioned being Jonathan Swift and Henry David Thoreau.[11] The situation is quite different in German literature. Besides the well-known use of scatology in the *Schwänke* and satirical writings of the sixteenth century, as well as in some of the prose of the seventeenth century, many more recent German writers employ scatology in their works. The list includes a number of famous names, such as Büchner, Busch, Benn, Kafka, Thomas Mann, Böll, and Grass. Although scatology does not dominate the writings of any of these authors, several of them—for example, Böll, Busch, and Dürrenmatt—use scatological material to such a significant degree that detailed studies of the excremental elements in their works are necessary.

There were, to be sure, important periods in the history of German literature that exhibited very little or no penchant for the use of scatological metaphors. Not surprisingly, this lack of interest in scatology is particularly characteristic of German classicism and to a slightly lesser degree of German romanticism. The period from 1785 to 1830, which is generally referred to as the Age of Goethe, was the time of German idealism, and the classical German writers strove for perfection in their pursuit of an aesthetically pleasing and carefully structured form of art. Excremental allusions were poorly suited to play a role in the efforts of the classical writers to achieve ideal beauty. Even though the romanticists reintegrated irrational forces with rational ones, they tended to continue the classical pursuit of idealism, and thus they too exhibited little interest in scatological metaphors.

In contrast, when one reads modern German literature in search of scatological elements, one quickly discovers such a great amount that any initial study such as this one must limit itself to the identification and analysis of certain representative examples of the wide range of German scatology and cannot claim to be exhaustive. Extensive studies could be made of the contemporary underground alone. The increase in recent years in the use of scatological terms and actions by members of underground artistic and literary circles in German-speaking countries was sharply reflected in a performance in 1969 by one Günter Brus. Stripping off his clothes on the stage of a University of Vienna auditorium, Brus urinated, drank the urine from his cupped hand, and promptly vomited. For his finale, the artist turned his back to the audience and defecated; he then smeared the excrement on his nude body while singing a rousing rendition of the Austrian national anthem.[12] Articles in German newspapers and magazines in the late 1960s and early 1970s reported that similar events occurred in such cities as Hamburg, "where the Viennese art-anarchist Otto Muehl, naked of course, urinated into the mouth of a countryman during the showing of a movie on the Reeperbahn, in order to prove through experimentation the 'equality of all natural juices.'"[13]

Acts such as these certainly are representative only of the most extreme usage of scatology, and it seems appropriate to question their artistic quality and purpose. When the poet Gerhard Rühm was asked why the word *Scheiße* ("shit") appears so frequently in his poetry, he answered: "Shit has the lure of the unaccustomed. It produces an immense alienation effect in literature, and it causes insecurity in the reader. Furthermore, for me the releasing of taboos has always been an expression of freedom."[14]

By reducing artistic expression to the mere acts of defecating or urinating, the artistic underground attempts to shock and aggravate the establishment, thereby giving the artist a temporary feeling of liberation. Some contemporary artists in the Western world are so repelled and bored by modern society that there is little left to do except to defecate on the stage or to label practically everything in life as excrement. In addition, their emphasis on the primitive excremental act displays their intense feeling of helplessness (assuming, of course, they had serious intentions to begin with); their scatological outpouring serves as a kind of primal, expressionistic scream, their last hope of being heard. Convinced that centuries of serious attempts to improve the world by more traditional artistic means have produced no noticeable change for the better, the artists who feel themselves imprisoned in a meaningless world finally express their independence in the same fashion as many a powerless child: "There is a direct connection between the bed wetter, who protests against parental treatment, and the students' [and artists'] anal rebellion . . . Shit has always been the weapon of the unarmed and the suppressed, a means of nonviolent resistance."[15]

Most critics and observers would question the designation of "art" for the works of Brus, Muehl, or Rühm; they see in them nothing more than a childish ideological revolt. For the literary underground itself, however, the whole aesthetic question of what should or should not be considered art has become irrelevant, "For in the underground there are no distinctions; there everything is one. The distinction between the production and the consumption of art that has been in use since the Renaissance has been eliminated, criteria of quality are no longer valid, scholarly disputes (art–nonart–antiart) have become untenable."[16]

THE RELATIVE ABUNDANCE of scatology in German literature is at least partially a reflection of the extensive use of scatological expressions and metaphors by Germans in general. There is ample evidence of the Germans' interest in the excremental. An article in *Die Zeit*, for example, suggested that Americans of the upper social strata are much more puritanical in their response to obscenities than are the Germans, who are relatively unruffled by such expressions as "Scheiße!" The same article also referred to the observation made by Reinhold Aman, an expert on profanity, that the obscene expressions used by Americans emphasize sexual elements, whereas Germans stress the scatological; it is Aman's view that almost all of the sexual obscenities so prevalent in the United States, if translated into German, would have to be rendered "in the scatological insults that are typical of the German language."[17]

That the acknowledged current German fascination with the word *Scheiße*, which is now being attached as a prefix to anyone or anything that one despises, is really part of a long tradition of scatological profanity can be seen by reading Martin Luther's *Table Talk* or by recalling the famous scatological reply from Goethe's *Götz von Berlichingen*.[18] In the early twentieth century, educated Germans were still carrying on the tradition; from his own days as a student at the Royal Academy of Art in Dresden, George Grosz recalls Professor Richard Mueller's remarks about Emil Nolde: "And, to the delight of the more progressive-minded among us, he made a scornful, sharp 'extermination' speech against such rot and scribble. 'What—Where—Such a fellow sticks his finger in his ass and smears it on paper! Such a lummox! He sketches like a drunken pig with a dung fork!'"[19]

Just as in abusive language, the Germans also frequently turn to scatology in their jokes. When Germans gather socially over a few glasses of wine or beer or for a game of cards, excremental punchlines to their jokes are not at all uncommon. This appears to hold true for the upper as well as the lower social strata. Acknowledging the dangers of generalizations, Peter Farb, in his book on language structures, nevertheless identifies the Germans as the champions of scatology: "Yet many Germans seem so extraordinarily susceptible to scatology that it dominates all other themes when they talk dirty." Comments Gershon Legman in the first of his two encyclopedic volumes on the dirty joke: "A clever joke teller can bring the usual German audience to quite a high pitch of screaming entertainment, rolling out of their seats, and so forth, just by *preparing* to tell a joke of which the inevitable punchline must include the word 'shit' (sometimes built up to the reduplicative *Scheissdreck*), without ever even beginning the joke."[20] Although these claims are probably a bit exaggerated, basically they do characterize German dirty jokes correctly. In contrast, Farb finds that the blue humor of other nations places less emphasis on the bathroom: "French dirty jokes are usually concerned with seduction, adultery, and sexual technique; British with homosexuality and incest; American wtih oral-genital themes and the debasement of women."[21]

The German indulgence in scatology is by no means restricted to the adult world but is also very apparent among children. A study by Peter Rühmkorf, for example, has called attention to the strong fecal emphasis in German children's rhymes.[22] The examples amassed by Rühmkorf reveal that scatology is employed by German children for a surprisingly large number of purposes. Many times, especially in the counting-out rhymes, one finds merely playful, humorous, nonsensical scatology:

> An elephant from Sierra Leone
> Let a fart into the telephone.
> It bounced back out,
> And you are out.

Other children's verses reflect the medieval identification of the devil with excrement:

> Ho, ha, heart,
> The devil let a fart.
> He let it in a butter churn,
> The stench would make your stomach turn.

Also not uncommon are rhymes that reveal the child's tendency to disrupt by scatological means the orderly world of adult authoritarian figures, especially parents:

> 1 2 3 4 5 6 7 8 9 10
> What's the name of your little friend?
> Herbert!
> Herbert shit in bed
> Right on the fancy spread.
> Mom saw what he'd done,
> And you can run.

In the following example cited by Rümkorf, the children reverse the negative feelings about excrement that adults, particularly their parents have tried to teach them:

> Johnny B.
> Has shit on his knee.
> He licked and ate,
> It tasted great.

Finally, one also finds scatological objects as metaphors for humanity:

> You're not a man,
> You're not a mole,
> You're just a toilet paper roll.

In his *Life Is Like a Chicken Coop Ladder: A Portrait of German Culture Through Folklore*, Alan Dundes has cited numerous examples of the use of scatology in the above-mentioned areas of German profanity, humor, and children's rhymes, as well as in German folksongs, folktales, riddles, children's and adults' games, medicine, food preferences, and other sources of folklore data.[23] Although Dundes does not give a great number of illustrations from each one of these categories, the wide range of his study and the unambiguous nature of many of his examples would seem sufficient to persuade most readers that scatological motifs are abundant in German society. His evidence leads Dundes to conclusions about the German national character that are, however, far less convincing—but more about that later.

Dundes has given scant attention to a highly visible example of scatological motifs in everyday German life: the field of advertising. The relevance of advertising as a measure of the importance of scatology in German thought lies in the fact that, before a public relations firm embarks on a costly campaign, substantial market research and psychological studies are done to determine which format will present the product in the most attention-getting, persuasive way. Inclusion of excremental allusions in the works of a single writer or artist may indicate only the eccentric bent of that individual, but the presence of similar elements in a number of advertisements for a wide range of products suggests that these motifs have significance for a reasonably large segment of the general population.

Indeed, readers of popular German periodicals will find that scatological elements appear openly and regularly in German advertisements. Whereas American advertisements for laxative products speak discreetly about "regularity" and seldom are illustrated, German laxative ads, such as that shown in figure 1,[24] often include a drawing or photograph of a toilet and mince no words about their product's effectiveness on the "sluggish intestine." When American toilet paper manufacturers try to sell the softness of their product, their ads go no further than the well-known "Don't squeeze the Charmin." In contrast, a German ad for Servus toilet paper (fig. 2) shows buttocks outlined in soft white on a blue background; along the curvature of the behind runs the wonderfully enticing line: "Velvety soft Servus turns a dissatisfied butt into a satisfied face."[25]

It is surprising that scatology appears from time to time in German advertisements for products having nothing to do with the anal region. An advertisement for Erdal silicone shoe spray shows a photograph of a little boy in position to urinate; the picture supposedly expresses the concept, "It rains more often than you think" (fig. 3). A drawing of a donkey excreting a pile of five-mark coins (fig. 4) is used to entice Germans to open savings accounts.[26] In order to sell its services to the public, the Bundesverband des Deutschen Güterfernverkehrs contrasts its modern methods of transport with an old-fashioned caravan that, because it is the "most natural" way of moving cargo, has the disadvantage of littering the highway with a trail of animal droppings (fig. 5).[27] Moreover, the fact that a product is of a scholarly nature does not necessarily prevent its advertisers from using scatology as a selling point. For example, a 1983 advertising brochure for the new edition of the *Illustriertes Lexikon der deutschen Umgangssprache* by Heinz Küpper featured as its most prominent illustration, covering sizable portions of the two center pages of the flyer, a reproduction of the entry for the word *Arsch* ("ass") (fig. 6).[28] Included as an illustration for the saying "at the ass of the world" was a bizarre photograph of a man in a gas mask and rubber boots sitting on one of two islands that are in the form of buttocks. Why, one may well ask, did the lexicon's publishers, Ernst Klett Verlag, having produced an eight-volume, 3,200-page compilation of 1,200 color illustrations and 120,000 German expressions, choose this particular entry as the focal point of their ad? Selling lexicons is their business, and at least some German advertisers seem to feel that scatology sells—anything.

There is yet another interesting difference between American and German advertisements: although in both countries many ads, if not most of them, are designed to have sex appeal for men, the emphasis in American ads is placed upon the usually only partly revealed curvature of the female breasts; in German ads, one frequently finds the exposure of the feminine posterior. Thus, a full-page ad for Creme 21 shows a large color photograph of totally nude female buttocks with the woman's hand applying cream to them; offering no explanation for this particular anatomical choice, the caption simply states: "Firm skin is more beautiful. Creme 21."[29]

In its preoccupation with scatology, German advertising has at times almost waxed poetic. A grandiose advertisement for Villeroy & Boch bathroom fixtures (fig. 7) was the centerfold for a 1977 issue of *Stern* that featured a three-page illustrated article on the phenomenon of the toilet. The central figure of the bathroom fixture ad is a man

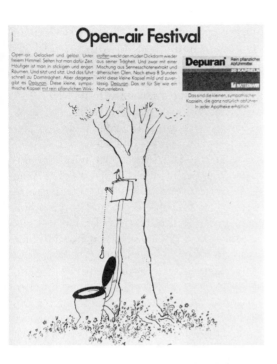

1. Advertisement: Depuran. Courtesy A. Nattermann & Cie. GmbH.

2. Advertisement: Servus toilet paper. Courtesy Feldmühle Aktiengesellschaft, Düsseldorf.

3. Advertisement: Erdal-
Wildlederspray. Courtesy
Erdal Rex GmbH, Mainz.

4. Advertisement: Sparkasse. Courtesy Deutscher Sparkassen-
und Giroverband e.V.

5. Advertisement: Bundesverband des Deutschen Güterfernverkehrs. Courtesy Bundesverband des Deutschen Güterfernverkehrs (BDF) e.V.

6. Advertisement: *Illustriertes Lexikon der deutschen Umgangssprache*. Reprinted with the permission of Ernst Klett Verlag, Stuttgart, Federal Republic of Germany.

7. Advertisement: Villeroy & Boch. Designed by Agency Lüders, Köln, for Villeroy & Boch, reprinted with permission.

sitting on the toilet as he peruses an enormous scarlet volume entitled *The Bathroom Philosophy of Villeroy & Boch*. The entire ad is designed like the pages of a well-studied textbook, complete with red and black underlinings of supposedly significant points. One of these highlights contains the philosophy of the designer of the advertised line of fixtures, Luigi Colani: "*Person, form and function should be unified.*" With this sort of deep thinking being applied to the creation of toilets, the bathroom is certain to become so warm and inviting that never again will a person using the facilities freeze "in her or his *innermost soul.*" After all, the ad suggests in what may or may not be viewed as hyperbole, "*An hour in the bathroom* can take the place of an hour with a psychiatrist." Even the fact that the Villeroy & Boch urinal has been designed to prevent stray drops of urine from splattering on the floor is given a philosophical justification: "For no husband has the right to degrade his lawfully wedded wife to the level of a restroom attendant." It may be indicative of the progress of the women's liberation movement in Germany in 1977 that this sentiment was not deemed important enough to underline. Or, considering the sensuous wording of another portion of the ad, perhaps the somewhat liberated "lawfully wedded wife" has a rival: "It is always a special feeling when two bodies meet and touch: therefore the design of a toilet should conform favorably *to the human body* and its *needs*." Advertisements such as this would almost lead us to believe that the German is having a love affair with his toilet.[30]

WHAT IS THE REASON for the abundance of implicit and explicit excremental allusions in German society and its literature? Although a definitive answer to this question is beyond the scope of this study and is very likely unattainable in any case, let us consider two possible ways of arriving at an understanding of—as opposed to a fully proven explanation for—the phenomena we have been discussing.

In order to understand individual persons who seem to be fixated to an unusual degree on the processes of elimination or excretory matters, classical psychoanalysis has developed the theory of the anal personality. The prototype of the anal character structure was detailed by Freud in his 1908 essay, "Charakter und Analerotik": The people I am about to describe are noteworthy for a regular combination of the three following characteristics. They are especially *orderly, parsimonious* and *obstinate* . . . 'Orderly' covers the notion of bodily cleanliness, as well as of conscientiousness in carrying out small duties and trustworthiness. Its opposite would be 'untidy' and 'neglectful.' Parsimony may appear in the exaggerated form of avarice; and obstinacy can go over into defiance, to which rage and revengefulness are easily joined."[31] These characteristics are believed to be prevalent in adults on whose development the anal-erotic stage of sexual development had a significant impact. The anal-erotic stage follows the oral-erotic stage and generally occurs between the ages of one and a half to three years. During this stage of development, according to Erich Fromm, the products of elimination are "a source of intense pleasure. The child is proud of its excrement, which is its first 'possession' or expression of its productivity."[32]

This pride in and naive affirmation of excrement is drastically altered by the intervention of the child's parents, who insist upon toilet training and bodily cleanliness.[33] The parents not only say no to uncontrolled movement of the bowels or the bladder but even describe such acts as shameful and dirty. Although the child adjusts to these new restraints, he or she develops a complex, ambivalent attitude toward excrement: "As the child adapts to the demands of its training and learns to hold back its stool, e.g., to time the movement correctly, the retention of the stool and the physiological processes connected therewith become a new source of pleasure. At the same time the initial love of excrement is partially replaced by feelings of disgust; partially, to be sure, the primitive pride in excrement, or rather in the punctual evacuation of the stool, is reinforced by the reaction of the environment."[34]

In the adult, elements of anal eroticism are preserved, but they usually are redirected by reaction formations, in which the original drive is suppressed and an opposite attitude is adopted, and by sublimation, which in Freudian terms involves the substitution of nonsexual, culturally significant goals for the original impulses.[35] The totality of sublimations and reaction formations then makes up the anal character traits, which at times may appear to be contradictory because they originate in the child's ambivalence toward excrement; thus persons with anal personalities may exhibit not only the anal triad of traits but also their opposites. Ernest Jones has commented on this complex interplay of the anal-erotic character components, which vary from person to person and within individuals as well. It is Jones's view that some of the most valuable human traits, such as "determination and persistence, the love of order and power of organisation," can be found in the anal character; on the other hand, detrimental qualities also are linked to the anal personality, among them "the incapacity for happiness, the irritability and bad temper, the hypochondria, the miserliness, meanness and pettiness, . . . and the obstinacy which, with the other qualities, may make the person exceedingly unfitted for social relations." The ambivalence present in such individuals of course breeds feelings of insecurity, as Jost Hermand notes: "Consequently, these types in particular have a chronic fear of getting dirty and constantly wash their hands. Consciously or unconsciously, they struggle their entire lives against the feeling of inner and outer contamination."[36]

Although the basic triad of anal personality traits—orderliness, parsimoniousness, and obstinancy—and their more complex elaborations may be found in persons the world over, observers have been noticeably consistent in finding characteristics of this type in the Germans. Indeed, cleanliness, a firm belief in order, frugality, and a strong sense of duty all are traits generally associated with Germans. The strong emphasis on cleanliness in German society has been linked to its religious heritage, as is evidenced by Theodor Rosebury's claim that "the sense of guilt feelings pertaining to functions and emotions shared by everybody . . . reached its height during the Reformation."[37] At that time, many Germans were receptive to the Lutheran stress upon the body as dirt or filth. The biblical metaphor of the human being as dust moved into a central position in Lutheran theology and often became intensified scatologically in the words of Luther, as in the following example from *Table Talk:* "On that day he [Luther] had taken a bath and after eating he washed his hands and said: Why is water so dirty after a bath? Yes, I have forgotten that skin and flesh are made of filth; as it is said in the Scriptures: You are dust and ashes. Why are you proud, O human being?" (Gen. 3:19).[38] A similar concern for cleansing oneself of dirt and of all sinister forces was exemplified by the use of gargoyles on medieval churches. In addition to their practical function of draining off the rain water, they were thought to cleanse the church symbolically of all evil impurities. Particularly blatant in an excremental sense is the gargoyle on the Catholic cathedral in Freiburg im Breisgau (fig. 8), a figure that inspired contemporary sculptor Franz Gutmann in his creation of five scatological fountains for a site in the neighborhood of the cathedral (fig. 9).[39]

Twentieth-century German writers have used the motif of cleanliness, particularly an excessive preoccupation with cleanliness, in describing the Nazi personality and the tendencies in the German psyche that made many Germans receptive to Nazi propaganda. Jakov Lind, for example, portrays his negative reaction to the compulsively clean German housewife during World War II as follows: "The pictures of her handsome SS family disturbed me less (or more?) than the creepy clean silence in the house. You felt that even breathing might have upset the arrangement of molecules in the muffy air. Germans quite often have this mortuary atmosphere at home. The rest of the world must indeed look to them like a pigsty in dire need of cleaning up." Fictional works in which this theme appears will be discussed later in this study, particularly in chapter 6. That the motif was deemed applicable even to postwar German society by at least one author is evident in Heinrich Böll's "Brief an einen jungen Nichtkatholiken" ("Letter to a Young Non-Catholic"), in which Böll laments over the "good, clean Catholic women" of his native country and the tragic tendency of German Catholics to prefer "the beaming, cheerful, clean, not particularly humble face of the Catholic military bishop" to a quest for peace.[40]

It is the theory of the anal personality that Alan Dundes cites to explain the many examples of German scatological allusions in his *Life Is Like a Chicken Coop Ladder.* Dundes ties his observations in with the

8. Postcard of gargoyle on
Catholic cathedral in
Freiburg im Breisgau

9. Brunnen am Bächle in Freiburg im Breisgau

theory of national character, which he defines as "the way people actually *are*." Noting, as we have remarked earlier in this chapter, that the traits attributed to the anal personality also happen to be characteristics often associated with the Germans, and viewing this observation in the light of the many examples he has collected of scatology in German life and culture, Dundes proposes the thesis that "anality would appear to be an integral part of German national character." In an attempt to determine the psychological origins of this alleged "critical facet of German character," Dundes discusses German child-raising practices, such as swaddling and toilet training.[41]

In the final section of his treatise, Dundes attempts to use his German anal character theory to "illuminate" certain phenomena of German behavior and history, including the development of anti-Semitism. Although he cautions that "it would be foolish to think that the anal eroticism of Germans could explain the ultimate causes of so complex a phenomenon," Dundes fails to deal with the complexities to which he has referred. His focus on the scatological ramifications of the German attitude toward the Jews provides the reader with a great deal of interesting folklore evidence but also with a one-sided perspective. "There is good reason to believe that the linkage of Jews with dirt culminated in the ideology of Nazi Germany," Dundes writes, adding that the "fanatic concern with racial purity is in part a logical extension of the reaction formation from severe infant toilet training."[42]

At this point Dundes' reasoning, problematic from the start (as any attempt to psychoanalyze an entire nation is bound to be), really runs amok. Citing examples of the scatological connotations of the Nazi extermination of the Jews, Dundes offers the anti-Semitic crimes as "de facto evidence that the specifics of such genocide are not incompatible with German national character." Hitler, seen from this perspective, becomes not an aberration but virtually a mirror of society: "Hitler's possible or probable anal eroticism is not germane, although I would argue that it is German . . . One individual's fantasy or nightmare cannot become a reality unless others in a culture are predisposed or willing to share it. . . . Adolph Hitler, like Germans centuries before him, saw the world through fecal lenses."[43]

Dundes' argument does not end here. Offering as proof only some observations about similarities between German and Swiss-German methods of training children for cleanliness and a reminiscence by Jean-Paul Sartre regarding his Alsatian grandfather's scatologically crude language, Dundes concludes that the anal character traits that he has attributed to the Germans are shared "in part or in toto" by

German-speaking peoples anywhere, including German-Americans and perhaps even Anglo-Americans.[44] By placing the stigma of Hitlerian anal aggression on, say, the average German-American immigrant living in Cedar Rapids, Iowa, Dundes has extended his theory *ad absurdum*. To be sure, there *may* exist in Cedar Rapids a German-American whose obstinacy, stinginess, and orderliness mark him as a textbook case of the anal personality; who during World War II found the Nazis' genocidal policies compatible with his own views; and who now spends his retirement years composing scatological verses and fighting chronic constipation. To raise the possibility, however, that all, or most, or even many German-Americans—or Germans—would in any way resemble such a grim caricature is ludicrous, insulting, and psychologically naive. One cannot hope to refute or explicate the Nazis' racist views effectively by playing their own game.

Although the anal personality theory may give us many insights into the role of scatological motifs in German life and culture, it cannot provide the final explanation for these phenomena. Part of the problem is that the theory itself and its ramifications are fraught with complications. Freud, on the one hand, indicated that there was an inborn predisposition to develop an anal personality; although others writing on the topic have not discarded this genetic explanation completely, the tendency in more recent times has been to stress environmental factors.[45] Many modern experts would agree with Otto Fenichel that the development of anal fixations is contingent on the nature of the toilet-training process. Going back to the originator of the theory, Seymour Fisher and Roger Greenberg accuse Freud himself of inconsistency, because his published clinical cases often depict life experiences as at least partial causes of anal fixations. Fisher and Greenberg conclude, "The most ambiguous and uncertain part of Freud's theory about anality relates to his concept of how anal traits evolve. . . . Without solid facts, we are left with all sorts of speculative possibilities. Overall, it would be fair to say that the historical part of Freud's anal character formulation is most in need of investigation."[46]

With Freud's views somewhat murky and the experts themselves throwing up their hands in dismay as to the origins of adult anality, it is not surprising that it is difficult to determine why German authors employ anal motifs in their works. Amid much guesswork about the anal personality, however, some scientific experiments have been conducted. After examining dozens of psychological studies completed since the days of Freud, Fisher and Greenberg came up with the following conclusions: first, approximately twenty studies completed between 1943 and 1969 "almost unanimously found it possible to isolate recognizable clusters of anal traits and attitudes. Repeatedly, these studies depict trait patterns quite reminiscent of Freud's anal character"; second, there is a significant correlation between the anal personality traits and the types of behavior that Freud presumed would arise from these characteristics; and, finally, there is little support for the hypothesis that certain toilet-training practices are responsible for anal character traits in the adult.[47] In our perusal of literature, then, it may be enough for us to know that the anal character Freud envisioned lives and breathes in reality as well as in fiction. The *why* remains unclear, however.

If we are to understand the German interest in scatology, we cannot listen only to the psychoanalysts but must turn to the historians and sociologists as well. Karen Horney, a psychoanalyst herself (who based her views not only on her practice but also on her observations of characters in literature), felt that the Freudian effort to explain cultural phenomena in terms of biological drives had led to "false generalizations" and "abstruse theories." In her introduction to *The Neurotic Personality of Our Time*, Horney pointed out that it is an oversimplification to label childhood experiences as the only causes of adult neuroses; rather, she felt that "the specific cultural conditions under which we live" are highly influential in generating neurotic problems and determining their forms.[48]

What cultural conditions, then, might have been conducive to the Germans' use of scatological motifs? When one consults the historical and sociological studies that have been made regarding the Germans, one finds consistent references not to the prevalence of the anal personality but to the traditional role of authoritarianism. Admittedly, a strong sense of obedience may be related to an anal interest in orderliness. In a society in which respect for authority is widely accepted, however, it is possible to be a part of the established system without necessarily being an anally fixated neurotic.

Gordon Craig points out in *The Germans* that "the habits of obedience that troubled me in 1935 were . . . the products less of that indefinable quality that we call national character than of a particular kind—indeed, a unique kind—of historical experience." Craig traces this experience far back into Germany's past, citing the movement toward bureaucratization in the seventeenth and eighteenth centuries and the authoritarian counterreaction against participatory government in the eighteenth century. G. M. Gilbert refers to the Germans' "centuries of subservience to the Junker aristocracy, church authority, and the military caste" and notes that even when this tradition was interrupted by the creation of the Weimar Republic, the Germans, in choosing a leader, "inevitably turned to the very embodiment of ancient symbols of authority—the aged Junker Field Marshal von Hindenburg."[49]

Some observers have depicted the German respect for authority as a stereotype. Emil Ludwig is an example of this tendency (although perhaps he may be forgiven his hyperbole when one considers that he was writing on the very eve of World War II): "The Germans are the only nation on earth who obey with passion, and not out of necessity"; and "Obedience is despised in France, worshiped in Germany." Even those writers who are exceptionally careful to avoid overgeneralizations, however, find authoritarianism to have been a salient feature of German life. Rudolf Leonhardt, after compiling a number of quotations attesting to the high value placed on obedience in Germany, reports that he had discussed this evidence with several other persons and they had reached agreement "on one thing: that we had arrived at one of the points where the secret of 'the Germans' could be found."[50] G. M. Gilbert, the prison psychologist at the Nuremberg trial of the Nazi war criminals, is extraordinarily fastidious in his attempt to present all the complexities of the difficult topic he treats in *The Psychology of Dictatorship*. He examines the Nazi phenomenon from the historical and sociological perspectives as well as the psychological, and, although he finds that the importance of obedience in German society played a major role in the Nazis' success, he is quick to point out that for at least some of the Nazi leaders "the conflict between authoritarian and humanistic values was quite apparent." Gilbert's efforts to be fair and his extensive testing and interviewing of the Nazi criminals should, then, lend credence to what is possibly the strongest assertion in his study:

> The cardinal principle in the value-system of aggressive ideological dictatorship is the "categorical imperative" of deference to authority. That which is right is that which is determined by higher authority in a given social hierarchy of power. Correct behavior is primarily obedience and loyalty to such authority; only disobedience and disloyalty are wrong. These attitudes are intro-cepted from the parents in earliest childhood and continue to provide the basis of social status, approval and disapproval, as the individual assumes the adult role.
>
> . . . Hitler expressed this philosophy in a thousand ways, and a culture long inured to authoritarian absolutism acquiesced. This cardinal value served as the principal justification for all admitted errors of omission and commission

among all the Nazi Germans we studied, from the lowliest *Blockleiter* to the top ranks of leadership. It overruled all other values and nullified the process of critical value judgment and reality-testing of even intelligent leaders.[51]

As Gilbert suggests, there is evidence that the authoritarian syndrome in German society has had its parallel in family life. Writing of the German family in the years following World War II, David Rodnick observed, "Obedience is so strongly conditioned in German children through the use of affection as reward and rejection as punishment that this pattern continues not only through childhood but also into adulthood." (One of the "rewards" to which Rodnick refers is the custom of giving a teaspoonful of sugar to a child whose bed has remained clean all night.)[52] Evidence that the Teutonic tradition of raising children strictly is a long-standing one is reinforced in the works of Immanuel Kant, who made note of the connection between the stern upbringing of German children and the German tendency to submit to despotism. In fact, when itemizing the qualities he considered most important to instill in a child, Kant did not mince words about his number one priority: "Above all things, obedience is an essential feature in the character of a child, especially of a school boy or girl." The philosopher felt that the need for obedience training in children compared unfavorably with the natural instincts toward acceptable behavior in other creatures: "It is indeed wonderful, for instance, that young swallows, when newly hatched and still blind, are careful not to defile their nests."[53]

It stands to reason that strict toilet-training practices would be part of authoritarian family life. Dundes has compiled evidence indicating that the Germans have practiced strict and early toilet training, with the process beginning at about the age of five months. The custom of training a child in infancy differs markedly from current American practices. In the most recent edition of his "Bible" on child care, pediatric guru Benjamin Spock states, "I don't recommend any training efforts in the first year." English and Pearson agree: "it has been shown by careful neuropathological study that the tracts of the spinal cord are not completely myelinated until the end of the first year."[54] In addition to physical maturity, emotional readiness also is crucial, according to Dr. Spock, who claims that an advantage of waiting until the second half of the second year to start training is that it lets children "feel that it is *they* who have decided to control their bowels and bladders, rather than that they are giving in to parental demands." In his study of 1,170 normal children, American pediatrician T. Berry Brazelton found 80 percent of them trainable at twenty-seven months.

Echoing Spock, Brazelton stresses that "the child's own motivation and autonomy are of primary importance to any real success in this area" and warns that one should beware of "too much parental control at a time when he [the child] seems to be searching for his own controls." Brazelton feels that his approach is consistent with American societal norms: "Our culture places emphasis on developing strong individuals who make their own choices in childhood, as preparation for an adulthood fraught with choices."[55] The American pediatricians' emphasis on autonomy and self-motivation presents a strong contrast to the traditional German patterns of obedience to parents and social conformity.

In the second half of the twentieth century, psychologists have stressed the importance of the concept of *internalization* in child raising. The goal is to have the child voluntarily incorporate important values as part of her or his basic *Weltanschauung* rather than have these concepts drummed into the child's head by stern authority figures who generally use threats and punishment. It is likely that many German parents of past generations took the stance of Immanuel Kant, who leaned toward the stricter approach. Kant contrasted an absolute obedience—the result of compulsion—with a voluntary type; the latter was considered by the philosopher to be important but the former "necessary, for it prepares the child for the fufillment of laws that he will have to obey later, as a citizen, even though he may not like them." With regard to the desirability of internalization of positive goals, Kant's response was "freilich gut, aber" ("all very well, but"), the caveat being that lifelong gains were to be achieved by the development of a strong sense of duty.[56] Although Kant may have been correct in saying that a strict upbringing prepares the child for life in a traditionally authoritarian society, this modus operandi has its drawbacks for the individual's emotional development. In the case of cleanliness training, the possibility arises that the child's ambivalence toward cleanliness may remain unresolved and may plague the person for the rest of her or his life.[57] The parent who takes a more patient attitude will find, according to Brazelton, that the two-year-old suddenly shows an almost instinctive interest in cleanliness that "seems to come from within and is part of his attempt to organize himself. The mastery of ambivalence is apparent in this symptom." Persons who do not internalize values and the desirability of certain forms of behavior may never fully mature: Alan Watts observed that those individuals who base all their decisions on the principle that "Mother is always right" have failed "to recover from being children."[58] (See chapter 6 herein for a discussion of Heinrich Böll's character Greck, whose conviction that his parents are always right colors his views of what is dirty and what is clean.)

The attitudes that we—as writers or artists, or as members of society—have toward cleanliness influence the ways in which we conduct our lives and deal with other people. For this reason, Dr. Spock feels that "toilet training plays a part in the formation of a child's character." Learning experts Nathan Azrin and Richard Foxx have devised a method of rapid toilet training based on observing the child's readiness to internalize the concept of the desirability of cleanliness; in this successfully tested program, it is emphasized that going to the toilet is only the *means* of reaching the satisfying goal of personal cleanliness.[59]

Lecturing at Oxford in 1947, John McKenzie (who rejects the concept of the anal personality) discussed the problems of individuals in authoritarian systems. Persons raised with a strict hand, according to McKenzie, may either rebel openly or stifle their rebellion in a meek servility. Sometimes, he feels, the emotional conflict masked by polite conformity leads to a breakdown, which may take the form of Tourette syndrome (see chapter 6 for a literary example of such a case). In terms of cleanliness training, McKenzie finds that the small child is often "under *authority* which he *must* obey; the authority is external and may be rebelled against. Not so when he grows up to appreciate cleanliness; he is still under authority, but it is the authority of his sense of rightness and beauty. . . . the authority is within oneself."[60] The outlook of the Freudians has been that the process of toilet training substitutes the reality principle for the pleasure principle. McKenzie and those who share his views would have the reality principle and the pleasure principle blend in an internalized appreciation of cleanliness.

The experts vary in their depictions of the dynamics of the rebelliousness–submissiveness polarity. Some seem to feel that a small child will be passive initially, only to revolt later in life; the opposite view is also held. Others feel that both tendencies are combined in one individual. Karl Abraham, writing of reactions to toilet training, described "those children (and of course adults also) who are remarkable for their 'goodness,' polite manners, and obedience, but who base their underlying rebellious impulses on the grounds that they have been forced into submission since infancy."[61]

The power play of parents over children in the area of cleanliness extends beyond the toilet-training process. English and Pearson give an overview of the entire programme: "getting the idea of keeping the body clean through bathing and hand washing and brushing the teeth; being neat about clothes; avoiding too much contamination with foreign matter in play; keeping the playroom clean and in some order. . . . The child is asked to do what the grownups want—to be a little lady or a little gentleman."[62] According to Heinrich Böll, the Germans have carried this process to an unhealthy extreme: "Compulsive washing in all its forms. Always impeccably coifed, always neatly dressed, always bathing twice a day if possible." One of the novelist's objections to the hectic Sunday morning dash to church is the anxiety about cleanliness: "if a person has five children, he has to check whether all five children have clean hands, clean stockings, clean shoes, pressed pants, and all that shit."[63] (Böll's use of the expletive *shit* as a summarizing term at the end of the four-item inspection list may be indicative of his own position in the submission–rebellion continuum.) Rodnick, who asserts that "German familial patterns tend to develop submissive and gentle children," illustrates his theory by relating the tale of a German schoolyard scuffle in which a small boy who had been knocked to the ground became distraught and would not stop crying. The other children attempted to find out why he was overreacting. "When he said that his mother would spank him for getting his suit dirty, all the children began to brush him off with their hands and to assure him that he was not dirty. It took about five minutes to convince him that his suit was clean."[64]

An American soul mate of the boy in Rodnick's account is a small girl named Joan whose pathetic case history, as described by Brazelton, may give us some insight into the function of scatology in German life and literature. The child of an emotionally disturbed mother, Joan was almost totally neglected until her toilet-training process began. This procedure, which involved sessions in which Joan was forced to sit on the toilet for several hours at a time, included many reprimands, along with spankings or being sent to bed. Although she was a withdrawn, passive child, Joan now asserted herself in a way that showed there were still "remnants of strength" in her: she withheld her bowel movements and became chronically constipated. With this behavior she was able to gain a modicum of control over her life and her relationship with her mother, provoking negative attention—which to some children is better than being ignored. Through her refusal to be trained, Brazelton tells us, Joan "protests her mother's desertion in a more effective way than any other so far, and draws her mother back into an effective interaction with her. Her sad, passive pattern of turning inward is being reflected in her body's physiology as well as her outward behavior."[65]

The "pattern of turning inward" is a syndrome that has often been observed in the Germans. Thomas Mann referred to "inwardness" as "that quality of the Germans which is perhaps their most notable one." Mann traced this trait as far back as Luther, whose "anti-political servility" the novelist blamed for "the centuries-old, obsequious attitude of the Germans towards their princes and towards the power of the state."[66] Gordon Craig also has commented on this trend in German society; he remarks that, as William II began a buildup of armaments, "the great majority of the country's novelists and poets averted their eyes and retreated into that *Innerlichkeit* which was always their haven when the real world became too perplexing for them." (Craig mentions some exceptions to this tendency, including Wedekind, Sternheim, and Heinrich Mann.)[67] Thomas Mann found inwardness a mixed blessing for the Germans, because it produced not only such expressions of depth of feeling as the *Lied* and in fact the entire German romantic movement but also the "morbidity" of romanticism. Carried to an extreme in the sense of becoming a mentality "of immaturity, of dull servility," the inclination to inner-directedness was, Mann felt, a contributing factor to the rise of National Socialism. Ultimately, however, Mann found at the root of German inwardness an indication that the Germans—like Brazelton's Joan and like all human beings everywhere—had "the wish to be loved."[68]

There would appear to be evidence, then, that the German tradition of authoritarianism, which in many cases has led to strict, early toilet training, could be responsible at times for a failure to internalize the principles of cleanliness training. Thus, for at least some Germans, coming to terms with their feelings about "doing their business" may be unfinished business. Seen in this light, the high visibility of scatology in folklore, art, and literature may be attributed to attempts to work through the complex agenda of ambivalence, to air unresolved struggles rather than dirty linen. In a slight variation on Joan's case, physiology becomes psychology becomes behavior. When they confront their readers with scatological references, German authors achieve the sort of interaction that is important if one is to deal with and master ambivalence.[69] Genteel attempts to look inward and examine one's attitudes toward the corporeal, such as Thomas Mann's novella *A Man and his Dog*, may meet with reader approval. Literary or artistic works that represent the polarity of rebelliousness, such as the creations of the Dadaists, will often arouse the wrath of reader or audience; but, as Brazelton noted, negative interaction may be preferable to none at all. By raising the taboo topic of scatology in a sort of public forum, German authors may be reaching for a personal or societal maturity that will enable them (or the culture in which they live) to come to grips with a process that many parents of past generations believed to have been complete when in fact it was only half-baked.

Neither of the two theories presented as possible rationales for the abundance of scatological allusions in German life and culture can provide a comprehensive solution. The anal personality theory, though it offers substantial insights, has many limitations. Not only does it represent the hopeless attempt to psychoanalyze an entire culture, but it makes the mistake of assuming a national neurosis. In addition to failing to distinguish the normal from the neurotic or psychotic, the theory pays scant attention to the fact that, as Horney points out, viewpoints vary within a culture from one era to another and at any one time from one social class to another.[70] Furthermore, any attempt to explain the vast abundance and variety of German scatological allusions as attributable to anal eroticism overlooks the many other possible motivations or explanations for these cultural phenomena. Without denigrating the impressive collection of German scatological references that Dundes has compiled, we should mention that one of the greatest shortcomings of his study is its failure to examine the wide diversity of outlooks or *Weltanschauungen* that the instances he catalogs represent. By concocting a cacophony of examples ranging from the writings of Goethe to toilet graffiti, from the letters of Mozart to the sexual practices of Hitler, and then labeling these figures and/or works as representative of "German anal character," Dundes is confusing the song with the singer and, moreover, neglecting to note the intricate harmonies and grace notes of the song itself. The topic of scatology, though universal in its relevance, has been treated by individual German authors in highly disparate ways, as this study hopes to demonstrate.

If the second theory, that of the effect of the German authoritarian heritage on the internalization of cleanliness principles, has any validity, it too may cast doubts on Dundes' national character theory. Erich Fromm has described his concept of "social character"—apparently tantamount to national character—as follows: "Any society, in order to survive, must mold the character of its members in such a way that *they want to do what they have to do;* their social function must become internalized and transformed into something they feel driven to do, rather than something they are obliged to do."[71] Because we can see in

German life and culture examples of both types of reactions symptomatic of uninternalized cleanliness training, German scatology may reveal just the opposite of what Dundes feels it does: it may be indicative of a variety of outlooks rather than of a fixed national character.

The internalization theory cannot provide a pat explanation for German scatology either. There is no total uniformity in German child-raising techniques, and the fact that cleanliness training has been such a private matter makes concrete data difficult to obtain. It should be noted that the authoritarian family structure, according to some observers, is rapidly disappearing from German society. The traditional system did prevail, however, during the years in which most of the authors discussed in this study were raised, and we may assume that at least some of them were affected by it. The argument may be raised that other societies with strict child-raising practices have not produced a culture so abundant in scatological references. A possible answer to this objection may be that the authoritarianism prevalent in German society in general over several centuries produced an especially strong stimulus to the tendency of particularly creative, expressive artists and writers to "let off steam" (as Gershon Legman observed; see note 20 to this chapter).

Though both theories have their flaws, they do provide essential background information for the understanding of scatology in German culture. The anal personality has been depicted repeatedly in modern German literature, especially in works dealing with World War II (see chapter 6). The reader finds not only characters with the anal triad of traits but also allusions to minor ramifications of the anal personality. An example of what might be termed anal literary trivia would be the theme of delight in recycling rubbish or converting waste products into useful materials: this propensity is depicted in, to name two instances, Dürrenmatt's *Hercules and the Augean Stable* (see chapter 3) and Böll's short story "Der Wegwerfer." The latter work is not discussed in this study because it is not openly scatological, but it would be of considerable interest to persons examining the anal character in literature.

Similarly, the theory of the internalization of cleanliness principles sheds light on German literary works. Thomas Mann's novella *A Man and his Dog* is told by a narrator who, as an individual, has not resolved his views of what is clean and what is dirty. The audience in the nightclub scene in Brecht's *Baal* is representative of a society that is ambivalent about the scatological. Böll, who made ample use of the anal personality theory, dealt not only with the internalization of the desirability of being clean, as we shall see in chapter 7, but also with the internalization of positive attitudes toward dirt ("consciousness raising about dirt and the acceptance of it"; "to propagate dirt or . . . to designate dirtiness as human"), which he preferred to a "super-hygienification" imposed on the individual from without by society.[72] In some cases, the author may be portraying her or his own unresolved conflicts; in others, it is society's ambivalence that is depicted; our task shall be to examine the motifs themselves rather than to attempt to psychoanalyze the writers.

Clearly, no authors worth their salt sit down to write a novel or short story with a psychology text open to a chapter on the anal character or any other psychological prototype. Writers base their characters not so much on their studies as on their life experiences and their observations of self and others. Böll made a telling comment while he was discussing in an interview with Karin Struck what he felt to be an abnormally strong emphasis on cleanliness in German society: "In classical psychology, as far as I know, it is an actual illness."[73] The novelist's cautious "as far as I know" underlines the fact that creative writers are not psychoanalysts (or historians or sociologists) and should not be viewed as such.

The German authors we shall examine in this study have tried to create realistic characters—not textbook cases, which seldom exist in real life. Their goal is to present life honestly. Because of their concern for truth, they acknowledge the fact that scatology is part of being human and thus present this portion of human existence in their works, sometimes with an almost Lutheran negativism and at other times with a humorous or serious affirmation. Many German writers have followed Freud's wish: "Civilized people conceal their scatologic functions and excretions from their fellow-men though every one is aware of their existence in others. Assuredly, it would be wiser to recognize their presence candidly and to devote to these earthy parts of our persons as large a measure of refinement as their nature permits."[74] Similarly, Franz Josef Bogner, a German mime and clown who blows his nose in his own program as part of his act, told us that art, if it is honest, must be "human art," as opposed to idealistic art, which is often an escape from reality. Bogner rejects scatology if it exists for mere sensationalism but not if it gives greater insight into the nature of human life.

Heinrich Wölfflin, in his comparison of Italian and German Renaissance art, makes some very important observations that also apply to German literature. The Italian, according to Wölfflin, is overcome by nature's perfection: "Not only does nature contain the precious store of forms that constitute the material of art; she also envelops in her womb, with greater or lesser concealment, perfect beauty. And to seize this beauty is the noblest task of art." In contrast to this outlook, for Germans "perfection has to have arisen out of the soil of imperfection; and they are capable of enjoying this beauty only as beauty in a state of becoming and not of fulfillment."[75]

Many German artists or writers find it very difficult to represent perfection in their works, because they tend to perceive dichotomies in all of life. Should they momentarily think only of their noble souls, they are quickly reminded of their carnal tendencies; Christian Enzensberger describes this polarized thinking in terms of what is considered to be "above" (*Oben*) and what is viewed as "lower" (*Darunter*):

> anything above, however high it aims, however low it bends, must have its lower part; consequently the individual finds himself in a dirt relationship not only with the outside world but also with himself, both equally hopeless. Even if at first it is only certain parts of his body which he finds impossible to accept, very soon it is the whole body, and eventually nothing is left but a refined, insubstantial breath, something which is entirely above, entirely clean, entirely timeless, certainly not divisible and not susceptible to decay—and then what happens? For the sake of this breath of spirit the rest of the individual is pronounced dirt and from then on this spirit, contrary to all its desires, is encased in an eternal state of inferiority, in crumbling decay, even worse, it immediately proves to be extremely susceptible to defilement.[76]

Even Goethe bemoans the persistence of corporeal limitations when he writes in the angels' song in the last scene of *Faust II:*

> A castoff earthly hull
> Is our discomfiture;
> Were it incombustible,
> It still could not be pure.[77]

Probably most typical of the traditional German vision of the human dilemma are these lines from Grabbe's *Herzog Theodor von Gothland:*

> The human being
> Bedecks his head with eagles
> While his feet stick in the mire![78]

2

Wilhelm Busch: Dumping the Chamber Pot on Human Vanity

Like his impish creation, Klecksel the Painter, the late nineteenth-century artist/author Wilhelm Busch was a master of caricature, given to depicting such unattractive human specimens as old crones (4:111)[1] and probing beneath the surface to the alimentary tract(4:88), often inventing comical roles for the digestive system's end products. A figure whose influence on modern German humor was extensive, as Heinrich Böll acknowledged regretfully in his *Frankfurt Lectures*,[2] Busch based much of his jocularity on scatological allusions. Despite the frequent appearance of excremental elements in Busch's works, particularly in his drawings, scholars tend to shy away from an examination of the artist/author's use of scatology. Although occasionally a critic may mention one of these allusions in passing,[3] we have been unable to find any detailed analyses of Busch's excremental references.

In his poem "Oben und Unten" ("Above and Below"), Busch humorously and effectively states his view of the prevalence of man's baser desires over reason:

> For the head to guide our planet
> Would make humans grow much prouder:
> Then the tricks and fraud that span it
> Would be blown away like powder.
>
> But it's nature's fundamental

That the stomach and its chorus
In ways quite untranscendental
Settle all decisions for us. [4:327–28]

The image "the stomach and its chorus" implies the alimentary canal, which includes the intestines and rectum. Particularly important are the words "nature's fundamental" (in German the adverbs *wurzelhaft natürlich* are used), because they depict human beings as rooted in their earthy origins, suggesting that this is the natural or normal state. Thus, the dreams that people may have of their own nobility are destroyed in the second stanza, after having been declared unreal by the author's use of the subjunctive in the first stanza.

"Above and Below" reflects Busch's awareness of the fundamental role played by digestion and elimination in human life and is also indicative of the similarity of his *Weltanschauung* to the position of the nineteenth-century materialists (e.g., Ludwig Büchner, Jacob Moleschott, and Karl Vogt), who had little confidence in the idealistic view of human beings as creatures made in God's image. However, as many scholars have pointed out, Busch's philosophy of life was heavily influenced by the pessimism of Schopenhauer. Josef Ehrlich has examined Busch's indebtedness to the philosopher in great detail and points out Busch's agreement with Schopenhauer that "the world is a place of constant worry, sorrow, and pain, of brutal accidents, indeed a playground for envy, meanness, and violence; as a result, one is more apt to believe in a devil as the creator of the world than in a god." A little later Ehrlich states: "Just as Busch's poetry reveals the spirit of the teachings of Schopenhauer, the same holds true for the master's drawings. They provide an impressive and humorous illustration of the Schopenhauerian 'will to live.'"[4] It is Ehrlich's view that the basic contrast in "Above and Below" is one between Schopenhauer's concepts of intellect and will;[5] because the poem seems rather to suggest a mind–body duality, however, Ehrlich's interpretation holds up only if one takes into consideration Peter Bonati's contention that Busch transmutes Schopenhauer's idea of the will from a metaphysical to a physical force. According to Bonati, Busch seizes upon the abstract concept of will as a moving force in the universe and depicts it in its specific manifestation as a "basic motivating drive" that is present in "the individual human being, the individual animal or object."[6] "Above and Below" thus reflects Busch's fusion of the theories of Schopenhauer and the materialists into his own distinctive view of the world.

Almost all of Busch's work, his picture stories, verses, and prose,

10. "The Good Grand-
mother" (Wilhelm Busch)

presents a world that is metaphorically ruled by the lower part of the
human body, as seen in "Above and Below." Excrement is, of course, an
important part of this realm, and Busch acknowledges this fact; however, he does not speak about excremental functions as directly and
openly as do many present-day writers. The few times that he does
mention excrement specifically, he always refers to animal droppings
and sometimes employs euphemistic terms such as "horse apples"
(4:223). This seemingly high degree of restraint in Busch's language is
deceptive, though, for a close examination of his drawings reveals the
unabashed depiction of human and animal posteriors, toilets, and excrement. Busch has a tendency to lead the unsuspecting reader of his
verses along with a fairly straight face, until suddenly an illustration
delivers a scatological punchline, and one cannot help but note the
discrepancy that often exists between the innocent and sweet, almost
idyllic Buschean couplet and the drawing that accompanies it. An example of this technique is the illustrated couplet "The Good Grandmother" (4:346). The rhyme reads: "Granny likes to do everything/
For Johnny, who's her little king." The accompanying drawing (fig. 10)
shows a pudgy-faced, broadly smiling baby boy sitting on his potty
chair, sucking his thumb. The viewer immediately notices that the
door at the back of the chair stands open and sees the long-suffering,
stooped grandmother carrying the potty out of the room. Thus Busch,
in his humorous realism, undercuts the romantic notion of the innocence and purity of young children, while simultaneously portraying

the adult as a slave of the excremental. This technique of unexpectedly contradicting his verses with his illustrations is not unlike Heinrich Heine's tendency to use the last line or two of many of his poems to dismantle the seemingly noble romantic imagery that he used in earlier lines.

When Wilhelm Busch employs excrement in his works, he often does it in a veiled and indirect manner. Instead of confronting the reader directly with waste matter, Busch frequently makes use of an object or place that is clearly linked with the excretory functions. Thus, one encounters numerous references to the posterior in Busch's works, often with the intention of conveying gentle humor. Near the beginning of *Mr. and Mrs. Knopp,* for example, the reader learns that Dorothea likes to look at the seat of her husband's pants:

> Gladly Frau Doris turns her glance
> Toward the seat of Knopp's (her husband's) pants,
> Which always brings her special cheer
> With its most expressive soft veneer.
> One minute it may look quite grim,
> Then sorrow makes the visage dim.
> Next comes a pride beyond compare,
> A noble face with nose in air.
> But soon these vanities depart,
> Replaced by the glow of a tender heart;
> Then finally, after a little time,
> It beams with cheerfulness sublime.
> [3:89–91]

Interspersed between the lines of verse are drawings of the seat of Knopp's pants, and in each illustration the creases in the pants resemble a different facial expression, as described in the text. Although the humor is clearly gentle here, the roles of face and behind have been reversed by implication, so that the posterior has become "a noble face." The suggestion is also present that people think and act with their rear ends rather than their heads.

More frequently, Busch employs the derrière in a strikingly pungent manner. In his works one finds numerous examples of how vulnerable our posteriors are, and these instances serve as reminders of how large a measure of human suffering stems from this category of injuries. In infancy, the villain may be the hot curling iron that was forgotten (intentionally or unintentionally?) inside the diaper by the nursemaid

(1:559–67). As a youth, one is susceptible to such accidents as becoming frozen to the rock on which one is resting (1:290). The adult backside faces such perils as falling on a fork (1:450), being bitten by a dog (1:473), or landing on a pitchfork (1:457).

Because we are so vulnerable in this part of our anatomy, it is possible for people to vent their spleen on others by wounding them in this sensitive area. Busch frequently depicts human malice by portraying one individual's assaults on another's posterior. Often these attacks are carried out with great vigor and with obvious sadistic glee. A recurring example of such inhumanity is that of fathers beating their children simply out of principle:

> Druff has strictly kept this saying:
> There is nothing like a flaying;
> Character building, given in time,
> 'Specially before the crime. [3:30]

Similarly, wives attack their adulterous husbands with brooms (3:59–61), children throw riding boots at the rear ends of animals (3:304) or burn their tails (2:249–50), and the artist attacks his critic's backside with an umbrella (4:121) and a sharpened pencil (4:125–26).

Finally, it is noteworthy that Busch frequently deliberately indicates the anus in his drawings of animals (e.g., 1:171, 420, 445, 485). Thus he assures that the viewer's attention will be directed to the excremental part of nature. Just as Busch depicts human beings as living, breathing individuals rather than as cardboard heroes, so he shows animals as creatures possessing normal anatomical equipment rather than as noble beasts.[7]

Busch's preoccupation with excremental functions leads him to depict in numerous situations the chamber pot, an object with universal appeal in his day because it was in every home, whether in the form of a humble pot or an elegant *chaise percée*. The artist/author gleefully perceived the infinite comic possibilities of this handy receptacle, and it became one of his most frequently employed props. In fact, in his drawings of beds or bedrooms the chamber pot is included in most cases, so that it essentially constitutes a leitmotiv in Busch's works and becomes as such a continuing reminder of the earthiness of the human race (e.g., 1:369–74). Furthermore, the chamber pot quite often assumes an important role, sometimes helping, sometimes hindering an individual. One may be fairly certain that the unobtrusive chamber pot shown in the first illustration of a Busch story will be spilled or

11. "The Handsome Knight" falls into a chamber pot (Wilhelm Busch)

otherwise involved in the action before the final drawing. On several occasions when one of Busch's characters attempts to prove his superiority over others by displaying ostentatious airs or by outwitting someone else, he ends up instead in, under, or next to the chamber pot. This ironic fate is suffered by the rich student of "The Handsome Knight." A suit of armor, the very object that was to gain him the admiration and envy of the others present at a masquerade party, becomes the means of his final undoing when its weight causes him to crash through his bed and land in his own chamber pot (fig. 11). An interesting reversal has occurred: what was to have symbolized his "manly" qualities before his friends becomes the means of reminding him that he really is no more impressive than a pile of waste matter. As is quite often the case in Busch's works, the chamber pot is not mentioned in the text, but the entire incident is vividly portrayed in the drawings (1:518–19). Only by examining both text and drawings can one experience the total effect of Busch's caricatures.

The use of the chamber pot becomes much more derisive and is coupled with another excremental incident in Busch's parody of a *Bildungsroman, Scenes from the Jobs Epic.* Again the author begins with the theme of human beings' false conceptions of their own worth and importance. Humanity's pretense to greatness is symbolized by the dream that Mrs. Jobs has three weeks before she finally gives birth to a son, after previously having had nothing but daughters. Her dream vision that she will bring forth "a celestial watchman's horn" rather than a baby parodies the biblical prophecy of the birth of Christ

12. Mrs. Jobs's dream,
from *Scenes from the Jobs
Epic* (Wilhelm Busch)

in Luke 1:68–69: "Blessed be the Lord God of Israel; for he hath visited and redeemed his people, and hath raised up an horn of salvation for us in the house of his servant David."[8] Once more the accompanying drawing adds a great deal to the text (2:298). The viewer sees Mrs. Jobs lying in bed, while a huge, radiant horn that appears to have a halo around it floats above the bed and dominates the drawing. Yet, ironically, in the deep shadows under the bed there clearly stands a chamber pot (fig. 12). The entire picture story that follows revolves around the question of which one of these objects is more prophetic of the boy's development. The line of the text describing the dream as *seeming* "so real, lifelike, and true" is a strong hint; so is the drawing, which shows the horn to be an apparition whereas the chamber pot has very real substance.

Although a considerable volume of evidence quickly accumulates indicating that the boy, Hieronymus Jobs, is a lazy, stupid, and malicious child, he and his parents continue in their vanity to believe in the glorious omen of Mrs. Jobs's dream. Thus, Hieronymus is sent to the university to become a clergyman. At this point Busch swiftly deflates Hieronymus's conceit by employing excrement and reintroducing the chamber pot from the opening scene. First Busch makes a coy but devastating use of horse excrement. After having lost most of his money to a cardsharp, Hieronymus seems to have found new happiness in the person of a young lady who is riding in the coach with him; although the text describes the "charming" encounter in exaggerated,

13. The horse's commentary, from *Scenes from the Jobs Epic* (Wilhelm Busch)

sentimental, romantic terms, the illustrations reveal that at this very moment the horse drawing the coach raises its tail and proceeds to move its bowels (2:308–9). Even though Hieronymus is oblivious to the animal's defecation, to the reader the horse's action is eloquent commentary on the falseness of the romantic scene narrated in the text. When the hero discovers a little later that his lovely Amalia has disappeared with his watch, the horse's judgment is vindicated. While Hieronymus laments his fate, the horse once again defecates (fig. 13) (2:310), a sardonic comment on humanity's stupidity and an indication of the blunt simplicity of the animal world in contrast to unnecessarily complicated human strivings. Scenes such as this one, in which an animal defecates unabashedly at the precise moment when a customarily revered human activity is taking place, are not uncommon in Busch's works.

Prior to giving up all claims to a higher calling in life, Hieronymus on two occasions falls victim to the ominous chamber pot that was present in the original prophecy. At one point he angrily tears apart the drain spouts of the ironically named inn, the Golden Angel, because the owner has dared to kick him out after closing hours; in the midst of Hieronymus's efforts, a most effective and sobering ablution showers upon him from above: "Just then the proprietress of the hotel / The vessel of anger pours out, aiming well" (2:312). This time the text only feebly disguises the scatological event by using the metaphor "The vessel of anger," and again the illustration is clear and unambiguous (fig. 14).

Hieronymus's final scatological disgrace comes a few chapters later, when he has been hired as a village schoolmaster. Dissatisfied with his

14. "The Vessel of Anger,"
from *Scenes from the Jobs
Epic* (Wilhelm Busch)

job performance, the peasants storm into his bedroom one night and
rudely remove him from office by shoving a pitchfork into his rear end
and throwing him out the door. The accompanying drawings reveal
that the peasants have knocked over Hieronymus's chamber pot and
spilled its contents. Finally, the peasants' victory celebration includes
a public procession in which they hold aloft the trophies of their conquest, including the chamber pot (fig. 15) (2:338–39). Such a public
exhibition of a most intimate and usually unmentionable object
approaches the ultimate scatological ridicule. Having thus suffered
through numerous humiliations, several of which were of a scatological nature, Hieronymus drops his pretensions to fame and accepts his
real calling, that of night watchman. Ironically, one discovers the
mother's vision was actually correct, although she should have interpreted it as an ordinary watchman's horn and not a celestial one. It is
clear that the chamber pot does win out, reflecting Busch's conviction
that human beings would often do better to accept themselves as they
basically are rather than to put on false airs.

Although the chamber pot usually functions in Busch's works to
ridicule and destroy human delusions of grandeur, in at least one example a chamber pot actually saves a person's life. In the chapter
"Nighttime Politics" from *The Birthday*, we find the village mayor in
bed anguishing over the news he is reading in the newspaper. Though
he clenches his fist as a sign of his distress, he is totally unaware of the

real danger that awaits him. After he has fallen asleep from the effects
of the brandy he had previously consumed, the tassel of his nightcap is
ignited by the candle next to his bed. Suddenly he awakens to find the
top of his head on fire and frantically searches for a pan of water. Unsuccessful, he finally sticks his burning head into his own chamber pot
and effectively extinguishes the fire (fig. 16) (2:393). Of course, Busch
is again deriding human foibles in this scene, but he is also humorously pointing out that there may come a moment when one gratefully
turns to that part of oneself that has too long been held in contempt:
"Afraid, one does without a twinge, / What normally would make one
cringe" (2:393).

In addition to the chamber pot motif, Busch occasionally makes humorous and effective use of the themes of the toilet and the privy; their
impact, too, can be relatively gentle or very scathing. As an example of
the significance sometimes assigned to the privy by Busch, one need
only examine the chapter "Alas!" from the first part of the Tobias
Knopp trilogy, *Adventures of a Bachelor.* The first oblique reference
made to the toilet is the ludicrous name Klotilda Piepo, designating a
character who is the daugher of a friend of Knopp. (*Das Klo* is the Ger-

15. Triumphal march, from *Scenes from the Jobs Epic*
(Wilhelm Busch)

16. Dousing the fire, from *The Birthday* (Wilhelm Busch)

man equivalent of "the john" or "the W. C." *Piepo* suggests *Popo* ["rear end"] and possibly *Pipi* ["pee pee"].) At first it appears that Klotilda Piepo will agree to become Knopp's long-yearned-for wife, for she quickly responds to his overtures by picking a rose for him. As it turns out, however, it is ironically the "Klo" that destroys this relationship, or, more precisely, it is the attitude that human beings have toward the toilet that causes Knopp's hopes to be shattered. The real humor of this little episode is contained in the dichotomy existing within the characters, who on the one hand accept the name Klotilda Piepo as perfectly natural and beautiful but cannot speak of the toilet without using euphemisms. Thus, when Klotilda's father shows Knopp, his overnight guest, the rooms of the house, he euphemizes the toilet by stating: "Here's our own *sanctum sanctorum,* / Lauded mutely, with decorum" (3:69). The words "Lauded mutely, with decorum" express precisely the human ambivalence toward the toilet. It is a place to which everyone really likes to go but whose existence everyone tries to conceal. Busch proceeds to satirize this attitude by showing us the fate suffered by Knopp. First the protagonist decides to visit the toilet during the night:

> Knopp cannot stop fondly dreaming—
> Svelte Klotilda he's esteeming—

> And, although it makes him smart,
> Grips her rose so near his heart.
> "O Klotilda, you alone
> Must be mine, my very own."
>
> Something else, though, he is needing:
> Knopp, you still must do some reading.
> Gladly he fulfills his urges,
> Softly from his room emerges,
> Candle lighted lest he fall;
> Off he wanders down the hall.
> [3:70–71]

It is implied that Knopp gets the urge to go to the toilet as a result of his infatuation for the slender Klotilda. Thus love has been equated with a laxative and stripped of its usual nobility. Busch then has Knopp sublimate the bowel movement into the desire to read, satirizing the human tendency to suppress the excremental to such a degree that one cannot be honest even with oneself. The absurdity of Knopp's claim that he has a desire to read is evident, because he could do that in his own room. The secret pleasure with which Knopp regards his trip to the toilet is expressed in the line, "Gladly he fulfills his urges." Thus we see Knopp heading for the toilet in the accompanying drawing. He is wearing his nightshirt, carrying a newspaper under his arm and Klotilda's rose in his mouth (3:71), a picture of heavenly contentment.

In the privy, Knopp's happiness comes to an abrupt end. Busch's objects often display an uncanny will of their own and turn humans into their victims, as seen earlier in the case of the armor in "The Handsome Knight." Similarly, Knopp becomes the prisoner of the toilet, because he falls asleep on it: "Fighting sleep, one may just lose, / As one sits and starts to snooze" (3:71). Ironically, although "snooze" (in the original German, *einschlummern*) usually means to fall into a light, short sleep, Knopp does not awaken until eight o'clock the next morning. He appears to have been fooled by the toilet, which made him feel so comfortable that he slept all night long. He is finally jostled out of his sleep by the laughter of the girls who are decorating the hall that separates Knopp from his room. After waiting a considerable time, Knopp decides to make a run for it, hiding himself totally under his nightshirt and the newspaper, but again he is foiled by an object:

> Swift his steps along the floor, 'til
> Knopp comes to the chamber's doorsill,
> Finding there some stumbling blocks.

Whoops! Defoliation shocks!
Secretly he flees this place,
To go where no one knows his face.
[3:72—73]

Knopp's attempt to conceal his stay in the toilet has ironically resulted in nothing less than his total unmasking in front of the hysterical girls, and therefore he flees out the window (3:73), completely humiliated. Clearly, this episode ridicules humanity's attempt to suppress or at least euphemize a perfectly natural part of life.

Busch allows the toilet to assume a more blatant role in the chapter "Love and Conversion" from the picture story *Saint Anthony of Padua*. Here, too, the privy is employed in connection with love, but in addition it is used as a weapon against religiosity. (Furthermore, the drawings in this episode are much less subtle than those in "Alas!") As is so often the case in Busch's works, at the beginning of the chapter it appears that Anthony has finally succeeded in touching the heart of his long-desired Julia, who is married to another man. However, one day Anthony is discovered in a compromising position by the wronged husband, and the would-be lover heads into the privy. Here he man-

17. The paramour's escape, from *Saint Anthony of Padua*
(Wilhelm Busch)

18. Arrival at the monastery, from *Saint Anthony of Padua*
(Wilhelm Busch)

ages to escape the sword of Julia's husband only by jumping right into
the opening and landing in the pit below (fig. 17) (2:85). But Busch
does not stop here; in the final drawing, he shows Anthony arriving at
the gate of a monastery, still totally covered with and dripping human
wastes (fig. 18) (2:86). This scene may well imply that Busch viewed
monasteries as receptacles for the dung of human society, a last resort
for those who could not succeed at worldly games like adultery.

Busch was well aware that precisely placed or timed animal droppings are nature's perfect response to human pretensions to greatness;
hence the vulgar counterbalance of romance and horse manure in
Scenes from the Jobs Epic, a technique that Busch employed on several
occasions. Although some of the human activities that become defiled
with animal wastes are such sensual pleasures as the enjoyment of
wine (3:26–27), even the loftiest, most sacred human values are not
spared. For example, the romantic view of nature as idyllic and inspi-
rational is humorously, scatologically assailed in the sixth chapter of
Balduin Bählamm, the Obstructed Poet. After a considerable search,
Bählamm is finally convinced that he has found the perfect spot for his
poetic genius to bear fruit, a pristine pastoral setting. Just as he is
ready to transfer his feelings onto paper, the unexpected reversal follows: "Oh yecch—a fleck! The poem's a wreck. / The bird, relieved, for-
gets the speck" (4:46). The accompanying drawing (fig. 19) shows a
bird depositing its droppings on Bählamm's open book. In addition to
defiling the supposedly idyllic setting, this occurrence also degrades

19. The bird's relief, from *Balduin Bählamm, the Obstructed Poet* (Wilhelm Busch)

Bählamm's poetry. Furthermore, there is a significant contrast between the reactions of the bird and of the poet to the bird's act: the poet feels that his masterpiece has been ruined, whereas the "relieved" bird has no regrets whatsoever about what it has done. In this dichotomy Busch again satirizes human reticence concerning excrement by having the bird deposit its wastes openly and naturally and fly happily away, revealing that the natural world shares neither human beings' inhibitions about excrement nor their illusions of greatness. The very same idea is presented in Busch's little verse "Carefree":

The wisest, they can't
View a thought-house that is vacant
Without dejection.
The raven lacks their introspection.
[4:391]

The accompanying drawing (fig. 20) shows a raven depositing its droppings on a skull that is sitting on top of a book bearing the initials W. B. Thus, the caricaturist who has poked such fun at those around him admits that he, too, belongs to the human race and, surrendering any pretensions to immortality, accords himself and his works the ultimate insult.

Even religion cannot escape excremental profanation in Busch's short picture story "The Top Hat" (2:481–88). The first few illustrations depict a very pious young man who has taken great pains to look clean, neat, and devout as he goes to church to pay tribute to his pa-

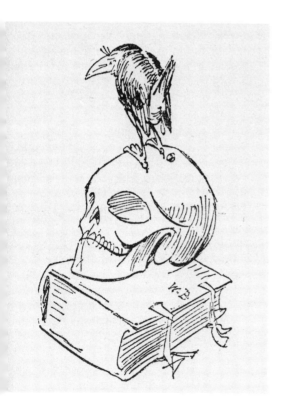

20. "Carefree" (Wilhelm Busch)

21. The dog's sacrilege, from "The Top Hat" (Wilhelm Busch)

tron saint. However, this peaceful, harmonious picture is quickly destroyed. Outdoors, the wind blows the young man's top hat away and, while he chases after it, he leaves his Bible (or prayer book or hymnal), rosary, and white gloves lying on the stoop of a house. Then a double defilement occurs. Joseph, the young man, trips over a rock in the road and lands full-length, swallowtail coat and all, in the street muck that is being swept up by two women; simultaneously, in the background of the drawing, a dog urinates on the book, rosary, and gloves (fig. 21). Again, one must note Busch's slyness in employing excremental elements; it is a full page later before the urinating dog is mentioned in a deceptively simple couplet: "Just safely out of range is found / An old gentleman with his pet hound" (2:486). Then, like a cameraman who suddenly zooms in on a fascinating detail, Busch shows Joseph returning to the stoop to recover his religious paraphernalia; the text tells us: "Toward home heads Joseph, swift of gait, / No longer such a fashion plate" (2:488). The incredible understatement of the last line is revealed in a drawing (fig. 22) that shows the dripping items held gingerly by the now filthy, tattered, scarecrowlike Joseph, who is walking home behind the man and his dog, the latter of whom glances back at Joseph with a Buschean smirk on its face. Once again a person with pious pretensions has been reminded of his human limitations, and the vitiation of the rosary and sacred tome constitutes a mockery of their validity.

Although there undoubtedly is a great deal of pessimism in Busch's *Weltanschauung,* he places a positive stress on the idea that human be-

22. Disheveled Joseph, from "The Top Hat" (Wilhelm Busch)

ings should accept and acknowledge the excremental parts of their lives instead of concealing them. Those persons who deny the excremental side of human nature often become engulfed in human wastes, as does Joseph in "The Top Hat," or they are simply laughed at, as in the following section from *Edward's Dream:*

> On the grounds of the nursery, which was located near the bridge, two women are strolling, the First Lady and her daugher. The latter had bought herself some plums. "Oh, Mama!" she says anxiously, "I'm getting such ——." "Shame on you, Pauline!" interrupted her refined mother. "One doesn't speak of such things!" "Good morning!" rasped the gardener's tame raven. "Oh, look, Mama!" called Pauline, once again cheerful. "What a heavenly bird! Please, dear little parrot, speak again!" "Crrrrap!" rasped the raven.—"Come here, my child!" said the indignant First Lady. "Now he's becoming vulgar!"
>
> From these proceedings it became absolutely clear to me that I was no longer in the territory of the relatively uninhibited expression of feelings but rather in the vicinity of a fine and highly cultured metropolis. [4:176–77]

By crying "Shame" before Pauline even mentions any intestinal disorders and then by commanding her daugher to come away from the bird with its explicit language, Pauline's mother is attempting to block out a side of life that she finds disgusting. Busch's oeuvre seems to suggest, however, that stopping one's ears to the fundamental rumblings of human life can result in the breaking of hearts. This is definitely the case with Knopp (*Adventures of a Bachelor*) who, as was described earlier, loses his deeply desired Klotilda because of his inhibitions.

Again and again Busch attempts to show his readers that the farther they stray from their corporeal home base, the greater the likelihood that life will hand them their comeuppance. Pretensions are rife with pitfalls. The artist/author's goal is for his readers to see themselves and the world around them without delusions of grandeur. Thus, although the romantic view of the pure, idyllic qualities of nature is excrementally dispelled by nature itself (the bird) in *Balduin Bählamm, the Obstructed Poet,* Busch a little earlier in the same picture story humorously substitutes for it the truly earthy side of existence as it is proudly and happily affirmed by the peasant Krischan Bopp:

> He puffs his pipe with relish pure, while
> He stands atop his dear manure pile:
> For Krischan Bopp enjoys indeed
> The caressing fragrance of his weed.
>
> Bopp seeks Ulrica Crappifinch,
> A girl who from no task will flinch.
> She's tidying the goats' old stall
> And peace is reigning over all.
> [4:31]

The juxtaposition of such lofty terminology as "caressing fragrance" and "peace . . . reigning over all" with references to a dunghill and a dirty goat pen clearly indicates Busch's intention to parody those nineteenth-century poets who idealized peasant life. Through the gentle humor of his bucolic idyll, Busch points out the potential contentment that any of us could find in this world, if we only were sufficiently relaxed to accept all natural functions unreservedly, as Krischan does, proudly standing on top of his manure pile.

As an extension of this theme, Busch sometimes depicts the way in which natural, uninhibited persons or creatures can gain real profit at the expense of overly refined individuals. Whereas the latter, due to their constant suspicions of the impurities of life, often hesitate and even refuse to partake of the good things offered by this world, the former enjoy themselves unabashedly. This is demonstrated humorously in the poem "Devil's Sausage," in which a dog, with its worldly Epicureanism, triumphs mockingly over an anxiety-ridden clergyman: the latter refuses to eat sausage that he fears may have been made by the devil, but his pet spitz gladly accepts the discarded meat without agonizing about its origin (4:321). Similarly, the person who does not turn away from excrement but rather is interested in it and inspects it may find himself greatly rewarded, as we learn in *Edward's Dream:*

Simple and sensible, his basket filled with the products of his artistic skill, the broom and switch maker comes strolling down the road. As is to be expected in his line of business, he reflects a great deal about the upbringing of the human race. His eyes gaze down at the ground. Consequently he chances to notice an object which the casual observer probably would take to be nothing more than a horse apple in rather squashed circumstances. However, the observant friend of nature, accustomed to investigating any occurrence carefully, realizes immediately what it actually is. It is a brown leather wallet. He glances around, and, since the coast is clear, he picks it up and lets it gently slip down inside his boot. [4:174]

Busch's ironic message, then, is that those of us who gaze haughtily toward heaven will end up wallowing in excrement, whereas those who look earthward may indeed strike gold.

3

Friedrich Dürrenmatt and Siegfried
Lenz: Mirth in the Manure

In her book about Friedrich Dürrenmatt, Elisabeth Brock-Sulzer points out that modern dramatists' tendency to attempt to shock their audiences is a reaction to theatergoers' nonchalance toward classical plays. Drama that has become socially acceptable is, according to Brock-Sulzer, "a disinfected form of art: nonthreatening, soothing, something decorative for one's living space. No wonder that modern dramatists are searching for new ways to create shock effects in order to prevent the public from experiencing this fake euphoria of pleasurable theatergoing."[1] The disengaged audience or reader presents a problem to the satirist in particular, for satire cannot succeed unless theatergoers or readers arouse themselves sufficiently to respond to the author's attacks and concur with her or his judgments. Of course, satirists are keenly aware of the fact that frequently the very people they are attacking compose a good part of their audience. In order to call attention to the world's vices and follies, satirists must have the courage to offend and shock their public; one of the very few means by which most contemporary audiences can still be shocked is the use of scatological elements. Thus, it is not surprising that Friedrich Dürrenmatt makes frequent excremental references in his dramas.

In several of his works, Dürrenmatt includes only small scatological touches; these details are rarely trivial, however, and usually add an important dimension to the plays. For example, there is the makeup containing crocodile droppings worn by Telesia in the radio play *The Trial Concerning the Donkey's Shadow*, which may satirize simultaneously the extremity of human vanity and modern audiences' qualms about the use of ingredients that would be acceptable to a primitive society.[2] Scatological references have a deeper significance in *The Visit*, which deals with physical and moral impurity in the fictitious city of Güllen (in Upper German, *die Gülle* means "liquid manure"); an outhouse is a prominent part of the set in the drama's opening scene.[3] Finally, in *The Meteor*, Dürrenmatt presents the audience with the excremental *Weltanschauung* of his main character, the Nobelist author Wolfgang Schwitter, who declares that his life "stinks to high heaven."[4] Schwitter's inability to cope with the earthy side of human existence is revealed in a scene in the studio where he has chosen to die; the agitated author rips down a clothesline full of diapers, exclaiming, "I can't stand to smell that damp odor of little kids' behinds and pee-pee anymore! I want mustiness, I want the air of the grave, I want the smells of eternity!"[5] The character in the play who points up for Schwitter the contrast between the lofty ideals of art and the stark realities of life is Frau Nomsen, the restroom attendant at the Hotel Bellevue.

In one drama by Dürrenmatt scatology literally moves to center stage: the comedy *Hercules and the Augean Stable*, which appeared first as a radio play and then in a theatrical version in 1963. Although certain differences exist between the two works, the use of excrement is essentially identical in both; therefore this analysis will confine itself to the longer stage version. This parody of one of the less aesthetic tasks of Hercules satirizes many of the shortcomings of Western civilization, using as an example the dung-embedded democracy of Elis. Although piles, even mountains of dung appear on the stage, this drama never turns into a bitter, sarcastic satire of human shortcomings, as was often the case in the works of Busch; Dürrenmatt's satire remains gentle, and the play concludes with the hopeful observation that human effort can turn dung into manure and use it to create new, healthy life. Not surprisingly, the play was strongly rejected by refined urban critics and audiences, who saw nothing but an insult to themselves in Dürrenmatt's use of dung on the stage (see fig. 23). Elisabeth Brock-Sulzer offers a perceptive explanation for this adverse criticism:

City dwellers have a negative relationship with manure. For the farmer and for the gardener it is something precious. City dwellers have lost sight of the fact that the transformation of manure into fertile soil is a basic necessity of human life. . . . Nowadays the splitting of the atom, a transformation that can obliterate humanity, has become socially and theatrically acceptable; in con-

23. "Hercules and His Critics" (Friedrich Dürrenmatt). Copyright © by Diogenes Verlag AG, Zürich.

trast, the former process, which nourishes humanity, seems beneath the dignity of the stage. Seen from the asphalt, manure is simply something that smells bad, nothing more.[6]

The play begins with a prologue in which Polybios, Hercules' private secretary, addresses the audience while the curtain is open, revealing a stage full of dung. The potentially explosive reaction of the audience to the ordure is humorously defused by Polybios's understated remarks: "There is only one answer to the slight displeasure that our stage, which is intended to symbolize the world, may arouse in you, ladies and gentlemen: from a dramatic standpoint, there is no other way. We are trying to tell a story that no one up until the present has ever dared to present on the stage, because of the fact that in this story, if I may express myself plainly, two basic human drives—the desire for cleanliness and the need for art—are at loggerheads" (361).[7] Very slyly, Polybios has first acknowledged human aspirations to cleanliness, which would of course include a revulsion against filth on the stage; however, he then points to the equally important need for art, which, it is implied, cannot always avoid ordure. Once again, Dürrenmatt is presenting the audience with the contrast between art and reality, as he did in *The Meteor*.

Polybios is able to tease the audience because it is clear that they knowingly have come to see a play about the well-known fifth task of Hercules. The viewers cannot claim that they have been unsuspectingly tricked by a misleading title into viewing a scatological play; in fact, they must have come with at least some interest in what was bound to be a somewhat excremental show. Psychologically, Polybios clearly has the upper hand.

Throughout the rest of the prologue, Polybios continues to fluctuate between shocking the audience and assuaging it. For example, at one point he risks offending the theatergoers' finer sensibilities by referring to the manure on the stage as the "primordial landscape of cow chips." This remark is quickly counterbalanced by an appeal to the urban audience's fondness for status symbols (especially those with the patina of the antique) and for highfalutin language: "this legendary compost—to use a more horticultural expression—is nothing less than the fertilizer from antiquity which has been collecting in the nation of Elis for centuries . . . and thus we do have a consolation of sorts: we may be presenting you with manure, but at least it is renowned manure" (361). The description of the stage set as the "primordial landscape of cow chips" pokes fun at the ancient theory that the world was flat by associating this view of the earth with the image of a pressed cake of cow manure; Polybios's allusions to the buildup of the manure over the centuries intensifies the historical jest by conjuring up a gentle scatological parody of the descent of the Western democratic world from its Greek origins. Yesterday, today, and tomorrow, manure—even "legendary compost"—will always be manure. Indeed, by using the term *legendary* Polybios raises the possibility that what the audience is seeing may be myth rather than historical truth, and thus perhaps the play itself is nothing but *Mist* (in the sense of the English expletive "bullshit"). This cynical tone reaches its fullest intensity when Polybios reflects on the fact that, like all human beings, the citizens of Elis sought their "place in the sun"; as to the results of that earnest quest, well, "The condition of our stage says it all" (362).

The fourth scene of the play takes us to the dung-ridden civilization of Elis. The situation is so bad that the town hall is buried under the manure, and thus the members of the national security council are meeting in Augias's stable instead. This caricature of an emergency meeting of a national security council opens with Augias and his ten-man board stuck up to their waists in dung. In this most appropriate setting for a meeting of bureaucrats, they finally acknowledge that an emergency exists:

> First Person: It stinks so bad in our country that it's unbearable.
> Second Person: The dung is piled so high that generally one can see nothing but dung.
> Third Person: Last year one could still see the roofs of the houses, but now one can't even see them anymore.
> Fourth Person: We are totally encrapsulated.
> All: Encrapsulated.
> Augias [*rings the bell*]: Quiet!
>
> [*Silence*]
>
> Fifth Person: But we are encrapsulated.
> Sixth Person: Up to the neck. And above.
> Seventh Person: Begrimed and beshat.
> Eighth Person: Entrenched and enstenched.
> All: Enstenched. [372]

Although the initial result of any emergency meeting of a national security council is bound to be such total unanimity in identifying the dilemma, in a free democracy there is usually dissent regarding the implications and dimensions of the problem. The ninth and tenth council members proceed to offer a number of reassuring thoughts, including a reference to the proud democratic tradition of Elis, in order to offset the negative situation in which the nation finds itself; however, each time the others respond, "But we're still encrapsulated."[8] This refrainlike reminder of the fundamental state of the republic, a sort of scatological litany, has the effect of neutralizing all the attempts to present an optimistic view of Elis's predicament.

In arguing for the rosier interpretation, the ninth and tenth members begin each of their statements with the word *dafür*, the double meaning of which is particularly significant in a line that relates to health: the sentence could be understood as meaning "On the other hand, we are healthy [in spite of being 'encrapsulated']," or it could be interpreted as suggesting, in view of the abundance of manure in Elis, "That's why we are healthy" (372–73). This is the first remark in the main body of the play that could conceivably be seen as referring to dung in a positive way, and it provides a transition to the arguments that will soon appear as to why the manure should not be removed.

The evidence in the drama appears to indicate that good natural manure is not incompatible with a healthy country, a fact that is becoming more and more evident not only in fiction but also in reality, as we discover the detrimental consequences to our environment and to human health of the "clean" new products created by modern technology.

Despite the few reservations, everyone firmly agrees that an end must be put to the dung and the country must be cleaned. New problems arise, however, when the security council decides to stop talking and begin taking the necessary actions to achieve the objective. A bureaucratic solution is suggested, namely, the appointment of a Chief Manure Remover (here Dürrenmatt pokes fun at the Swiss love of titles) who will "radically get rid of the crap." However, it is feared that this solution may present new complications, because it may prove easier to get rid of the manure than of the new official (374). In a more ominous vein, the words "radically get rid of the crap" conjure up images of revolution or a *coup de merde;* furthermore, a threat to the economy also exists, because the citizens would have to neglect their cows while devoting all their energies to cleansing their country, thus causing their butter and cheese exports to drop. A good proletarian answer to this problem is found:

> The Others: Let the rich pay for the dung removal.
> Sixth Person: They produce the most dung! [374]

This is the first indirect indication in the play that the manure is coming not only from the animals but from the people themselves, who are of course the targets of Dürrenmatt's satire.

The answer to all the above dilemmas appears to have been found when the citizens turn to an outsider, the hero Hercules, to do the job for them, thus allowing them to continue to concern themselves with their daily matters. The fact that a Greek hero would agree to perform such a filthy task is humorously exploited by Dürrenmatt. Hercules at first has no intention whatsoever of lowering himself by accepting this task, even though his lover, Dejaneira, sees no such degradation: "It's not important what a person does, but *how* he does it. You are a hero, and thus you will also remove the manure heroically. What you do will never be ridiculous, because it is you who are doing it" (385). Hercules has so many debts that he is almost bankrupt and finally agrees to go to Elis when Dejaneira threatens to bring in the necessary money through prostitution. Dejaneira and Hercules present a humorous contrast in their attitudes toward the dung. She, having already been a successful hetaera, is unabashedly ready to undertake any task without worrying about loss of dignity. This lack of inhibitions Dejaneira shares with Heinrich Böll's Leni in *Group Portrait with Lady*. In contrast, Hercules, the son of Zeus, who has successfully conquered all sorts of powerful and horrible beings, for the first time encounters an almost insuperable opponent in the enormous piles of dung.

In a hilarious and grotesque scene we see the mythological hero arriving in Elis "in an indescribable state" (387). The citizens of Elis, having lived in the dung for hundreds of years, do not notice any defilement of their hero and receive him with great pomp. Hercules answers them by describing his unforgettable trip to Elis in words that clearly bring to mind the Swiss landscape: "I marched through a hell with my entourage. I trudged through horrible swamps, I traversed dreadful passes between piles that loomed toward the heavens, climbed over gigantic chips, startling millions of cackling hens, dung beetles in my beard and my body covered with flies" (388). By inserting verbs normally associated with a military expedition in Hercules' speech, Dürrenmatt perhaps is suggesting a satirical explanation for Switzerland's centuries of peace: because of the inconveniences caused by its abundance of manure, the country may present would-be invading forces with obstacles almost as great as a Russian winter!

Having managed with great difficulty to arrive in the excrement-ridden land of Elis, Hercules, like any respectable hero, is determined to clean out the dung quickly and elevate Elis into a more noble society. He expects to accomplish this without befouling his own grand person, for he has no intention of removing the excrement himself but will redirect two rivers to Elis so that they can flush out the dung. Meanwhile, an unexpected reversal has occurred. Although at first Hercules wanted no part of this assignment, he is now obsessed with the need to cleanse. The citizens of Elis, on the other hand, have begun to have second thoughts. The first definite indication of the change is the scene in which Augias, the president of Elis, finds peace and contentment while he is in the stable milking his cows; the ambience of the barn enables him to relax and forget the problems of government, for, after all, "in our country, too, the worst bullshit is not always produced in the stables" (394). Two humorous but important changes have occurred in Augias. First, he has discovered that it is enjoyable and relaxing to work in an environment of animal manure, and second (and most important), he realizes that the worst ordure is produced by the people themselves. Because it is the citizens' own dung that is to be removed, Augias is now aware of the fact that it will not be an easy task to remove it, and it certainly cannot be done abruptly, for the people are far too attached to their own waste products.

Hercules has no such understanding of human nature and can think only of the immediate flushing out of all the manure. The difference in the attitudes of the two men is underscored as the impatient, increasingly frustrated Hercules arrives at the stable and observes Augias and his farmhand, Kambyses, calmly milking the cows. There is a striking contrast between the raging Hercules, who cannot understand why he is unable to get the necessary permits to flush out the dung, and the composed Augias; while the hero fumes ("A trail of shit leads to you" and "I'm trampling your farming paradise, I'm sending your dung republic to hell"), Augias remains unruffled and invites Hercules to take a seat:

Hercules: Between the cows?
Augias: They won't hurt you. [395]

In this scene Augias is clearly the superior character because of his keen insights into human nature and his patient level-headedness. Hercules, on the other hand, has been reduced to an ineffective bungler whose chief skill is throwing temper tantrums. His agitation becomes most ludicrous when he refuses to sit down among the cows. The extent to which Augias's understanding of psychology overshadows that of Hercules becomes apparent as they speak of the proliferation of bureaucratic departments that demand that Hercules secure a permit from them:

Hercules [*wiping his sweat*]: Even though you're so encrapsulated, you still
    have a bureaucratic officialdom.
Augias: That's precisely why we have it.
Kambyses: We have a Dung Department too.
Augias: You have to appear before them also. I'm sorry, I would have liked to
    spare you all this, but that's what was decided last night by the main national council. [396–97]

This scene in the stable includes several classic components of the theory of the anal personality, and thus it may serve as an illustration of the way in which an author can utilize psychological insights to further the thematic development of a work. Dürrenmatt highlights the contrast between Augias and Hercules and portrays the ambivalence of the citizens of Elis in one fell swoop by having the bureaucrats and the Greek hero dramatize the vacillating behavior patterns typical of persons troubled by anal fixations—with Augias cast as the voice of sanity. According to Ernest Jones, the person with an anal character structure alternates between procrastination and action, a tableau that mirrors the small child's wish to postpone and retain its bowel movement until it can no longer resist what one might term "the urge to purge." Thus one type of behavior of the anally fixated adult is motivated by retentive tendencies and may be described as "the inhibitory phase of inactivity, brooding, delay, and postponement."[9] The leaders of Elis, so well understood by Augias, illustrate this polarity. Reluctance to act, according to Jones, alternates with the desire to rid oneself of the task at hand, as indicated by "a spell of feverish and concentrated activity," a plunging "into the work with a desperate and often almost a ferocious energy which nothing is allowed to thwart, any interference being keenly resented."[10] Hercules plays this role to perfection, and the impediment that he finds so annoying and perplexing is the bureaucracy of Elis. The leaders' hierarchy of officialdom is, however, consistent with their anal fixations, and Augias reveals by his perceptive "That's precisely why we have it" that he is well aware of the passion that such persons have for organizing their lives. Seen from the perspective of classical psychoanalysis, being "encrapsulated" and being highly bureaucratized are not contradictory but compatible characteristics.

The playwright's use of human psychology adds to his audience's growing impression that the removal of the citizens' own dung is the crux of the problem. With this realization, Hercules' failure seems inevitable, because it is extremely unlikely that the citizens will tolerate a hero who not only speaks of removing but actually undertakes the flushing away of their most personal contribution to this world. Augias is aware that one cannot bring about change in a democracy, or in the human psyche, with a swift and powerful flush. He realizes that progress can be achieved only by first accepting the piles of excrement and then by patiently finding some beneficial use for them. The time when heroes could quickly change the course of the world is past, and Hercules, together with all heroes, has become an anachronism; furthermore, he is amusingly depicted here as a person suffering from the same neurotic attitudes toward excrement shared by many human beings rather than as an omnipotent colossus from the pages of classical literature.

Augias's prediction of the people's refusal to part from their own dung comes true in the twelfth scene, at the reconvening of the national security council in Augias's stable. Although all of the ministers, in the typical fashion of politicians, first make assurances that they are still solidly in favor of the dung removal, they then proceed to bring up a number of possible complications. What is particularly ludicrous is the fact that the minister of culture, Pentheus vom Säuliboden, voices the first concerns. He speaks of great art treasures buried under the dung and forsees the possibility of their destruction by the hydraulic pressure of the manure removal process (411). Never before had the citizens of Elis spoken of a cultural legacy hidden under the ordure, but now, when threatened, they sublimate their love of their own excrement into a love of buried art treasures. The fact that they really are concerned about the loss of their dung rather than the loss of any art works becomes clear when Kadmos von Käsingen suggests the possibility that there really is no such artistic treasure trove under the dung:

> Kadmos von Käsingen: In that case, gentlemen, the dung removal would be a great misfortune, yes, really a betrayal of our most sacred possessions.
> The Others: Betrayal?
> Kadmos von Käsingen: Whatever hope the nation might have of finding them under the manure would go down the drain. [412]

The clear implication here is that excrement *is* the cultural heritage of Elis, and the sly comparison of art to the production of feces adds to the satirical irony of this scene.

With these developments, Hercules' attempts to rid Elis of its ordure are doomed. It is impossible to cleanse or exalt a civilization that is so deeply rooted in and tied to its dung. The meeting in Augias's stable ends with an appropriate decision in favor of excrement:

> Sixth Person: Let's appoint commissions that will test whether once the manure Is removed the depth of our religion will be eliminated.
> Seventh Person: Or whether the numbers of the livestock will be decimated.
> Eighth Person: The women of Elis lured into excesses.
> Tenth Person: The rich impoverished.
> First Person: Our economic stability destroyed.
> Second Person: The villages urbanized.
> Third Person: The spiritual life of our children atrophied.
> Fourth Person: Because we will be lacking the primal congeniality of the manure. [414–15]

The citizens have become so accustomed to their centuries-old dung that they feel comfortably at home in it and, in their anal retentiveness, do not want their surroundings altered any more than a small child wants its diapers changed. Attachment to dung thus carries the day in Elis, and the hero hired to remove it becomes a circus performer in the end to avoid bankruptcy. He never does carry out his task in Elis but leaves for his next assignment, which appears no more promising than the present one: he is asked to rid a northern country of birds that produce particularly disagreeable droppings (424).

The final message of this play is not so pessimistic as it may seem. Although the ordure has successfully defeated the hero and is openly embraced by almost everyone in Elis, there is some hope in the distant future. During Hercules' disgruntlement and departure, Augias has been patiently and diligently at work. He has succeeded in turning manure into soil and is growing a flower garden among the excrement. Augias himself explains the meaning of this garden to his son:

> I am a politician, my son, not a hero, and politics cannot perform miracles. It is as weak as human beings themselves, a reflection of their frailty, and destined to fail again and again. It can never promote goodness if we ourselves do not do what is good. And that is why I did something good. I changed dung into humus. These are difficult times, in which one can do so little for the world, but one should at least make the small contribution of doing one's own thing. You aren't able to bestow the blessing of brightening up the world, but you can create the right conditions so that grace—when it comes—finds in you a spotless mirror for its light. [428]

The imagery of illumination recalls the prologue, and the point is made that one can find one's "place in the sun" without a Herculean sanitization program; ironically, the "condition of our stage," as decried by Polybios, can in fact provide a hospitable setting for the improvement of human life.[11] Thus, the end of *Hercules and the Augean Stable*, not unlike Goethe's *Faust*, presents us with an affirmation of humanity's continual slow striving. Faust's last deed was also that of gaining soil for the future of humanity. Although the time for traditional heroes is over, individual persons still may have a positive impact on the world; according to Dürrenmatt's scenario, however, the bringer of change will not be the transcendent *Übermensch* but rather the life-affirming *Mensch*.

SIEGFRIED LENZ, in his gently satirical short story collection *So Tender Was Suleyken*, uses scatological elements in a manner similar to Dürrenmatt's. Many of the lusty peasants who appear in the stories, as well as the Southeast Prussian towns in which they live, bear names with excremental connotations, such as Hamilkar Schass, Edmund Vortz, Kulkaken, and Schissomir; these appellations are based on the roots *Scheiß* ("shit"), *Furz* ("fart"), and *Kacke* ("crap"). The behavior of the characters reflects their earthiness, as when two peasants on their way to market in "Schissomir's Great Day" urinate together in a spirit of camaraderie (59).[12]

Reminiscent of *Hercules and the Augean Stable*, excrement acts as a stimulus to action in the story "The Racing Shoemaker." The weakling Karl Kuckuck has almost lost a swimming contest to husky Valentine Zoppek when a floating cake of horse manure electrifies him; unlike the approach–avoidance conflict in Elis, this is a case of unambivalent flight, as Kuckuck's horror of excrement elevates his adrenalin level, causing the race to end in a tie. Just as Busch depicted chamber pots that took on a life of their own, so Lenz personifies the "horse dropping, which considered it to be its natural right to swim around the horses' watering place" (89). Lenz builds the humor of the scene by imparting such vitality (not to mention a determined "personality") to the horse manure that it, rather than Zoppek, becomes Kuckuck's chief opponent. Despite Kuckuck's efforts to flee, the manure, "once it had gotten into motion, did not think much of the idea of being shaken off; it skimmed along close on Karl Kuckuck's heels and followed him doggedly through whirlpools and eddies" (90). Thus, thanks to his own inhibitions and the lively clump of excrement, Kuckuck is able to equal the efforts of a man who ordinarily would have easily defeated him.

Particularly rampant with scatology is the story "So-called Intellectual Servitude." In this narrative School Superintendent Christopher Ratz, the epitome of all authoritarian, obsessively clean persons, confronts a sly, uninhibited, earthy teacher and his class of boys, who share their teacher's characteristics in every way. The humor of the story lies in the contrast between these two personality types, with Ratz finally being defeated by excrement just as Hercules was. Lenz begins by introducing us to the cunning teacher Eugene Boll, who believes in learning by doing and teaches geography by having his students rake through the terrain of the manure pile adjacent to his own stable (111). This technique of teaching his boys by the use of practical (and excremental) example, which surely will leave a most lasting impression in the minds of the students and which not altogether accidentally happens to benefit Boll as well, is put to use again when Boll decides "to have them deepen his wee latrine—with the goal of giving his students a critical overview of nature" (112). Because no one can deny that the toilet is an important part of life, Boll's rationale is not really invalid, and thus Lenz is able to laugh at the world's excrementality without allowing the reader to feel justifiably offended. The use of the diminutive "wee latrine" (*Latrinchen*) is also most effective, because it sounds so endearing that it dissolves the threatening or offensive connotations of the word *latrine*. The boys, who in a Buschean way are totally unaffected by the irrational fears of excrement felt by the "civilized" adults, quickly accept the teacher's invitation and several are lowered into the pit.

Just at this most undignified moment, Superintendent Ratz arrives for an inspection of the class, accompanied by a skinny, bespectacled lady (an excellent caricature of the prudishness of the establishment). Instead of panicking at this turn of events, Boll manages to outwit the straitlaced Ratz with a series of brilliant, humorous maneuvers that Lenz presents in rapid succession. Having been warned by one of his boys of Ratz's approach, Boll immediately lines up the pupils; by the time Ratz actually arrives, they are in the middle of a song in praise of spring. The quick-witted Boll presents a sharp contrast to the thorough, investigative, and cautious superintendent, who sniffs first the air and then the students, announcing dryly: "The pupils . . . they stink." Quickly concluding that the setting is the cause of this unpleasant aroma, Ratz questions the wisdom of choosing this locale for a celebration of spring: "why then, if I may ask, does this have to take place next to the wee latrine? Why not, as would be more proper, in one of God's beautiful open meadows?" (114). One can sense the outrage concealed behind these deliberate words, but because he is speaking in the presence of a group of children, Ratz is not free to let his anger erupt with thunder and lightning; instead, he is a prisoner of his own obsession with propriety. Furthermore, the presence of a lady is an inhibiting factor for a puritanical person. It is particularly amusing that Ratz, too, must use the diminutive "wee latrine" in front of the boys.

Boll, however, is not at all intimidated and has an immediate and appropriate answer ready: "The boys . . . they are tired from intellectual servitude. And besides, if I may be permitted to say so, they have grown accustomed to these conditions. No matter where one places them, they sing and greet spring" (114). Ratz, of course, cannot accept such a healthy, uninhibited attitude; he feels impelled to convince the teacher of the dangers of filth, without, however, being able to say what these dangers are: "But nevertheless, Instructor Boll, one should not seek out stench-ridden environs. For the pupils, upon my honor, could suffer harm as a result" (114). The "upon my honor" should have

brought the teacher into line, but instead a far worse shock awaits
Ratz. At this precise moment, loud noises are heard from below ground
and Ratz, who is beginning to show signs of strain, discovers the boys
in the pit of the latrine. The following exchange ensues among Ratz,
Boll, and the lady:

> Called Ratz, "What sort of state of affairs is this? I see various pupils in dis-
> tress. Why, if you please, are they poking about in the wee latrine?"
>
> Eugene Boll, our teacher, sadly shrugged his shoulders and spoke: "Pos-
> sibly, Mr. Superintendent, one of them lost his pants in it."
>
> "But such a pair of pants," the distraught little lady joined in, "would no
> longer be fit to wear."
>
> "A pair of pants is a pair of pants," said Boll. "But perhaps there are, let's
> say, ten pennies in them. Not to mention a pear that could be in them, or a
> red-cheeked little apple. The students doubtless have their reasons. I know
> these youngsters." [115–16]

In addition to Boll's incredible ability to come up with an immediate
explanation for even the most incriminating evidence, the humor is
heightened in this case by Boll's audacity in linking a highly respected
symbol of wholesomeness, the red-cheeked apple, with excrement (a
connection that is established in colloquial German by the use of the
word *Roßapfel* to describe horse manure) and in implying that this
"little apple" has not suffered at all from its supposed fall into the
latrine pit. By suggesting that the boys have jumped into the pit to recover such an apple or pear, Boll is playing two characteristics of anal
personalities, frugality and disgust at filth, against each other; Ratz
and the lady would feel forced to commend boys who would risk anything to keep a nutritious piece of food from being wasted, but they
must inwardly recoil at the idea of eating fruit that has been sullied by
human sewage. Boll has shocked and confused the visitors so much
that they are incapable of pursuing the matter any further. Instead,
they pull the boys out and bring them all back to the schoolhouse.

One would expect that as a result of the change of location from the
manure pile to the classroom Ratz would now gain the upper hand
and take control of the situation. This does not happen, however, and
the superintendent continues to be roasted slowly on a scatological
spit. Perhaps in order to gain revenge for his earlier unsettling experience, Ratz proceeds to test the boys. The second boy he questions is
Titus Anatol Plock, and the nature of the query reveals the extent of
the impression that the scene of the latrine pit made on Ratz's subconscious mind: "Tell me, Titus Anatol Plock, where and under what con-

ditions a gentleman jumps into the water in order to dive for a ring? And include the full last name of the poet." After fifteen minutes of careful thought Titus's face lights up and he replies, "Dear sir . . . my seatmate is breaking wind, and in addition I've gotten a splinter in my toe. It's bleeding, and therefore I can't think straight" (117). Just as in the works of Busch, even the noblest thoughts are scatologically ridiculed here. Because the offensive remark is followed slyly by the reference to the student's pain from the splinter in his toe, Titus is saved from any further questions, as the sympathetic nature of the skinny lady (as well as her desire to conceal her embarrassment) causes her to busy herself with the careful removal of the splinter.

The narrator, one of the boys in the class, continues humorously, "Whoever thinks that at this point it was all over has underestimated the boundless patience of Superintendent Ratz." Ratz now calls on Joseph Jendritzki, a boy with a blue milk can next to his seat, whom he asks to tell him something about clouds (118). The adroit Joseph goes to the window and stares at the sky. Then he climbs out the window and into a chestnut tree and continues his contemplation. Finally he returns with a bunch of chestnuts and everyone smiles at him in anticipation of a good answer. Just as he is ready to speak, Joseph looks down and shouts, "Dear sir . . . someone has peed all over my milk can. It must have happened while I was sitting in the tree for the purpose of observation." As great confusion breaks out, the totally nonplussed Ratz excuses himself "for just a wee minute" (119).

Caught in a continuum of scatological humiliations that even Busch would find hard to surpass, Ratz does not seem to want to return: "Well, when distant cries for help rang out, Instructor Eugene Boll went out and found the superintendent locked up in the wee latrine" (119). Thus, the ultimate humorous reversal has occurred: Ratz himself has become entrapped in the latrine, where his own excrementality is publicly exposed. Just as in the cases of Dürrenmatt's Hercules and many of Busch's characters, Ratz's filth phobia turns out to be his undoing. The final comical blow is delivered by Boll, as he demonstrates to Ratz that the newly installed bolt jams easily and suggests that the door should be lifted a little. In the course of the demonstration, the bolt becomes inordinately jammed. Knocking, pushing, and drumming with their fists on the "wee door" all prove useless, and the two restroom captives fittingly take a seat and ponder their fate until it is evening. Their release is achieved only when the refined lady overcomes her inhibitions enough to unlatch the door of the latrine containing the two men. Thoroughly shaken, the lady presses for a speedy departure (119). It is not surprising that this class of boys never faced another inspection. As Busch and Dürrenmatt knew, there is no greater weapon against pretentiousness or excessive inhibitions than "manure power"; here, once again, a straitlaced stereotype has inadvertently become a prisoner of the privy.

4

Scatology and Self-knowledge in

A Man and his Dog by Thomas Mann

Persons who find the excretory processes disgusting and would like to deny their very existence are among the favorite targets of such satirical authors as Busch, Dürrenmatt, and Lenz. However, German literature and art reveal far more complex attitudes toward scatology than those portrayed in the works of the satirists. Positive and negative views can in fact be held simultaneously by one person; they may come to light in the form of approach–avoidance conflicts, or they can exist fairly comfortably side by side, as is the case in Thomas Mann's 1918 novella *A Man and his Dog*.

In this work, the genteel and fastidious Mann does not allow traditional prudery to impede the detached, almost scientific manner in which the narrator observes his dog, Bashan. Further tempering the narrator's outlook is his tendency to take a fond, romantic view of peasant life: the noble savage, the good earth, the rich manure.

Throughout the novella the narrator speaks of "hunting blood and peasant stock" (219)[1] in his descriptions of Bashan. The narrator's family first found their pet in the kitchen of a mountain inn, where he had been existing on a diet of garbage—specifically, potato parings. Because the imagery of refuse is closely related to that of the body's waste products, it is only a stone's throw to Mann's use of scatology to point up the dog's lowly origins. One recalls Busch's peasants' march with the chamber pot trophy when reading of the family's trip home ("scarcely a triumphal procession") with Bashan, who had to make frequent stops because of "an apparently chronic diarrhœa" (227). The refinement and civilized scruples of the narrator and his family become apparent when we learn that they felt it necessary to form a circle around Bashan so that the villagers would not observe his embarrassing dilemma.

The dichotomy of the natural or primitive and the civilized or cultivated permeates *A Man and his Dog;* but instead of a conflict one generally finds a peaceful coexistence of the two. One sees this even in the trees in the narrator's neighborhood: the ornamental shrubs and "rows of French poplars standing erect in their sterile masculinity" share the terrain with the ash trees, "aborigines" that grow "like weeds" (246–47). The contrast is even more striking in the narrator's comparison of Bashan with his previous dog, Percy, whom he describes as a "harmless, feebleminded aristocrat" (224). Bashan, on the other hand, has a peasant soul. Percy was delicate, but Bashan is hardy; Percy was self-disciplined, but Bashan lacks any inhibitions. The controlled, fragile Percy spent his nights indoors, but Bashan, who suffers from a weakness of the bladder, must of necessity be left outdoors even on the coldest nights.

The narrator takes pains not to pass judgment. Such differences are part of nature, and Bashan is nothing if not natural: "Whatever seems to him natural and right and necessary, that he will do" (257). Maintaining his role as a cool, detached observer, the narrator describes in gruesomely clinical detail Bashan's devouring of a mouse; the narrator feels "rather chilled by what I have seen, yet inwardly amused by the crude humours of life. The event was in the natural order of things" (268). Although we perceive not only in the content of the novella but in the precision, one might even say elegance, of its literary style that the narrator represents the civilized, fastidious side of the two polarities, he rarely loses his objectivity. His preference does show through in both the tone and the wording of a remark about Bashan's early days with his family; the dog had a tendency to get lost in the forest, "where, being quite on his own, he would certainly have reverted to the condition of his wild forebears. Our care preserved him from this dark fate, we held him fast upon his civilized height and to his position as the comrade of man, which his race in the course of millennia has achieved" (229).

His lofty view of humankind does not prevent the highly civilized narrator from being intrigued by the "natural" world that Bashan reveals to him; he wonders at it, admires it, approves of it. On their morning walks, the dog jumps on its master and slavers all over his arm; instead of expressing disgust, the narrator describes this routine as Bashan's "Morgentoilette,"[2] his way of ridding his coat of straws.

The narrator describes with fascination and meticulous detail the routines that Bashan follows when he is in a state of boredom; when all else fails, there is one last pastime:

> He can go down again and lift his leg against one of the little formal arbor-vitæ trees that flank the rose-bed—it is the one to the right that suffers from his attentions, wasting away so that it has to be replanted every year. He does go down then, and performs this action, not because he needs to, but just to pass the time. He stands there a long time, with very little to show for it, however—so long that the hind leg in the air begins to tremble and he has to give a little hop to regain his balance. On four legs once more he is no better off than he was. [234]

By avoiding the use of the word *urinate* (or even coarser terms) and depicting only the motions of Bashan's legs, Mann gives the impression of a sort of canine ballet, albeit one that is universally comprehensible. The stylistic restraint of this passage reveals clearly the point of view of the narrator and contrasts sharply with the artless indelicacy of an animal who does not hesitate to relieve himself on shrubbery that is as carefully, formally structured (Mann uses the adjective *pyramidenförmig*,[3] suggesting one of the wonders of human achievement) as the narrator's prose.

Even more interesting to Bashan's owner than his pet's methods of interrupting tedium are the rituals that dogs go through in their encounters with each other, tokens of a primitive world that human beings cannot hope to understand. His description of a typical confrontation between the "peasant" (238) Bashan and a fenced-in dog reminds one of the two peasants in *So Tender Was Suleyken* who urinated together on their way to market: "He advances, then, and with a modest and inscrutable bearing performs that rite which he knows will soothe and appease the other—even if temporarily—so long as the stranger performs it too, though whining and complaining in the act" (241). Similar tribal "laws" (240) are in effect when an unleashed dog approaches Bashan, and both pause at a tree "to perform the accustomed rite" (242). As is suggested by his use of the word *rite*, the narrator assigns an almost supernatural significance to these scatological acts: "He is under a spell, he is bound to the other dog, they are bound to each other with some obscure and equivocal bond which may not be denied. . . . they stop flank to flank and sniff under each other's tails" (243).

Again, as in so many other cases, scholars have paid little attention to the scatological elements in this work. The scatological rite that

Bashan performs when meeting with another dog is the one excremental allusion in the novella that has received a modicum of critical notice. Joachim Müller, who like many scholars sees *A Man and his Dog*
merely as an animal story, very briefly mentions this mysterious "rite."
However, Müller does not even describe the act and includes it only as
part of a highly superficial analysis in which he sees the passage in
question as indicating a degree of alienation between human being
and pet; thus, such rites stand apart from the empathy the owner feels
for the dog and the latter's adaptability to human ways, leaving the
owner "bewildered."[4] Müller's reluctance to risk dirtying his hands
(and hence perhaps vulgarizing his prose) with a more frank analysis
ties in with his grandiloquent interpretation of what Mann is attempting to depict in the novella: "The noble animal with masculine dignity
and distinguished bearing, perfect nature in beautiful simplicity, the
dog as a person and as a citizen in the domestic realm—that is the
goal of the narrative."[5]

Frank X. Braun's comments on the same scene are equally sketchy.
Braun sees the narrator's attempt to describe the ritual that the latter
finds so curious to be a sign of inconsistency:

> The temptation to analyze the behavior of his four-footed companion at times
> leads Thomas Mann into inconsistencies. Thus, for instance, he will, by way of
> introduction, carefully point out the chasm of communication that separates us
> from the canine. He will then describe with subtle earthiness that frightful
> circumstantiality attendant on the meeting of dog with dog. Admitting on the
> one hand his inability to enter into the feelings and behavior of the partici-
> pants, or to understand the tribal laws which govern their strange ritual, he will
> proceed, most inconsistently, to interpret the canine encounter analytically.
> And when, in doing so, Mann endows these dogs with such emotions as men-
> tal anguish and distress, with profound embarrassment and scruples of con-
> science, he very definitely enters into the realm of anthropocentric
> assumptions.[6]

Braun, accusing Mann of anthropocentricity, and Müller, similarly
concluding that Mann portrays the "dog as a person," fall short of the
mark in their interpretations of the novella. The narrator's real preoccupation is not so much with the human characteristics of his dog as
with the primitive tendencies in his own psyche, which are at times
aroused by his observations of Bashan and for which the dog may even
be seen as a symbol. The fact that the narrator finds Bashan's scatological rites cryptic is inevitable, for the former is a product of a highly
advanced civilization; his game determination to describe the dog's

acts is not an inconsistency but simply an attempt to probe the workings of the fascinating natural world from which he regrettably finds himself at some distance.

At times scatology loses its mystical fascination for the narrator and becomes downright unpleasant. We have already commented on the diarrhea of Bashan's earlier days, an ailment perhaps induced by the same sort of anxiety as that felt by a pheasant flushed by Bashan, which "drops its excrement into the brush and takes flight" (268). An even greater repugnance was felt by the narrator toward the discharge of blood that once issued from Bashan's nose or throat. This emission, according to the narrator, caused the dog to revert to the dismal physical and spiritual state in which he had originally been found. Eventually, the narrator took Bashan to a veterinary clinic, which he characterizes as a sort of dung heap of unhealthy animals presided over by a keeper, "busy with rake and shovel" (272).

In the passage on the veterinary clinic, one becomes aware of what might be termed a "secondary scatology" that may appear in the writings of an author as subtle as Mann: the depiction of the type of unpleasantly oppressive atmosphere that stifles the senses in late sequences of *Death in Venice*. The sense of smell plays at least a minor role in *A Man and his Dog* as well, and thus the narrator observes in the veterinary clinic the odor of the excrement of sick animals coupled with the inevitable human efforts to cover up the smell of ordure: "The medium-sized room I found myself in reminded me of a carnivorahouse—a similar atmosphere prevailed. Only here the menagerie odour seemed to be kept down by various sweetish-smelling medicinal fumes—a disturbing and oppressive combination" (272). The mixed aroma lingered in the dog's coat long after his return from the clinic and wore off very gradually as the dispirited pet was subjected to many baths. Bashan, who in good health enjoyed sniffing under another dog's tail, failed to display his former inquisitiveness and joie de vivre for a long time after his incarceration in the sickening, putrid atmosphere of the infirmary.

The odor that resulted from Bashan's hospitalization stands in contrast to other aromas that the narrator observes in the course of the novella. There is the smell of the sheep manure on the idyllic eastern slope where the narrator strolls with his dog; the narrator finds this scent "strong enough to me, though not unpleasant" (253). In the wilder region of the river, where nature is not so romanticized and the gulls scoop up "unappetizing-looking morsels" from the brown streams of the sewer pipes (282), "the water is deep, it has a smell of decay—that is the Lagoon, that is Venice" (261).

Nevertheless, the odors of nature are preferable to those of human beings: after guests have visited the narrator's home, he finds that "the breath of the strangers still hovers on the air" and he feels the need to step outdoors and inhale deeply. The narrator describes his process of restoration in terms reminiscent of the Buschean "Oben und Unten" dichotomy that one finds so often in German literature: "I look up into the sky, I gaze into the tender depths of the masses of green foliage, and peace returns once more and dwells within my spirit" (263). Unlike the cynical Busch, however, Mann appears to be suggesting that a balance of the spiritual and the material may be not only a healthy outlook but also an achievable goal—at least at some moments in life.

The narrator's quest to identify with and involve himself in the world of nature interestingly parallels Bashan's obsession with the hunt. The dog's absorption in digging rodents out of their holes causes him to immerse himself in filth, and by the time he finally admits defeat, one finds him "with soil sticking to his nose, and his legs black to the shoulder" (267). The 1961 German television film production of *A Man and his Dog* accentuates this process; the camera zooms in on the dog's hindquarters as he kicks clumps of dirt directly into the lens.[7] Though his quests for game are futile, except for the occasional capture of an inept mouse, Bashan has at least proved himself in his owner's eyes. At one point, the narrator, when describing himself and Bashan, uses the phrase "for hunter and hound"; he quickly corrects his terminology, however, to "for the hunter and his master" (282). When he teases Bashan for his lack of success, the narrator asks himself if he is not doing so out of feelings of guilt because he was not man enough to shoot the hare, as many other masters of hunting dogs would have done. A certain self-loathing because of his own overly refined temperament seems to arise from the narrator's continued fascination with Bashan's untamable nature.

The narrator's guilt over his own excessive degree of civilization reaches a climax in the scene in which the narrator and Bashan observe a hunter shoot a duck. The sportsman strikes the narrator as merely picturesque, but to Bashan, the dog from hunting stock, it is a moment of revelation in which his whole body seems "to be crying out: What! What! What was that? Wait a minute, in the devil's name! *What was that?* He . . . listened within himself and heard things that had always been there. . . . I got the impression that he was trying to look at himself, trying to ask: What am I? Who am I? Is this me?" (287). On their way home, the narrator senses that Bashan views the hunter as more manly and as a more desirable master than himself. His reply to the dog is defensive, angry, condescending, and, for a person fond of formal diction, a bit colloquial: "Get out with you! Go to your new friend with the blunderbuss and attach yourself to him! . . . he is only a man in velveteens, to be sure, not a gentleman, but in your eyes he may be one; perhaps he is the right master for you, and I honestly recommend you to suck up to him—now that he has put a flea in your ear to go with the others." In this moment of emotion an allusion to filth comes to the surface when the narrator suggests to Bashan that the hunter may not have a license and thus if the dog joins him they may "both get into fine trouble some day at your dirty game" (289). In the original German the wording is more fastidiously ironic, as Mann uses the words "bei eurem sauberen Treiben";[8] clearly, at this point the narrator is anxious to side with civilization rather than with the noble savage.

Six months after this crisis in the master–dog relationship, things supposedly return to normal. The reader, however, now faces the question of whether the narrator is so highly civilized and deeply inhibited that he can never regain his original state or, on the other hand, is at heart the "natural man" who earlier referred to Bashan as "mein Zuhause" ("my home"),[9] suggesting that his pet is in fact a sort of guide dog who leads him back to his authentic inner self. Is a person's true identity the one that emerges in moments of emotional intensity or the one with which he or she feels comfortable the other 90 percent of the time—or perhaps a combination of the two? The scatological attitudes revealed in *A Man and his Dog* supply at least part of the answer to Bashan's, the narrator's, and ultimately the reader's questions, "What am I? Who am I?"

5

"Unideal Nature"

The peaceful coexistence of the "natural" and the "civilized" had been under attack in certain German literary and artistic quarters for some time prior to Mann's writing of *A Man and his Dog* in 1918. The early years of the twentieth century were marked by a rebellion on the part of some artists and writers against prevailing aesthetic standards and the tastes of bourgeois society; changing views of both human nature and the external world figured prominently in the upheaval.

Part of this process was a revolt against what were perceived as the stylistic niceties of Jugendstil art. Werner Hofmann states, "[Jugendstil] maintained a closed system of aesthetic regimentation, an island of beauty shutting itself off from 'The Other Side' about which Kubin wrote his novel of that name. Beyond this retreat blew the winds of disorder and decay."[1] Artists and writers who believed that art should be primarily truthful rather than ennobling or aesthetically pleasing sought to depict human beings and nature more realistically. Their aim was not a photographic realism but rather a frank portrayal of life in which ugliness and squalor would not be denied. In their pursuit of candor, a number of artists and writers made use of scatological references—not surprisingly, for if one is going to attempt a blunt depiction of life in its entirety, one cannot omit such basic physiological functions as the processes of elimination. Karl Kraus has offered the following illustration of the standpoint of these "honest" artists: "Adolf Loos and I, he verbally and I linguistically, have simply shown that there is a difference between an urn and a chamber pot, and it is precisely this difference that enables culture to grow. The others, however, the Positivists, either use the urn as a chamber pot or use the chamber pot as an urn."[2]

The targets of the rebellion extended beyond the art and literature of the day to society in general, as Martin Esslin has described: "In Germany more than elsewhere the artistic temperament was driven into opposition to the established way of life. Respectable society was not only stuffy, stupid, and hypocritical, it was, above all, utterly without grace or wit, ugly and unaesthetic."[3] Repelled by both aesthetic standards and the bourgeois life style, these young writers and artists turned to an examination of nature. Here, too, they were disappointed. They found the world that the romanticists and even many of their contemporaries had idealized to be malevolent and harsh, a dung heap riddled with decay. Human nature fared no better in their view, and they often portrayed human beings not as noble creatures but as apelike, instinct-driven barbarians.

The nineteenth-century work that anticipates more than any other the frank and honest view of man and nature demanded by Karl Kraus and those who shared his opinions is Georg Büchner's *Woyzeck*. This drama defied aesthetic standards, the social milieu, and traditional views of humanity and nature just as startlingly as did many literary and artistic works in the early twentieth century, and it served as an extremely strong influence on the creative minds of that era. As Max Spalter has noted, "among modern movements, it [*Woyzeck*] anticipates epic theater by projecting characters and situations which challenge our total response to bourgeois society and bourgeois attitudes toward life."[4] That Büchner shared the twentieth-century rebels' dislike of bourgeois facades and values is evident in the first scene of *Woyzeck:* the Captain has just told the lowly protagonist that he is lacking in virtue, to which Woyzeck replies: "if I could be a gentleman, and if I could have a hat and a watch and a cane, and if I could talk refined, I'd want to be virtuous, all right. There must be something beautiful in virtue, Captain, sir. But I'm just a poor good-for-nothing!" (40).[5]

In Woyzeck we find a "natural" man who is an outsider to society's conventions. Although he is more sensitive, thoughtful, and imaginative than the other characters in the play, Woyzeck nevertheless has not lost touch with his instincts and is brought even closer to an animalistic state by the Doctor's use of him as a guinea pig for medical experiments. As a consequence of his "naturalness" or his debilitated physical state or both, Woyzeck does not hesitate to relieve himself in public if that is what his body urges, as we learn in the "At the Doctor's" scene:

Doctor: I saw it all, Woyzeck. You pissed on the street! You were pissing on the wall like a dog. And here I'm giving you three groschen a day plus board!

> That's terrible, Woyzeck! The world's becoming a terrible place, a terrible
> place!
> Woyzeck: But, Doctor, sir, when Nature . . .
> Doctor: When Nature? When Nature? What has Nature to do with it? Did I or did
> I not prove to you that the *musculus constrictor vesicae* is controlled by your
> will? Nature! Woyzeck, man is free! In Mankind alone we see glorified the
> individual's will to freedom! And you couldn't hold your water! [47]

Although critics generally have a tendency to overlook references to the excremental in literature, the scatology in *Woyzeck* is so blatant and so significant to the thematic development of the drama that it is virtually impossible to ignore. Some critics have been more willing than others to sully their hands with an analysis of this scene. Spalter briefly states that "At the Doctor's" reveals Büchner's "revulsion" at a "kind of scientism" and then, using the distancing effect of a footnote as one would the proverbial ten-foot pole, adds, "Juxtaposition of the process of urination with such idealistic pronouncements tells its own story."[6] One finds a slightly more detailed examination of just what story is being told in Herbert Lindenberger's study, *Georg Büchner;* Lindenberger interprets Woyzeck's urinating in public as a negative assertion of his "naturalness" in response to the Doctor's cruelty: "His urinating against the wall is a reaction analogous to that shown by a cat which bites him as he picks it up after the doctor has thrown it out of a window." Furthermore, observing the comic implications of the scene, Lindenberger feels that this is one of a number of instances in which Büchner presents Woyzeck as a sort of Charlie Chaplin figure in order to avoid sentimentality: "[Woyzeck's] method of defending himself against the doctor ('But Doctor, when Nature calls . . .'), despite the cruelty we feel in the doctor's treatment of him has an indubitably comic effect for us. To the degree that he is continually beaten down he has something of the external clown about him."[7]

A more detailed and perceptive analysis of this scene is found in Ronald Hauser's *Georg Büchner.* Hauser reveals a better understanding than Lindenberger of the free will–involuntary nature motif, and his interpretation stands in contrast to Lindenberger's suggestion that Woyzeck's public urination is a deliberate act of vengeance against the Doctor:

> The most fundamental error of the knower (the "scientist") comes into focus
> here. Surely there is no one alive who cannot feel, within their own organs,
> the ludicrous wrongness of the Doctor's "proof" of the human will's control over
> the *musculus constrictor vesicae*. Shocking as it is on the stage even today,
> Büchner could not have chosen a clearer symbol to drive home the point of his

argument. No amount of reasoning could better demonstrate man's precarious position vis-à-vis nature. Although the human will certainly does exercise some control over the muscle under discussion, the strict limitations of these powers are evident to all. Behind the Doctor's chatter about will power, a rather precise, almost painful message comes across the boards. Rather than making man the master over nature, the human intellect—the very quality which distinguishes him from the "lower" animals like the dogs "pissing on the wall"—is only strong enough to bring him into a most unfortunately disharmonious relationship with it. The image of man that emerges is that of a rebelliously stubborn, but still heavily shackled, slave who sometimes, in his fantasies, mistakenly thinks that, simply because he has the power to think, *he* is the master and *nature* the servant.[8]

Hauser has touched upon a number of the purposes that scatology serves in this scene. Surely Büchner, like the contemporary German underground writers, included scatological details for their shock value; it was necessary for him to use strong words and images in order to convey the intensity of his moral outrage. This ribald element was, of course, an affront to bourgeois society. Lindenberger was correct in sensing comedy in this scene, but there is not only the gentle humor of Woyzeck as a bumbling clown but also the sharply satirical portrait of the Doctor (considered to be a parody of one of Büchner's medical school professors).[9]

As Hauser implies, the excremental references help the audience to identify with the character of Woyzeck. There is no question that scatology has a universality that is virtually unrivaled. Not everyone may have a love affair or commit a murder, although it is common to feel the urge to do so at one time or another; but everyone must take part in the processes of elimination. Thus, though the audience may be shocked on a conscious level, subconsciously they must side with Woyzeck rather than with the Doctor, who might be characterized from the audience's point of view as a sort of super toilet-training figure of the kind they learned to resent, if not to hate, when they were children. Strikingly, Büchner emphasizes the episode, using a technique that might be likened to running film backward through a projector: although the doctor has just criticized Woyzeck for urinating, moments later, anxious to get on with his experiment, he wheedles like a parent about to take the family on a Sunday drive, "Woyzeck, couldn't you just *try* to piss again? Go in the other room there and make another try" (47).

In addition to its function as a means of portraying character, the "At the Doctor's" scene, with its scatological motif, serves to advance the thematic development of *Woyzeck*, as Hauser has pointed out. The question of free will is essential to the drama, and through Woyzeck's offstage act and the grotesque caricaturization of the leading exponent of free will in the play, the Doctor, Büchner is lampooning the attitude of those who naively believe in the freedom of will. Like Woyzeck, human beings are shaped and driven by their physical needs, passions, and the forces at work in the environment, and in certain domains of their experience, such as the one represented in "At the Doctor's," free will is of little if any importance.

Rather than making pronouncements on issues such as volition, however, Büchner as a playwright was more interested in painting a portrait, creating an atmosphere, conveying a *Weltanschauung*. The world that he portrays in *Woyzeck* is not so much a jungle as a zoo or circus in which the human beings are not a great deal higher on the evolutionary ladder than their animal forebears. In *A Man and his Dog*, the scatological habits of dogs are described by the sublimating narrator in terms such as "rite," "bond," and "laws"; in *Woyzeck*, written more than eighty years earlier, the main character is accused of "pissing on the wall like a dog." Hauser had added in a footnote to his comments on the "At the Doctor's" scene, "As anyone who knows dogs well will realize, man's intellectual superiority over this animal, to which the Doctor so contemptuously compared Woyzeck, is not so very great in the specific context under discussion."[10] This was Büchner's point precisely, and not just in the context of the processes of elimination.

The similarities of human beings and animals are emphasized in the carnival scenes in *Woyzeck*. First one encounters the monkey dressed in a soldier's uniform, then "the astronomical horse," of whom the Proprietor says, "This is no dumb animal. This is a person! A human being! But still an animal. A beast" (44–45). After the horse relieves itself, the Proprietor informs the audience, "As you can see, this animal is still in a state of Nature. Not ideal Nature, of course! Take a lesson from him! But ask your doctor first, it may prove highly dangerous! What we have been told by this is: Man must be natural! You are created of dust, sand, and dung. Why must you be more than dust, sand, and dung?" (45). If, as the Proprietor claims, the horse is "a metamorphosed human being" (45), the implication is that human beings are merely metamorphosed animals. The playwright is using mirror writing again. Hauser elaborates, "Büchner's point is not just that monkeys resemble people, and people monkeys. The comparison is made not with the healthy monkeys in the jungle, but with the sick, *denatured* specimens that blow trumpets in carnival sideshows."[11]

As in the "At the Doctor's" scenes, Büchner is not only philosophizing about human nature in general in the carnival scene but is hurling satiric barbs at specific targets in his society. The monkey, without his clothes, would be nothing, claims the Barker, but dress him up with a coat, pants, and a saber and he becomes a baron (43). So much for aesthetic refinements and social strata! The horse, the Proprietor informs the audience, "is a member of all the learnèd societies—as well as a professor at our university" (44–45). We can only assume that, had they not been subjected to the same sort of "training" that domesticated animals receive, scholars too would give in to unideal nature and relieve themselves in public. As Spalter points out, "Büchner's target is once more the idealist for whom reality is insufficient; he suggests that there is more truth in an animal's spontaneous behavior than in the refinements of artists who keep actuality at a safe distance."[12] Years before Karl Kraus (and Jugendstil), Büchner perceived the folly of interchanging chamber pot and urn.

The bestiality of some of Büchner's characters is reflected in their vulgarly scatological language; for example, in scene 16 the Sergeant exclaims, "You watch or I'll see you drink a pot of your own piss" (58). The most animalistic figure in Woyzeck, the Drum Major, reveals his nature in scatological diction: "I'll screw his nose up his own ass!" and "You want I should leave enough wind in you for a good old lady's fart?" (59). Spalter has observed that Büchner's overriding interest in creating a very vital type of drama led him to develop

a prose containing linguistic elements for which neoclassical drama had no place. This prose was as evocative as it was down to earth; it was plastic enough to take in complex subjective experience as well as states of mind expressive in the most vulgar epithets; it availed itself of imagery that was often shockingly concrete and direct, and at times salaciously outspoken. This prose, for all its lowness, was charged with poetic force; it could be true to the idiom of the gutter without doing violence to the sensibilities of the poet.[13]

One might argue that some of the cruder language in Woyzeck deliberately assaults poetic "sensibilities" in the same way that the vulgarity of life does. Nevertheless, Spalter is essentially correct. Büchner uses his sometimes dissonant, sometimes melodious prose to convey his bittersweet Weltanschauung. Spalter, who declares that "Woyzeck's world is muck," and Hauser stress Büchner's pessimism; Hauser finds that "Woyzeck's romantic conception of love as the inseparable union of two people joined together by the forces of nature within man is as fallacious as the Doctor's theory about man's control over the musculus constrictor vesicae. Here, too, nature will not be controlled and made to conform to the patterns of human dreams. Nature is the master and man the servant: what it joins together it can tear asunder."[14] For Büchner, the universe is indeed harsh, but it is also complex. As Woyzeck philosophizes, "What is Man? Bones! Dust, sand, dung. What is Nature? Dust, sand, dung. . . . What a beautiful place the world is! Friend! My friend! The world! [*Moved*] Look! The sun coming through the clouds— like God emptying His bedpan on the world. [*He cries*]" (58).

IF A PERSON reading Bertolt Brecht's *Baal* after having read Büchner's *Woyzeck* experiences a sense of déjà vu, it is not surprising. Brecht, a typical representative of the young rebels of the early twentieth century, was strongly influenced by Büchner, and the scatological imagery quoted above from *Woyzeck* is closely paralleled in Brecht's first play. Max Spalter observes, "The early Brecht has much in common with the Büchner of *Woyzeck*. Both felt the challenge to write a drama in which humanitarian sympathies would not keep them from confronting the world at its coarsest—a drama in which every temptation to sentimentalize or romanticize would be resisted and every opportunity to underline the hell of life exploited." In his statement that both Brecht and Büchner created scenes characterized by an "aggressive concreteness and vividness in areas where so much of literature until recently has refused to be concrete or vivid," Spalter implies that both playwrights were noteworthy for their disregard for societal taboos, both sexual and scatological.[15] Just as Büchner's frankness aimed to shock the establishment of his day, so Brecht and his contemporaries sought to challenge the "respectable" ruling class.

In order to achieve the strongest possible impact on their audiences, both Büchner and Brecht created characters that were anything but stock. Woyzeck and Baal have often been compared in the sense that they are both outsiders, but clearly there is not an exact parallel between the two figures. Spalter suggests that "Baal is a sadistic inversion of Woyzeck, relishing the very malevolence built into the nature of things that keeps Woyzeck on the rack."[16]

Looking at it another way, one might find in Baal a mixture of virtually all the characters (and animals) in *Woyzeck*. Certainly he shares with the Drum Major his uninhibited sexuality and crudeness; one is reminded of the Drum Major's unthinking, vulgar remarks by Baal's answer to the teamster who declares, "A man could *use* a head like that": "Don't overrate the head. You need a backside too and all that goes with it" (32).[17] Outrageously unconventional even on his deathbed, Baal asks a man who has just spit in his face to wipe the spittle away, and then he laughs; when asked to explain his mirth, Baal replies, "I like the taste" (94). In addition to being as much the sensual, scatological man as the Drum Major, Baal uses people as callously as the Doctor uses Woyzeck for his experiments, and he relishes the process of tormenting others just as the Captain enjoys hinting to Woyzeck that Marie has been unfaithful. Like Marie, Baal is promiscuous. Hauser has noted that Marie, like many Storm and Stress heroines of the 1770s, is "'a child of nature,' under the control of her momentary impulses. . . . But whereas nature was idealized by the Storm and Stress writers, Büchner had 'unideal nature' in mind when he created his Marie."[18] The same could be said for Baal. One might even liken Baal to the child in *Woyzeck*; there are many instances in *Baal* in which the main character's similarity to a child is noted. Although Baal lacks the pristine purity that the romanticists attributed to children, he does have an infant's reliance on instinct and is as untouched by "breeding" and "good taste" as a burping baby. His refusal to "grow up" according to society's norms enables him to be openly sexual and scatological, and his vulgar language is thus, in terms of characterization, a means of indicating his lack of inhibitions. For Baal is really no worse than the rest of the world, merely less inhibited. Furthermore, he can verbalize his feelings; he is a philosopher of sorts and a poet. This is his closest tie to Woyzeck himself; both are thinkers who can see things in nature that are not revealed to others. Their ability to understand humanity's position in the universe makes Baal and Woyzeck more than monkeys in uniform.

A strong link between *Woyzeck* and *Baal* is the predominance in both plays of animal imagery. Baal is consistently described in bestial terms; for example, a ranger declares to his colleague, "A man like that has no soul. He belongs to the animal kingdom" (to which the second replies, "And with all that, he's like a child" [91]). Even the rowdy teamsters must concur, "You're an animal, Mr. Baal" (34). In *Baal*, however, the emphasis is more on wild, unrestrained beasts than on the "trained" animals depicted in *Woyzeck*. Even when Baal imagines himself as a circus animal, he envisions the sort of uncivilized behavior to which the "astronomical horse" reverted: "I want to be an elephant in the circus and make water when everything isn't just right" (74).

Many critics have noted the similarity in the earthy, pungent language used by Büchner and Brecht. Both playwrights had declared war on bourgeois values, and language was one of their weapons. They found the lofty diction of classical literature, held in such high esteem by many of their contemporaries, to be inappropriate for depicting the world that was crumbling about them. Brecht complained to Lion Feuchtwanger, "When Horace expresses even the most common thought and the most trivial feeling, it always has a glorious ring to it. That is because he worked with marble. Today we work with dirt."[19] In order to make the German language a richer medium for expressing his iconoclastic thoughts, Brecht drew upon oral traditions. One influence on his literary diction was the street ballad. Martin Esslin notes, "Brecht turned to this 'vulgar' style in protest against the gentility and respectability of the bourgeois society he abhorred." Included in the sources of Brecht's inspiration, according to Esslin, were "the entertainments of the common people, the songs of kitchen maids and the pleasures offered by the sideshows of fair grounds and beer gardens."[20] These are, of course, the same kinds of sites that Büchner exploited for *Woyzeck*.

Another source of Brecht's language was the Bible, and the traditional German hymns inspired him as well. If this seems inconsistent, one must recall the frequency of crude, scatological language in the theological writings of Martin Luther, who translated the Bible into German and authored a number of robust hymns. By sacrilegiously paganizing these traditional forms, Brecht was able to arouse in his audience the sort of shocked reactions for which he hoped. *Baal*, for example, begins with a "Chorale" that sets the tone of the entire drama; it contains a couplet that might well serve as Baal's personal motto: "And your shit's your own, so sit and have a ball / Rather than do nothing, lads, at all" (21). Later in the drama, Brecht "metamorphoses" the traditional hymn form into one of the most blatant scatological tributes in German literature, as Baal entertains the crowd in the barroom with a paean to the privy:

> Orge said to me:
> The dearest place on earth was not (he'd say)
> The grassy plot where his dead parents lay:
>
> Nor a confessional nor harlot's bed
> Nor a soft lap, warm, white, and fat (he said).
>
> The place which he liked best to look upon
> In this wide world of ours was the john.
>
> It is a place where you rejoice to know
> That there are stars above and dung below.

A place where you can sit—a wondrous sight—
And be alone even on your wedding night.

A place that teaches you (so Orge sings):
Be humble, for you can't hold on to things!

A place where one can rest and yet where one
Gently but firmly can get business done.

A place of wisdom where one has the leisure
To get one's paunch prepared for future pleasure.

And there you find out what you are indeed:
A fellow who sits on a john to—feed! [31–32]

Aside from its obvious shock value and its role in revealing Baal's vulgar nature, the hymn to the toilet supplies important information to the audience about the *Weltanschauung* that Brecht is depicting in this drama. The couplet "It is a place where you rejoice to know / That there are stars above and dung below" is of particular interest. In the original German, the person on the toilet is described as *zufrieden* ("content") rather than rejoicing;[21] this adjective, the root of which is the German word for peace, suggests that one can achieve a state of tranquility by accepting one's position in the *oben–unten* duality described in Busch's poem. As viewed through the eyes of Baal, the human situation is one of being so firmly grounded in the physical that any efforts to transcend one's corporeal nature constitute a threat to one's inner peace. The stars are beyond a mortal's reach, but one can still admire them (if one gets too close, one might find, as did the orphan in the grandmother's story in *Woyzeck*, that they are only little golden flies). There is a realism in this hymn that goes beyond its blunt language. Most persons would have to admit the truth in the notion that the bathroom is the ideal spot for privacy (at least in some households) and also the perfect place for achieving a feeling of humility. Where but on the toilet does the king behave the same as the peasant or even become as lowly as the animals? If one can reach this realization (a goal earnestly desired by proletarian Brecht), then the bathroom is indeed a "place of wisdom."

The last two lines of the hymn to the privy, in which the processes of elimination are juxtaposed with the wolfing down of food, epitomize the unappetizing view of the life cycle that is a major theme in *Baal*. The Darwinian concept of the world as a place in which one devours or is devoured appears often in Brecht's works, and in *Baal* it is tied in with a sort of scatological metaphysics; that is, we devour others and cast them off like waste products, but eventually we too are consumed and become part of the earth's excrement. This pessimistic outlook is conveyed throughout the play (and in Brecht's *Hauspostille* poems as well) by means of a series of "dark" images—in contrast to the use of "white" terminology to describe what is pure and unsullied. Frequent references to excrement add to the atmosphere of decay and decomposition. Charles R. Lyons feels that "Baal's song of 'Orge's' glorification of the 'john' is an outrageous variation of this basic image, relating the use of Johanna and the rotting of her corpse in the river to the process of the consumption of food and the production of excrement, a grotesque statement of the self-devouring Nature of the play."[22]

Baal's view of human beings' attitudes toward each other can be summarized in three lines from his song, "Death in the Forest," in which a dying man is told by his friends,

> You no-good beast! You're mangy, you're nuts!
> A bum! A heap of pus and guts!
> With your greedy gasping, you grab our air, lunkhead! [82]

It should be noted that the original German version of this passage includes the word *Dreck* ("dirt");[23] the same term was used by Büchner in Woyzeck's similarly negative "Dust, sand, dung" speech. An even stronger echo of the earlier play may be heard in Baal's expression of his *Weltanschauung* near the end of the drama:

> Baal: . . . I see the world in a mellow light: it is the Lord God's excrement.
> Ekart: The Lord God, who sufficiently declared his true nature once and for all in combining the sexual organ with the urinary tract!
> Baal [*lying on the ground*]: It is all so beautiful. [78]

In the satirical works of Busch, a dog urinates on a sacred tome and a wayward saint falls in the latrine; the greater pessimism (or, at least, more earnest approach) of Büchner and Brecht conjures up visions of the Deity showering all his creation with excrement of cosmic proportions.

As might well be expected, *Baal* has drawn varying responses from the critics. Brecht's emphasis on excrement has not prevented Max Spalter from admiring the uninhibited Baal, whose "unabashed instinctualism has about it something refreshing. . . . For him the world abounds in urine, mud, vomit, dung, and bile; why not enjoy the stench?"[24] A critic whom Baal himself might have applauded, Herbert Luthy, has waxed lyrical over Brecht's celebration of the scatological; he describes the theme of *Baal* as corruption itself, decomposition in all its forms, mould, mildew, urine, excrement, scurf, scabs, and caries, stagnant pools, carrion, rotting wrecks—the whole flora and fauna of decay. . . .

And yet all this is not morbid at all. Under a thin protective layer of wild posturing, it is really careless, joyous, and with genuine spiritual depth. What is presented here in the language of decomposition is the life process itself, the great, orgiastic metamorphosis of nature.

. . . The Brecht of *Baal* and *Hauspostille* is no nay-sayer. His poetry has a curious, quite this-worldly piety hidden at its core—he calls Baal "pious" and the word is not a sarcasm. It is the piety of an uncompromising acceptance of the natural world because it is natural.[25]

Lyons is more reserved. There is some truth to such criticism, he feels, and it is his opinion that Brecht does not explicitly pass judgment on Baal in the drama. However, "in the recurrent emphasis upon the metaphors of decay, the pervasive obsession with the natural process of the pure becoming the sullied, in the notion of the universe as a self-consuming animal—there is an implicit fear—a horror which is part of his [Brecht's] fascination with this world but which is also an emotional response which qualifies that acceptance." Lyons points to Baal's demise as at least approaching a negative judgment on him: "Deserted by his companions, Baal crawls toward the open door and the sky, whose vultures will consume him, committing himself to that universal digestive process, in which he will become part of the excrement of the created world."[26]

Walter Sokel explains this divergence of critical opinions in terms of the ambivalent way in which the spectator views Baal: "Seen by the social self in all men and women, Baal is a 'degenerate beast' and deserves full contempt. Seen by their nostalgia for a pre-social state of freedom, Baal wears the halo of eternal childhood and arouses hopeless admiration."[27] There are as many Baals as he has beholders; an inhibited person will surely regard him differently than a self-indulgent one, and a person's attitude toward the scatological will certainly have a bearing on her or his opinion of the drama. Furthermore, as Sokel suggests, individual persons may find themselves experiencing an approach–avoidance conflict regarding Baal. Brecht portrays this ambivalence in the scene in which Baal sings an indecent song in a café and is forced to retreat to the lavatory:

Chanteuse: Taking the guitar to the john with you? You are divine!
Members of the audience [*putting their heads through the curtain*]: Where is the pig?—Go on singing!—What a pig! [*They withdraw*]

Mjurk [*enters*]: I talked to them like a Salvation Army major. We can count on
the police. But these people are clamoring for him again. [52–53]

Baal's fictional audience, then, had the same love–hate relationship
with him as have the drama's real audience and critics. Such emotions
are confusing, but at least they are real. As the beggar tells Baal and
the rest of his grotesque compatriots, "No one understands anything.
But you can feel some things. Tales that can be understood are just
badly told" (71).

THE COMMOTION that Baal raised in the café was not unlike the up-
roar caused in similar nightspots in Zurich, Berlin, and other European cities by Brecht's contemporaries and sometime collaborators,
the Dadaists. The performances of these young iconoclasts, however,
were even more chaotic and unrecognizable as "art" than Baal's songs,
and the "reviews," in terms of the audiences' reactions, were definitely
not mixed. The Dadaists were a small and disparate group of artis-
tically gifted individuals who, like many intellectuals of their time,
were nauseated by bourgeois society in general and particularly by
the horrors of World War I (Brecht wrote *Baal* in part as a reaction
against the inhumanity he had witnessed during the war). The response of the great Berlin director, Erwin Piscator, to the First World
War was typical; after his return from the trenches, Piscator

turned away from "establishment" politics and politics' subservient hand-
maiden, Art. He rejected, as did most of the intellectual, aesthetic elite, including, of course, Brecht, everything connected with the old and discredited
Establishment. Art (with a capital "A"), in all its forms, had clearly been a part
of that establishment and went into intellectual exile. . . . An enormous wave
of "anti-artists," labelling themsclves Dadaists, Futurists, etc., ridiculed and
denounced any art form that did not permit, indeed demand, "unlimited artistic anarchy." . . . the slogan "Art is Shit" might be given as the suitably provocative watchword of the whole movement."[28]

There is no question that scatology served the purposes of the anti-
artists well, and the terse motto *Kunst ist Scheisse* (or *Dreck*) adorned
a number of the writings of the period, including Piscator's *Das politische Theater* and Richard Huelsenbeck's *En Avant Dada: Eine Geschichte des Dadaismus.*[29] Although there is still disagreement as to
which of the antiartists came up with the name "Dada," it was agreed
by all at the time that it was suitable because of its connotations of
infantilism—and, like Baal, the Dadaists glorified the small child's re-

24. *The Match Vendor I* (Otto Dix). Courtesy Otto Dix Stiftung, am Schrägen Weg 2, FL 9490 Vaduz.

liance on instinct. Naturally, this uninhibited abandon, particularly in its scatological manifestations, did not impress the establishment. Huelsenbeck has remarked that the nonintellectuals laughed at Dada: it "was a powerful reminder for them of their own baby bottles of a generation ago, of their honorably soiled diapers."[30]

The outrage of the Dadaists and their contemporaries was artistic, moral, and political. On the political level, most of the young artists and writers were procommunist and antiwar. They were furious about society's neglect of the poor and particularly of those who had been permanently disabled in World War I: consequently, the maimed war veteran and others in the throes of poverty were common figures in the art works of the postwar period. A rendition of this theme in scatological terms is *Der Streichholzhändler I* (*The Match Vendor I*) by Otto Dix (fig. 24).[31] The painting depicts a match vendor who is blind and has lost both arms and both legs (it is not clear whether he is a war veteran or simply a representative of the oppressed masses). The central figure sits on the sidewalk hawking his wares, while hurrying passersby to his left and right, shown only from the waist down, turn their heels and derrières toward him. Meanwhile, the crowning indignity is being suffered by the Streichholzhändler, as a dachshund urinates on one of his stumps. Dix's choice of the dachshund is particularly poignant, because this breed of dog looks as if it were at least partially a quadruple amputee itself. Squat and lowly though this typical German pet may be, it still can see and walk; here, in its ground-level world, it has perceived someone whose condition is worse than its own, and it does not hesitate to express its superiority. Through the dog's scatological act, Dix has conveyed the totally inhuman plight of those persons who constitute society's refuse.

Such victims and their victimizers were favorite themes of the anti-artists. The ugliness of German postwar commercial society has been pointed out by Martin Esslin: "Then the bull-necked, bloated financier, in his loud suit, his bowler hat, chewing enormous cigars in dreary nightclubs, listening to vulgar music, and leering at disgusting floor shows, really existed."[32] Esslin describes perfectly here the sort of figure that appeared so frequently in the drawings and paintings of George Grosz. In his painting *Pillars of Society* (fig. 25), Grosz depicted a number of these empty-headed types, one solemnly scowling with an overturned chamber pot on his head, another with the top of his head sliced off, revealing a steaming pile of excrement instead of brains.[33] "If the Workers Want to Stop Being Slaves, They Must Snatch the Knout from Their Masters," one of Grosz's drawings for Oscar Kanehl's *Steh auf, Prolet!* (fig. 26), is dominated by the figure of a wealthy member of the ruling class sitting on a pile of money in a way that is bound to conjure up thoughts of the anal personality's tendency to associate gold with excrement (see chapter 1, herein).[34] Grosz often expressed his revulsion at the vulgar excesses of the establishment in a pictorial rendering of the act of vomiting, as is the case in "Bellyache" (fig. 27).[35] And, like Büchner and Brecht, he did not hesitate to liken human beings to beasts, as in the drawing from *Das Gesicht der herrschenden Klasse*, "The Voice of the People Is the Voice of God" (fig. 28), in which one of the animalistic authority figures clumsily spills a receptacle that closely resembles a chamber pot.[36]

Caught up in their fervor for political and social reform, the Dadaists tended to deny that they had any positive artistic purpose and thought of themselves chiefly as antiartists. In 1936 Huelsenbeck asserted: "The

25. *Pillars of Society*
(George Grosz). Estate
of George Grosz, Prince-
ton, N.J.

26. "If the Workers Want to Stop Being Slaves, They Must
Snatch the Knout from Their Masters" (George Grosz).
Estate of George Grosz, Princeton, N.J.

eternal value of Dada can be deduced from the fact that in Germany an exhibition of 'Dadaist Works of Shame and Filth' was organized officially in order to frighten off the constructive burghers. Dada is forever the enemy of that comfortable Sunday Art which is supposed to uplift man by reminding him of agreeable moments. Dada hurts."[37] In his autobiography, George Grosz mused, "Perhaps there is no such thing as art any more. Perhaps the materialists are right when they say that art is just as much a natural function of man as going to the toilet."[38]

Their protests notwithstanding, the supposedly antiartistic Dadaists did produce works of art, and both the style and contents of these works had scatological overtones. Grosz, for example, based his technique in part on studies of toilet graffiti[39] and was indebted also to the "soap painters," itinerant artists of the day who, paradoxically, drew "dirty" pictures on barroom mirrors with soap.[40] Kurt Schwitters made collages and sculptures virtually out of garbage, combining assorted scraps and bits of junk that he found in his apartment or lying in the street. Ever mindful of the excremental, Dadaists carried with them stickers bearing slogans such as "Dada conquers" and "Dada, Dada above all else," with which they festooned, among other places, cabaret restrooms.[41] Furthermore, scatological insults supplied their usual shock value in the Dadaists' public performances. Beth Irwin Lewis describes an evening of readings in the Berlin gallery of J. B. Neumann; the climax of this soirée (which infuriated the audience) was Grosz's performance of "an obscene tap-dance in which he relieved himself in pantomime before a Lovis Corinth painting."[42]

Dadaism was an international movement, and antiartists of other nationalities shared the German enthusiasm for scatological satire (e.g., Marcel Duchamp's *Fountain*). What distinguished German Dada from the movement in other countries was the degree of moral outrage that seethed through many of its members. Elsewhere, Dadaists were chiefly concerned with artistic iconoclasm, and their philosophy, if it is possible to place a label on it, was predominantly a sense of the absurdity of life. The German antiartists, particularly Grosz, stressed the necessity for social change in order to alleviate human misery. Grosz once expressed his disillusionment with his countrymen in a conversation with Ben Hecht: "'They are fine people,' Grosz said, 'but they are quick to catch the disease of anti-humanity which is very close to many people, but my poor Germans are unusually susceptible. I think it is, on the whole, because of their poor elimination. Yes, I am sorry to say, I think Germany is a headquarters for constipation.'"[43] In

27. "Bellyache" (George
Grosz). Estate of George
Grosz, Princeton, N.J.

28. "The Voice of the People Is the Voice of God" (George Grosz).
Estate of George Grosz, Princeton, N.J.

29. Illustration from *Rosarote Brille* (George Grosz). Estate of George
Grosz, Princeton, N.J.

a more serious vein, Grosz wrote in his autobiography, "My drawings expressed my despair, hate and disillusionment. I had utter contempt for mankind in general. I drew drunkards; puking men."[44] The German Dadaists responded to the world's "unideal nature" as outrageously as Grosz depicted them in one of his illustrations for *Rosarote Brille* (fig. 29).[45] The person on the right-hand side of the drawing who has his posterior exposed for all to see recalls several lines from a poem that Grosz once wrote for a Dada poster:

> !!COURAGE: to AFFIRM the absurdity of existence!!
> !![to affirm] the GIGANTIC nonsense of the universe!!
> Accomplished by the rear-end of the world![46]

6

Of Battlefields and Bowels

Undoubtedly the greatest influence on German literature since 1914 has been the two world wars. The antisocial, antiartistic works of the Dadaists were just one type of response to and
outgrowth of the devastating upheavals of war. Many authors have
concerned themselves with serious examinations of the wars themselves and their effects on the individual psyche and conscience. The
works that have appeared following World War II often have treated
the issue of guilt, particularly regarding the extermination of millions
of Jews.

German authors whose works deal with the world wars have found
the use of scatological allusions appropriate for at least four major
reasons:

1. The actual, revolting physical conditions of life on the battlefield,
including the dysentery and typhoid epidemics of World War I,
could not be overlooked by any author who wished to deal honestly
with the war experience.
2. The dehumanization and brutality of the wars made the use of
crudely scatological terminology especially fitting.
3. The apparent contradiction between Germany's high degree of
civilization, in terms of both cultural achievement and fastidiousness of daily life, and the atrocities of the wars, particularly the
World War II concentration camps, prompted authors with a psychoanalytic bent to examine and depict Germans as anal personalities,
thus reflecting the views of such thinkers as Freud and Fromm (see
chapter 1, herein).
4. The no-holds-barred camaraderie of the trenches and the general
relaxation, even in civilian life, of niceties of speech and manners

during wartime resulted in authors' depicting this "naturalness" with varying degrees of approval—depending on whether the scatological speech or behavior arose from earthy "good guys" or from vulgar villains.

One of the most famous literary works to appear after World War I was Erich Maria Remarque's 1928 novel, *All Quiet on the Western Front*. Remarque, who fought at the front in the First World War and was wounded on several occasions, presents a realistic picture of the horrors faced by the common soldier. Through the eyes of his nineteen-year-old narrator, Paul Bäumer, Remarque demonstrates how wars reduce human beings to the level of animals and finally to excrement. As Jakov Lind has stated, the message of this novel is so overpowering that it leaves a lasting impression on the reader: "*All Quiet on the Western Front* taught me at the age of nine that war is shit, lice, mud, a trench full of foul-smelling bodies, gouged out eyes, and torn-off limbs, the ordinary soldier digging his grave while officers are having a great time in the casinos and brothels."[1]

All Quiet on the Western Front contains a number of scatological scenes through which the reader is continually reminded that war involves wallowing in ordure and that excrement gains a powerful and complex hold over the soldier. By means of the many different types of scatological references that are included in this work, the reader becomes aware of the numerous connotations that excrement has for the fighting man. Interestingly, Remarque depicts the two extremes of meaning in the first and the final scatological scenes in the novel: at the very beginning of the work one encounters an almost idyllic praise of the toilet, whereas at its end the soldiers have been metaphorically reduced to excrement. Throughout the rest of *All Quiet on the Western Front*, the tone of the scatological references fluctuates between the humorous and the brutal.

The novel's first reference to the scatological appears in the second scene of the first chapter. Here the narrator, Paul Bäumer, gives the reader a detailed description of the hours he and two of his friends spend sitting happily on three wooden toilet receptacles in the middle of a meadow, totally exposed to the view of others. This description continues for about three pages and is the longest scatological section in the book.

When one examines this scene carefully, it becomes clear that it is not included in the novel as bait for prurient interests but rather serves several very important purposes. (It is noteworthy that this passage, together with several other scatological sections, has been expurgated from at least one English-language edition of the novel.)² First, the reader is shown how and why a soldier's attitude toward the excremental becomes remolded. When a young man first enters the military, he brings with him the very typical feelings of shame toward excrement that society has instilled in him since his toilet-training period; as a soldier, he is suddenly forced to perform in a more public atmosphere what has been a very private and secret bodily function: "I still recall how embarrassed we were at first, as recruits in the barracks, when we needed to use the common latrine. There are no doors, twenty men sit in a row as if on a train. One can take them all in at a glance;—well, the soldier should always be under supervision" (12).³ This depiction of the common latrine demonstrates that the state reduces its citizens to an uncivilized level when they become soldiers. Ironically, it is precisely at the moment when an individual is being asked to give his life for his nation that the government finds it necessary to observe him even when he sits on the toilet. A second irony is contained in the fact that being forced to defecate publicly has the effect of reawakening within the soldier the infantile enjoyment of moving his bowels: "For us these very procedures, because of their compulsory openness, have recaptured the nature of innocence. Moreover, we have become so much at ease with them that we value their relaxed performance as much as one would enjoy knowing sure-as-shooting that he can execute a high-scoring hand of skat" (13).

The rediscovery of pleasure associated with the time spent on the toilet is strongly reinforced by the fact that it is only during these moments that the soldier is neither disturbed by commands and harassments from his superiors nor threatened by the need to enter into battle. Thus the toilet becomes for the soldier a temporary, peaceful escape from his harsh environment. It is these circumstances that make the narrator's inclusion of this rather lengthy excremental scene so appropriate. Only on the toilet does the soldier find "wonderfully carefree hours" (14). Furthermore, the latrine provides the soldier with a substitute for those very necessary opportunities to engage in small talk that had been readily available in civilian life: "these places are the gossip corners and the ersatz neighborhood hangout of the barracks" (13).

The combination of being forced to defecate in open view of others together with the discovery of the advantages of the time spent on the toilet finally causes the soldier to become fairly uninhibited in regard to his excremental functions. Thus Paul and his friends eventually prefer to use portable toilet receptacles out in the open air instead of the public latrine. Under the blue sky they can really relax and become a part of the idyllic beauty of nature. Remarque waxes more lyrical than Baal over the pleasures of an interlude on the privy: "And round us lies the blooming meadow. The delicate clusters of the grasses sway, cabbage butterflies whirl by, they float in the soft, warm wind of late summer, we read letters and newspapers and smoke, we remove our caps and lay them next to us, the wind plays with our hair, it plays with our words and thoughts" (14).

Even though Remarque emphasizes the positive value of the toilet and defecation in the first scatological scene in *All Quiet on the Western Front*, he by no means ignores the negative connotations. Through his narrator he informs the reader that war involves a continual association with filth, excrement, death, and other horrible and disgusting experiences. In fact, one reason why it is not too difficult for the soldier to lose his inhibitions regarding toilet functions is that he is witness to so many more revolting happenings: "We have learned more in the meantime than how to overcome a little bit of bashfulness. With the passage of time much worse things have become second nature to us" (13). The soldier finds no better means to express his frustration and revulsion than through excremental terminology. In this regard he simply follows the traditionally held view of scatological words as shocking and hair-raising. His counterpart in civilian life is only allowed to think of or to whisper to himself an appropriate excremental expression, but the soldier is free from all societal restraints among his peers at the front and may express himself clearly and loudly in the most scandalous words. Because the toilet and excrement also have certain positive connotations for the soldier, it is not surprising that he turns to scatological words to express both his greatest joy and his strongest disgust: "The soldier, more than any other person, is on intimate terms with his stomach and his digestion. Three quarters of his vocabulary is drawn from them, and the expression of highest joy as well as of deepest anger derives from this essential background. It is impossible to find any other way of expressing oneself that is equally clipped and clear" (13).

Throughout the rest of the novel, Remarque repeatedly demonstrates the soldier's strong propensity toward the use of excremental phrases and actions and the reasons for this tendency. Not surprisingly, encountering a particularly painful and hopeless situation will lead to an excremental curse as the most immediate form of release for the soldier's frustration and agony. One finds an example of this right after Paul and a few others have visited their dying comrade,

Kemmerich, in the military hospital: "Suddenly little Kropp throws his cigarette away, stamps it out fiercely, looks around with a haggard face that seems about to dissolve in tears, and stammers, 'Damn shit, this damn shit'" (21–22). Similarly, the soldiers occasionally manage to take revenge against their tyrannical and stupid superiors through excremental means. The primary target of their anger is the obnoxious, loud-mouthed Sergeant Himmelstoß (literally, "Heaven-thrust"). This man with the rather ironic name is a totally inhumane machine who does not hesitate to use the most brutal means to train the recruits assigned to him. When one of his charges turns out to be a bed wetter, the sergeant claims that the cause of this disorder is mere laziness and decides to cure it by matching the young man with a second person with the same infirmity; they are made to sleep in bunk beds with wire bottoms. One night one must take the top bunk, the next night the other, so that both receive retributive showerings (46). It is perfect poetic justice when the recruits manage to return the excremental lesson one Sunday as Himmelstoß prepares to leave the barracks, "spruced up immaculately." Bäumer and Kropp, carrying the latrine bucket, feign a pratfall just as Himmelstoß asks them how they are enjoying their work, and the bucket's contents cover the furious sergeant's trousers (28).

Scatological humor is an essential element of life at the front. The only way for the soldiers to keep their sanity somewhat intact and to maintain the will to keep going is by turning the entire nightmarish environment into a vulgar joke: "The somberness of the front recedes if we turn our backs on it, if we attack it with vulgar, bitter jokes; if someone dies, then we say that 'he pinched his ass shut,' and that's the way we talk about everything, that saves us from going crazy" (131). This description of death by means of the metaphor of "pinching the ass shut" is based on the grisly truth that the war with its rampaging dysentery is manipulating the soldiers in an extremely cruel way, first by accelerating their intestinal processes because of their disease, then by stopping *all* bodily functions abruptly with their death. The extreme degree of the war's excremental impact is most vividly described in the final scatological scene of the novel, which will be discussed later.

Although the narrator informs us that with worsening conditions the humor becomes more and more bitter, there is an occasional lighter touch in the soldiers' jests. Thus one day, as one of the soldiers breaks wind very loudly (not surprisingly, for the army diet includes a great deal of beans), he adds appropriately, "Every bean on the spoon/

Squeezes out a little tune" (42). Another amusing remark is made at the time of the kaiser's visit to the front. In preparation for the visit, the entire area has been cleaned until it almost sparkles. The kaiser is such a lofty figure in the eyes of the common soldier that they cannot completely imagine him; however, their awe is abruptly destroyed when one of the soldiers makes the following observation: "Look . . . I simply can't grasp the fact that the kaiser has to go to the latrine just as I do" (184). The recognition that scatological functions act as a great equalizer allows the soldiers to laugh and gives them a moment of comic relief from their horrible world. Because they see themselves as very excremental creatures, this remark also temporarily establishes a link between themselves and the kaiser.

Most of the remaining excremental material in *All Quiet on the Western Front* is quite brutal and shocks the reader into an awareness of the dehumanizing and destructive nature of war. Throughout the novel, the debasement of the individual is symbolized primarily by the helplessly defecating soldier, an image that is slowly intensified in its shocking clarity until it reaches its height in the final scatological scene. These defecation scenes are consistently linked in one way or another to death. Initially, it is the fear of possible death that brings on a bowel movement when an inexperienced recruit faces his first rocket attack. After the attack, the embarrassed soldier is consoled by the more seasoned narrator: "That's no disgrace, there have been plenty of people besides you who have soiled their pants during their first bombardment. Go behind that bush there and throw your underpants away. Forget it" (60).

As the war progresses, conditions on the front continue to deteriorate, and the soldiers' rations become insufficient in quantity and less than edible in quality. The consequence of the unsanitary conditions is the spread of dysentery with its accompanying diarrhea and passing of blood, bringing a slow death to its victims. The very first to succumb are of course the prisoners of war; but by the end of the novel the soldiers themselves are afflicted, and the dysentery has evolved into an all-encompassing symbol of the degradation of war. This last, terribly grotesque excremental scene stands in stark contrast to the first, relatively positive scatological passage. Again the soldiers are sitting on the toilet, but this time they are there not of their own free choice but because the war has turned them into a mass of helplessly defecating objects. All hope of an escape from death is gone, and the only recourse left to them is to vent their anger on those at home who are escaping their fate: "The factory owners in Germany have become rich people—

our intestines are racked with dysentery. The latrine poles are constantly full of tightly jammed together, squatting forms;—one should show the people back home these somber, yellow, miserable, resigned faces, these twisted figures, from whose bodies the colic has squeezed the blood to such an extent that the most that they can do is to sneer, their quivering lips contorted with pain: 'There's no point in pulling your pants back up'" (250). With this all too vivid image, Remarque ends his use of scatological elements.

Earlier in the novel, there is a scene that depicts with particular poignancy the degree to which war estranges its participants from civilized manners and forces them to speak as well as act from the bowels. The incident takes place as the narrator and a friend, both having been wounded, are being sent home by train to recover. During the night, Paul needs to go to the toilet, but because of his cast he is unable to do so without assistance. When a nurse appears, Paul finds himself incapable of telling her what he wants: "She looks at me with her bright eyes, she is clean and wonderful, which makes it even harder for me to tell her what I want" (223). Paul feels himself inferior to this clean woman; he has become so immersed in the excremental world at the front that he can no longer remember how to express his needs in polite terms. When his friend tries to help him, he too fails at first: "but Albert too no longer knows how to express himself acceptably and properly. Among ourselves out there it's said with just one word, but here, face to face with such a lady—." It is only when Albert recalls his school days that he remembers a proper way to state his friend's dilemma: "He'd like to leave the room, Sister." Paul, however, is still psychologically incapable of functioning in the civilized world. When the nurse says that there is no need for him to get out of bed and asks him to indicate to her what he has to do, Paul is horrified, "because I have no idea what the technical term for the thing is." Paul has been so completely overwhelmed by the vulgarly excremental life at the front that a chasm separates him from the clean civilian world. Finally, the nurse helps to resolve his dilemma by asking pointedly, as if Paul were a child, "Number one or number two?" (224).

This scene forces the reader to reflect on the scatological conflicts that can affect a person in wartime. The novel earlier had revealed certain advantages to the loosening of the societal standards taught to children during the toilet-training process; as the conditions at the front worsen, however, the disadvantages of a lack of civilized niceties become ever more apparent. Here, for the soldiers on the train, toilet training, like clean sheets, means home. Their inability to recall the powder room etiquette their parents had taught them, coupled with their shame at not being able to do so, illustrates touchingly the military men's alienation from a world they cannot completely forget.

Scheißkrieg ("shit-war") is the all-encompassing term used by one of the army officers in Heinrich Böll's antiwar novel of 1951, *And Where Were You, Adam?*, a book that paints as bitter a portrait of World War II as Remarque did of World War I.[4] Remarque, however, took the reader to the main battle lines at the front to witness the horrors of war, whereas Böll directs one's attention to seemingly insignificant places and events. Focusing upon lesser group actions allows Böll to present the senselessness and absurdity of war by portraying in detail the merciless destruction of individual men and women. Instead of the heroic actions of wartime, Böll depicts tiredness, filth, disease, and death.

Like Remarque, Böll makes use of scatological elements in his novel. There are, however, some important differences in the way these two authors use scatological material. Remarque employed excremental allusions to demonstrate that, during wartime, life for the soldier revolves around his stomach and bowels. This scatological environment takes on both positive and negative chatacteristics for the soldier. In *And Where Were You, Adam?* excrement is used strictly in a negative sense to underscore the view of war as a filthy, stinking, deadly disease. The lighter excremental humor, as well as the peace and quiet the toilet provided in Remarque's novel, is totally absent here.

The view of war as a disease is the most important metaphor in *And Where Were You, Adam?* Böll directs the reader to this image even before his narrative begins; the second of two quotations that precede the text as epigraphs ends with the words, "War is a disease. Like typhus." The likening of war to typhoid fever leads Böll naturally to the use of scatological allusions, because typhoid fever involves the digestive tract and the bowels. Until shortly after World War II, typhoid fever was an important killer, resulting in death for approximately 10 percent of those who contracted it. Although no one in *And Where Were You, Adam?* actually contracts typhoid fever, this distasteful disease is a symbol for the filth and death associated with war. In keeping with this symbol, Böll on several occasions links an excremental object with references to dirt and death. Very early in the novel there is an especially harsh description of the unsanitary and diseased world that engulfs the soldiers during wartime: "Next they halted at a grimy school standing among half-withered trees. The foul black puddles, with flies buzzing and darting above them, looked as if they had been standing there for months between rough cobbles and a chalk-scribbled urinal that gave out a nauseating stench, acrid and unmistakable" (6).[5] Similarly, the injured in the field hospitals cannot escape this deadly atmosphere: "the room was shadowy, the air fetid, there was a slight smell of cowdung, and even with closed doors and windows there were swarms of flies; at one time cattle had been kept in the basement beneath" (24).

The same hospital becomes the setting for the gruesome slaughter of two decent, dedicated individuals, the surgeon Schmitz (who symbolically holds the title of Sanitätsunteroffizier as a reflection of his moral purity) and Sergeant Schneider. The sickening insanity of their death is emphasized by the excremental setting and·grotesque circumstances under which it occurs. Orders have been given to evacuate the hospital because of the advance of the Russian troops. As so often is the case in Böll's works, a clue that something is about to transpire is an abrupt change in the usual mechanical routine of life: "In the calendar of routines, Thursday was the day for washing the senior M. O.'s car," but suddenly the ritual has been moved up to Wednesday (26). Despite the impending disaster, the chief doctor's driver is adhering to his fastidious routine, as Böll puts it, "painstakingly" (25). The chief doctor and his family manage to clear out swiftly in their gleaming car, almost mowing down a group of refugees. As they are stalled temporarily by the human traffic jam, the hospital's janitor, who (again symbolically) resided in the bathhouse and whom his chief of staff has left behind like a pile of refuse, throws stones at the car in frustration. When he realizes his protest is useless, the janitor despairs, and Böll tells us: "the tears were clearly visible on his grimy cheeks" (37). The novelist's inclusion of this incident serves to illustrate his view of Nazi officials as callous and to establish the themes of the anal personality and excessive obedience to authority as described in chapter 1 of this study. Both of these theories of personality and behavior figure prominently in *And Where Were You, Adam?*

In contrast to the degenerate chief doctor are Dr. Schmitz and Sergeant Schneider, who decide to stay behind with the patients who cannot be moved. In fact, there was no need for the patients to be in this state, because the chief doctor knew a move was forthcoming and could have postponed the operations; official orders for the withdrawal had not been received, however, and so the surgery was allowed to proceed. Here again we see the theme of the anal insistence on orderliness combined with that of the authoritarian tradition. The reaction of Schmitz to this perverse behavior is to cry in disgust, "Orders! Orders!" (30).

The only hope that Schmitz, Schneider, and their patients have for survival rests in the Russians' comprehension of their humane action. Death, however, awaits them in a most perverse fashion. Because the field hospital had previously been an agricultural school, there is a cesspit nearby. This site is chosen as the safest dump for all remaining weapons at the hospital, although a live mine has been left lying nearby for several months. Despite numerous requests from the chief doctor's wife, fearful for her children's welfare, to have the rusty mine removed, no concrete action has ever been taken. The rusty mine lies next to the cesspit as another indication of the inhumanity and sickness of the Nazi world.

Sergeant Schneider passes the cesspit twice during the last moments of his life. The first time, he is heading toward the railroad embankment to try to spot the advancing Russian tanks. As he comes to the cesspit, he notes that there is not a single ripple on its surface to indicate that a machine gun had been thrown into it. Although Schneider gets past the dangerous spot unharmed this time, it is most significant that he notices the resettled "green, greasy smoothness" of the liquid manure (43). This sight is a grotesque foreshadowing of his coming extermination, and once again excrement is linked with death. Soon the filthy, excremental sickness of war will swallow Schneider up without a remaining vestige, just as the machine gun had disappeared in the liquid manure without the faintest trace.[6]

A little later Schneider returns to the vicinity of the cesspit, carrying a Red Cross flag in front of him as a signal to the approaching Russian tanks. He seems to be controlling his anxiety at first, but then fear gets the best of him, and he blindly steps on the mine and is blown to bits. The rusty, dirty mine has become, as it explodes, the catalyst that brings about the extinction of everyone in the hospital. Because the Russians misinterpret the explosion as an attack against them, their tanks furiously pound the hospital until it comes crashing down, all its occupants dead. Only then do the Russians realize that not a single shot had been fired at them.

The slaughter of Schneider and Schmitz is attributed by the novelist to the moral and psychological sickness of those who created and were in charge of the war. Indeed, Böll's entire portrayal of war as a sickness is largely based upon his depiction of the unhealthy persons who are engaged in it, especially the officers. Although one may find in the novel some decent, compassionate figures, among both the officers and the common soldiers, who have become sick as a result of the war, the author's spotlight focuses on several officers whose minds were sick long before the war began and who have in turn contributed to the pathology of the conflict.

The narratives describing two of these sick officers, Colonel Bressen (rhymes with *fressen,* a verb that pertains to the way in which animals eat and also means "to devour") and First Lieutenant Dr. Greck (rhymes with *Dreck,* which means "dirt" or "excrement"), contain a number of excremental references. It is in his portrayal of these two characters that Böll rings changes on the theories discussed in chapter 1 of this study. By examining Bressen and Greck, one can see not only how these two approaches to scatological matters can be used by an author but also how closely intertwined the two theories can become as they are reflected in human behavior and attitudes.

In Colonel Bressen, whose background is related to the reader first, Böll presents a figure who demonstrates the orderliness and obstinacy of the anal personality; at the same time, the colonel's love of obedience to rules links him with authoritarianism. Bressen is a fanatic officer, amply decorated with medals, who even after years of war still harangues his weary troops on the need for victory; when they fail to respond, he loses all control and accuses them of being a *Mistbande* ("bunch of manure").[7]

At the end of the first chapter Colonel Bressen becomes a victim of excremental revenge, reminiscent of Sergeant Himmelstoß in *All Quiet on the Western Front.* Here too it is implied that at times excrement can best be fought with more excrement. Himmelstoß literally drenched his men with urine and was doused in return, but in *And Where Were You, Adam?* the attack is verbal, albeit no less distasteful. Shortly after having presented himself to his soldiers as seemingly dauntless and confident, Bressen lies in a field hospital childishly screaming for champagne. He gets an immediate and well-aimed answer from one of the other wounded soldiers: "'Piss,' said the bald head calmly, 'drink your own piss.' Someone behind laughed, quietly and cautiously" (13). In this scene, Bressen's obstinancy becomes clear. He has withdrawn into a psychosomatic or, more likely, a faked state of semicatatonia and is angry that he has not been able to shut off his sense of hearing (20). The tendency toward finickiness that is related to an anal insistence on order also emerges as Bressen frets about the poor placement and lack of aesthetic quality of the pictures on the wall of his hospital room.

Through flashbacks, Böll reveals to us how this patient with his fussy, rigid outlook became the way he is. After having served as a major during World War I, Bressen used his knack for handling details and his military bearing in a job in a tony restaurant (in this position he acknowledged the status of the patrons by gestures ranging from a deep bow to a barely visible nod) and as a teacher of refined manners to the nouveaux riches. Although some persons were so cloddish that they could never learn to hold "a wine glass properly by the stem," other pupils outdid their teacher and soon treated Bressen with great condescension, much to his shock and discomfiture (17). Bressen's reluctance to share his social expertise may be indicative of his anal character structure: "Such people find pleasure in a possession only when no one else has anything similar. They have the tendency to view everything in life as property and to defend everything 'private' from outside intervention. This attitude pertains by no means just to money and possessions but equally to other human beings, as well as to feelings, memories, experiences."[8] In addition to anal traits, one also finds in this passage the suggestion that an overemphasis on the fine points of etiquette implies a disregard for one's innate instincts for doing what is right, a failure to internalize goodness: Bressen himself observes that his pupils were "people who could no longer bear to be the kind of people they really were" (16).

Finally, with the reestablishment of military activity in Germany, Bressen's aristocratic manners and anal punctiliousness became desired commodities again. Beginning as a training instructor for the "Stahlhelm" organization, Bressen enthusiastically participated in the military exercises: "The things he had always encouraged and considered of prime importance were: route marches, standing at attention, about-turns executed with maximum precision" (19). This orderly utopia does not last long, however, and soon we find the colonel lying in the field hospital with an insignificant head wound, aware that his regiment has been badly beaten. In an attempt to evade responsibility for the defeat and to escape the reality of the failure of his orderly world, the formerly aggressive Bressen goes into the state of withdrawal described above. The doctors speak to him, but he refuses to respond; "he never wanted to be reminded of it again, the regiment that had disintegrated in his hands like dry tinder; Horse Droppings, Sharpshooter, Sugarloaf—under the command of his staff known as Hunting Lodge—all finished!" (17). While other soldiers with terrible wounds desperately struggle to survive, the colonel retreats into his past and lies in bed calling repeatedly for "champagne and a girl" (18).[9] Bressen's obstinate refusal to respond to the doctors and his tenacious clinging to his former life are, of course, symptomatic of the anal personality.

A close examination of the character of Colonel Bressen clearly shows that Böll feels nothing but contempt for this outwardly clean and law-abiding individual. Morally and psychologically he is to be despised, and the vulgar reply made to him by the bald, wounded soldier is most richly deserved. Even the names that Bressen used for his three battalions, "Horse Droppings, Sharpshooter, Sugarloaf," reflect the sickening nature of this man as well as the entire Nazi Reich. In contrast, the compassion of such decent and humane figures as Feinhals, Dr. Schmitz, and Captain Bauer sets them apart from the colonel, of whom Böll writes, "He found status-differences so easy to recognize" (15). Bressen's highest priority was not kindness to others but adherence to regulations, whether in the form of military orders, aesthetic principles, or the rules of etiquette.

In Colonel Bressen, we find an authority figure who was given a second opportunity for fulfilling his ambitions by World War II; lying defeated in his hospital bed, he knows that life will not give him a third chance. First Lieutenant Dr. Greck, on the other hand, represents the type of person who acquiesces to being the authoritarian's victim. In addition to reflecting the potential for human failure in a system that overemphasizes obedience, Greck is a clear embodiment of the anal personality. In fact, virtually everything Böll tells us about the first lieutenant relates to these motifs, and thus Greck represents a more detailed and clear-cut development of the two themes than does Bressen. Greck's attitudes toward life are obviously those of the anal personality; this outlook of course influences his actions. Nevertheless, his behavior patterns also are those of a person raised in a strict authoritarian system: because he has not internalized his views of good and evil, clean and dirty, his behavior is not consistent but alternates between submissiveness and rebellion.

Böll combines the dual motifs succinctly when he introduces Greck at the beginning of the novel. The weary soldiers observe the first lieutenant, and Böll tells us, "As soon as he took command they knew what kind of man he was." The reader will soon know, too, for the narration continues, "they could read it in his eyes: 'It's a lot of shit,' said his expression, 'just a lot of shit, but we can't do a thing about it.' And then came his voice, with studied indifference, contemptuous of all regulation commands: 'Let's go'" (6). In these brief lines we find a condensation of Greck's tendency to think in anal terms, his meek submissiveness, and his occasional rebellion against regulations. In order to assure the reader that the soldiers were not mistaken in their impression, several paragraphs later Böll has Greck himself verify their observations with his eyes and his voice: "The lieutenant's face was tired and sad, and now when he looked at them he looked first at their decorations, then into their faces, and said: 'Good,' and after a brief pause, with a glance at his watch: 'You're tired, I realize that, but it can't be helped—we have to leave in fifteen minutes'" (7). Greck's words convey his sense of helplessness and his resigned obedience. His glance at his watch suggests the anal insistence on punctuality, but the movement of his eyes tells us even more: by looking first at the men's medals and then at their faces, Greck demonstrates that he places a higher priority on the accumulation of these pieces of metal than on human contact.

As the novel proceeds, we discover that gaining decorations has become an obsession with Greck, and he is plagued with feelings of inferiority because of his relatively unadorned uniform. The anal interest in garnering status symbols (or, more precisely, copro-symbols) has been passed on to him by his mother, who goads him about his lack of achievement. In her letters, she compares him unfavorably with a local boy who could not succeed as a butcher's apprentice but who now has been awarded the Iron Cross, First Class; perversely, she also implies that a soldier who has lost a leg has accomplished more than her son has (61). Frau Greck's attitude reflects two elements of the anal personality: the interest in accumulating trinkets and the tendency to be envious. The latter trait, as described by Fromm, "is the extreme envy that one finds in many people with anal personalities. They often waste their energy not on their own productive achievements but in envy of the accomplishments and especially of the possessions of others."[10]

Greck has been affected even more strongly by a third anal quality in his mother—her stinginess. Although his father was a physician "and they were reasonably well off," because of his mother's thriftiness "they ate poorly" (60). As a result of his diet, which consisted largely of potato salad, Greck has had chronic stomach trouble since the age of sixteen. In fact, a doctor once told him that his symptoms were similar to those of malnutrition. Greck's appearances in the novel are punctuated by bouts of heartburn, nervous stomach, vomiting, and spastic colon.

In chapter 4 we find Greck in a tavern in a Hungarian village, agonizing over the fact that he has sold a pair of his trousers to a "dirty" Jew. Because he has never internalized his concept of cleanliness, Greck cannot tell the difference between harmless outward dirt and truly disgusting moral filth. The recollection of having sold his pants in the tailor's untidy hut makes him feel that he has committed an ugly sin in the eyes of his family and the Nazis. He actually begins to worry that his "crime" may be discovered and starts to perspire profusely as he concocts an alibi. Everywhere he looks in the Hungarian village Greck encounters dirt, which repels him. He cannot stand these sweaty, unwashed people and feels uncomfortable around them; yet he cannot deny a desire for many things in their life, such as their women, their fruits, and their alcoholic beverages. The longer he stays, however, the more he feels threatened by this environment. His dirt phobia reaches its height when he sees two lovers sitting at a table in the tavern with dirty dishes in front of them. Driven by his reaction to his surroundings and by his increasing paranoia about his own "filthy" deed, he has an overpowering desire to wash himself. When he is directed to the toilet, he is amazed by its condition: "The cleanliness of the washroom surprised him. The washbasins were neatly cemented to the wall, the doors were painted white. Beside the washbasin hung a towel. The innkeeper brought a cake of green army soap. 'Here you are,' he repeated. Greck felt at a loss" (56). After having observed sweat, flies, and dirt everywhere, it is inconceivable to Greck that the restroom is clean. Coming as he does from a spotless German town, he cannot comprehend a country in which some types of dirt are accepted as "natural"; his supposition, based on his initial observations, had been that *everything* in the Hungarians' lives must be filthy.

Although Greck's emotions are those of a person with an anal character structure, it is clear that his personality also has been affected by the rigid authoritarianism with which he was raised. Greck's values have not been internalized, and he allows himself to be manipulated like a puppet by his parents. He studied law (a most appropriate profession for such a person) because his father had recommended he do so:"He followed his father's advice to the letter, much as he hated him" (61). Even Greck's sexual life is determined by his father's wishes: "It was a stupid idea to go to a woman in the middle of the day in this heat. But he had been following the advice of his father, who had told him he must be sure and have a woman at least once a month" (59).[11]

Occasionally Greck rebels but is quickly reined in by his parents' apron strings. One incident from his youth illustrates this pattern particularly well. As a present on the occasion of his graduation from the Gymnasium, his parents give him money for a three-week trip. In one of his rare moments of revolt, the young Greck travels to Frankfurt and spends all the money in one week, satisfying his long-imprisoned sexual hunger with prostitutes; upon his shamefaced return, his parents are stunned, and his father insists he submit to a physical. During the long examination Greck realizes he hates this man with his fat face. However, when his father finally grins at him and tells him, "You're crazy. A woman once or twice a month is plenty for you," Greck capitulates again: "He knew his old man was right" (61).

The two theories discussed in chapter 1, that of the anal personality and that of the influence of an authoritarian society, dovetail strikingly in Böll's account of Greck's ride on a swingboat. When the first lieutenant comes upon some swingboats in the Hungarian village, he views them as forbidden fruit: "Never in his life had he gone for a ride on a swingboat. Such pleasures had not been for him; they were forbidden in his family, first because he was never really well, and then because that was no way to behave, in public, swinging through the air like some silly monkey. And he had never done anything that was forbidden" (48). In an unaccustomed gesture of rebellion, Greck decides to take a ride. Although he finds the proprietor and his family dirty and repulsive, which causes him to have second thoughts, Greck does take the plunge. He quickly masters the technique of moving his body in rhythm with the swingboat in order to keep the device moving smoothly. The experience proves to be an exhilarating revelation for Greck: "All of a sudden he knew he had been missing something vital in his life: riding a swingboat. It was glorious. The sweat dried on his forehead, and the gentle coolness of the rocking motion even dried the sweat on his body: the air blew through him, fresh and exquisite, with every swing, and furthermore: the world was changed" (50). The sweat that had plagued Greck prior to his ride had been caused not only by the heat but also by fear and guilt. The cooling ride temporarily frees him from his neurotic symptoms, although soon he thinks of his transaction with the Jewish tailor and also of what his mother would think of his ride in the swing boat: "Mama didn't understand about things like that. Whatever life may bring: Always behave with dignity! was her motto. She would never understand how her son, an attorney, Lieutenant Greck, could take a ride in a swingboat, in the middle of a broiling hot day in a dirty Hungarian market square, in full view of anyone—anyone at all—who happened to be passing by. . . . it was no use trying to fight it" (50–51). As if conjuring up visions of his disapproving mother were not enough, Greck then recalls the messiness of the tailor's back room; he pictures in his mind a bowl of cucumber salad in which flies were swimming, and an attack of heartburn strikes, causing Greck to shout for the proprietor to stop the ride. Mentally as well as physically he is now out of sync with his pleasurable feelings, and as the brakes are applied he feels the "hard rhythmic jolting" (51).

In chapter 1 we noted that Ernest Jones found "the incapacity for happiness" to be one of the most disadvantageous characteristics of the anal personality. Considering it a sort of offshoot of anal eroticism, Jones described this tendency as "an inability to enjoy any pleasurable situation unless all the attendant circumstances are quite perfect. People who display this trait are extremely sensitive to any disturbing or disharmonious element in a situation; a satisfactory mood is readily impaired by slight influences." Among the moodbreakers Jones named were "the striking of a slightly discordant note, the thought of an important duty not attended to, the slightest physical discomfort."[12] Thus Greck, with his spoilsport memory, may be seen to have secondary anal characteristics as well as primary ones.

Greck's digestive disorders tie in with his (and his parents') anal fixations and also with his unusually strict upbringing. Reminiscent of Brazelton's Joan, Greck's organic symptoms mirror his mental distress. Unlike the little girl, however, Greck does not have "remnants of strength" that enable him to rebel for any length of time, and thus his symptoms are different from Joan's. Whereas she was able to manipulate her intestinal tract to the point of withholding her bowel movement from her mother, in Greck's case it is his parents who are in total control, just as the proprietor remained in charge of the swingboat, because "It's the law" (49); consequently, Greck's symptoms are those of a person who has scant power over his own body fluids or excreta: excessive sweating, heartburn, and diarrhea.

As was suggested above, the swingboat ride reveals Greck on a rare occasion when he is in harmony with the natural rhythms of life. Furthermore, the swingboat is a highly appropriate symbol for Greck's vacillation between submissiveness and rebellion. Because this grown man has never internalized his values, he remains ethically and emotionally immature, a victim of the "mood swings" that characterize adolescence.

Böll packs even more meaning into this loaded symbol, however. The terminology the novelist uses to describe Greck's perceptions while swinging to and fro is significant:

> the world was changed. One minute it consisted merely of a few dirty planks with broad grooves running along them, and on the downward swing he had the whole sky to himself. . . . This was the glorious part: to stand parallel to the earth as the little boat swung back—to see those dirty planks that signified

the world—and then, plunging forward again, to kick your feet into the sky, to see it overhead as if you were lying in a meadow, only this way you were closer to the sky, infinitely closer. Everything in between was insignificant. [50]

By contrasting the heavens—and the reader should bear in mind that Böll uses the word *Himmel*,[13] which means both "sky" and "heaven"— with the dirty (according to Greck) world, Böll places this passage in the "Oben und Unten" tradition of German literature. Thus Greck becomes a neurotic modern variant of the literary figure who reaches for the stars with one hand and the toilet paper with the other. The lines that bracket this passage are especially important when considered in the light of the *Weltanschauung* revealed in Böll's works. The author gives us an indication of his interpretation of his character's problem in the sentence "Everything in between was insignificant." (These words are followed by a few references to everyday life in the village.) Earlier German literature often used the *oben–unten* contrast to depict the tragic fact that our human limitations prevent us from attaining the ideal; it was Böll's opinion that the real tragedy is viewing life in terms of such dualities. Persons who divide their universe into a glorious heaven and a rotten earth, an absurd degree of organization and messy disorder, or hygienic cleanliness and disgusting filth are, according to the novelist, indulging in dangerous oversimplifications while missing out on the real stuff of life, which lies somewhere between these extremes. Had Greck's upbringing and resultant view of life been less rigid and judgmental, he could have attained oneness with the world instead of gliding parallel to it. By placing the traditional "Oben und Unten" imagery in the consciousness of a person as disturbed as Greck, Böll would seem to be telling us: Something is wrong with this type of thinking! The everyday reality between the two polarities is *not* trivial— it is what is ultimately significant!

The words that provide the lead-in to this passage, "the world was changed," call the reader's attention to the fact that the novelist is not just describing one neurotic individual or a German tradition that he feels needs to be reexamined but rather making observations universal in their relevance. Although clearly Böll felt that the bitter lesson taught by World War II had not ended the inclination of some Germans to obey orders unquestioningly, Greck serves as a negative example not only for Böll's fellow Germans but for all humankind. The desirability of relying on one's own best instincts rather than on external compulsion is a major theme in Böll's works, and it is one that knows no national boundaries. Truly ethical behavior, according to the author, is motivated from within, springing from human decency rather than from the fear of "getting caught." A relaxed appreciation of life, as opposed to an overemphasis on order and duty, is a necessary prerequisite for Böll's moral reforms. To change the world, one must start with oneself.

Just as a swing continues its back-and-forth motion for some time after its rider has jumped off, so Böll emphasizes the points of the swingboat scene in a sort of echo or ripple technique, as he stages several reprises of Greck's inner struggles later in the chapter. The reverberations may be observed in Greck's exchange with the proprietor of the swingboat after the ride has so abruptly ended. The Hungarian's wife offers Greck a drink that will calm his churning stomach; the first lieutenant stands, politely says "Thanks very much," but is embarrassed to discover he has no small change to offer them in payment for their kindness. The proprietor, who represents the relaxed unconcernedness of the local villagers, shrugs off Greck's predicament with a casual "okay," to which Greck, in a typical face-saving reversion to his role as an officer of the Wehrmacht, replies, "Heil Hitler" (52). This encounter reflects the earlier contrast between relaxation and rigidity; similarly, Greck's dilemma about what to drink in the tavern mirrors his vacillation between submissiveness and rebellion, as well as his anally related inability to enjoy life. "Nothing really turned him on," writes Böll,[14] and this statement of course is applicable to more than just the choice of beverage. The sole longing Greck had was for "Just a wash." He usually avoided alcohol, which aggravated his digestive disorders: "Not for nothing had his mother warned him against it, just as she had against riding swingboats" (52). In keeping with his "Mother is always right" philosophy, Greck orders coffee, but when the innkeeper, who has glanced at Greck's undecorated uniform, nods all too understandingly, Greck is shamed into rebellion and orders a schnapps: "What the hell, he thought, I've been a fool, I've been a fool all along. Always respectable and law-abiding, while everyone else— everyone else has been having himself a good time. What the hell." Greck's swing toward his rebellious side does not last long, however. For a split second he enjoys his daring leap off the wagon: "The schnapps was sharp and burning but felt good." The word used for "good" in the original German, however, is *wohl*,[15] a term with connotations of health consciousness, and in the next two sentences we find Greck lapsing into hypochondria: "He sipped it slowly, drop by drop. That was it: he must take alcohol like medicine, that was it" (54).

Greck's meek susceptibility to the views of others is quite different from Bressen's opinionated obstinacy. The contrast between the two officers is clear from the beginning of the novel, when the aggressive Bressen screams at his men, calling them a "bunch of manure," whereas the resigned, passive Greck says "shit"—referring to the war conditions in general—with his eyes. What connects the narratives describing the two men and prevents this part of the novel from being a series of isolated sketches is Böll's use of the adjectives *widerwärtig* and *widerlich*, both of which essentially mean "disgusting," "repulsive," or "revolting." Both Bressen and Greck use the terms, but each defines them differently according to his own outlook and experiences. To some extent Bressen shares Greck's aversion to dirt and recollects with disgust his early days in the high-class restaurant, where he had found it "disgusting" to have to take his meals in the "dirty" back room.[16] The unpardonable gaffe according to Bressen, however, is tackiness. This snobbish aesthete calls to mind American comedienne Lily Tomlin's caricature of "The Tasteful Lady," a pill in a pillbox hat who scorns those who fail to crook their pinkies at just the right angle. Decorative objects that are in poor taste and/or imprecisely placed offend Bressen; as he lies wounded in his hospital bed and views a picture of the Virgin Mary (with her feet on a globe, her eyes gazing toward heaven in "Oben und Unten" fashion) his reaction is clearcut:"He shook his head slightly and thought: revolting."[17] Böll frequently uses this technique of setting a word off by itself to underline its importance as a leitmotiv.

In *And Where Were You, Adam?* the theme of revulsion initiated with regard to Bressen is developed extensively in the account of Greck. There can be no question that what disgusts Greck most is dirt. As an anal personality, however, Greck defines dirt loosely to include anything untidy, disorderly, or not exactly as it should be. Thus he describes the inaccurately pronounced German of the swingboat operator as "repulsive" (49), he finds his own failure to accumulate medals to be "a revolting business" (53), and he notes that the innkeeper who should be his inferior but acts so superior has a face that is "repulsive" (58). It is the actual physical dirt of the Hungarian village that especially bothers Greck, however. There is the Jewish tailor's back room and its "repulsively large bowl of cucumber salad with drowning flies floating around in it" (51) and the inn, where he makes the following observation: "Swarms of flies were perched on the dirty plates, with remains of food, chop bones, little mounds of vegetables, and wilted lettuce in earthenware bowls. Disgusting, thought Greck" (52–53). As Greck's afternoon wears on and his digestive disorders increase, we find that *everything* disgusts him, even former sources of pleasure—a point Böll's style hammers across to the reader: "Everything was repulsive: the woman, the dirty Jew, even the swingboat, although that had still been a novelty, but that also was disgusting; disgusting, too, were the apricots, the innkeeper, the soldier."[18]

Just as Böll employs the words *widerwärtig* and *widerlich* to establish a link between Bressen and Greck, he also advances the plot of his novel through his varying uses of a single word—*Parole* ("password" or "motto"). Early in the novel, when the top brass, if not the foot soldiers, wish to maintain a semblance of optimism, we find that the password on the battlefield is "victory" (10). As the author continues his narrative with the tales of Bressen and Greck, we begin to understand why an effort directed by such leaders is bound to fail. When Böll tells us of Greck's mother ("Always behave with dignity! was her motto"), we get a glimpse of the superficial values that had been propping up the now crumbling Third Reich. Some pages later, as the Germans face total destruction in the locale in which the story has been unfolding, we hear one soldier respond when asked for the password, "The password's shit" (90). Thus the novelist has been playing an increasingly dismal game of Password in which the soldiers are doomed to defeat.

As might well be expected, one of the biggest losers of all is the perpetual victim, Greck. The above-mentioned excremental password ushers in a highly scatological scene in which Greck's intestinal disorders finally get the best of him. While the German soldiers are preparing to withdraw from a Hungarian village, Greck suddenly is overcome with stomach cramps so intense that they nearly paralyze him. In a slow, detailed, and anguishing scene that takes more than two pages to recount, Böll describes Greck's gruesome demise. This is by far the longest and most hideous excremental section of the entire novel. Again the setting is a cesspit. Just as Sergeant Schneider had earlier become aware of his fear of death at such a pit, it is here that Greck's sickness makes an end of him. Greck is desperately trying to reach the moving van that will evacuate the soldiers, but his stomach ailment will not let him go: "As soon as he straightened himself a gripping pain like a corkscrew in his stomach forced him to double up, and he felt the urge to defecate—he was squatting beside the low wall surrounding the cesspool, his stool came in driblets, barely a tablespoonful at a time, while the pressure in his racked abdomen was enormous" (94). Apropos Greck's anality, Böll uses strictly the most acceptable words in this scene; the words "a tablespoonful at a time" also remind one of doses of medicine and thus reinforce the reader's image of Greck as a sick man who even took a medicinal approach to drinking schnapps.

No fate could be worse for the obsessively clean Greck than to be dribbling feces while the village is under attack. One can well imagine his mother's reaction if she were to find out that, instead of heroically giving his life for his country, her son died in the most ignoble fashion imaginable. It is particularly ironic that just at this moment the major is calling Greck's name in order to present him with the Iron Cross, First Class, the medal that his mother had chided him for not having. This stingy woman's failure to nourish her son both physically and emotionally is responsible for his inability to attain any of the superficial or genuine rewards of life. As grotesque and perhaps exaggerated as this scene may seem, it presents a most appropriate fate for a person such as Greck.

The first lieutenant's death demonstrates that the Nazi ideology that dominated Germany for more than ten years reduced many of its adherents as well as others to the level of excrement. Just as the humane Schneider fell victim to the inhuman Nazi world, as symbolized by the explosion of the live mine, Greck too succumbs to the same system. In Greck's case, however, there is an internal explosion that is a travesty of the tanks' outward bombardment of "incredibly hard round balls" (95): "He held onto the wall, his naked bottom shivering, and in his bowels that grinding pain would form and re-form, like some slowly accumulating explosive that surely must be devastating in effect but, when it did come, was always minimal, kept accumulating, kept promising to bring final release while never releasing more than a tiny morsel of stool" (94).

A healthy man like Schneider can be felled by one bullet or one mine, but a sickness generally will destroy its victim in a much more leisurely and painful manner. Greck's death is a result not only of the battle but also of his upbringing and lifelong problems. Recall the significant words near the beginning of this scene—"barely a tablespoonful at a time," terminology characteristic of a polite dining room—and consider, too, the words at the end of the same paragraph: "a tiny morsel of stool." The use of terms reminiscent of eating in the context of Greck's personality and of what is happening to him in this scene lends the entire passage a particular repugnance. The reader's queasiness (not to mention Greck's catastrophe) is intensified when Böll continues, using an adjective that is by now familiar: "A shell landed in the cesspool, a wave splashed over him, soaking him with that disgusting liquid; he could taste it on his lips, and he sobbed more bitterly than ever." Greck had earlier found warm apricots "disgusting," but his present fate is a thousand times worse. The digestive disorders inflicted upon him by his anally oriented parents have finally peaked; he imagines himself encircled by all the doctors he had ever consulted, a nightmarish group headed, appropriately, "by his repulsive father." In what seems to be almost a Buschean fashion, whatever thoughts of his nobility that Greck could possibly still retain are doused by the liquid manure. He too will soon disappear without a trace, as did the machine gun and Schneider. As his tears run into the filth, "that muck he had tasted on his lips" (95), Greck is buried beneath a large wooden barn that has just been hit by the Russians.

It is striking that after this scene Böll includes no further major excremental passages in *And Where Were You, Adam?* After having used excremental allusions effectively in his descriptions of Colonel Bressen and First Lieutenant Greck, Böll does not belabor the point. The author may well have felt that scatological sections in the final third of the novel would have served only to weaken the dramatic impact of Greck's cataclysmic death scene.

Despite the paucity of explicit excremental references in the remainder of this work, Böll does, however, continue to elaborate on the theme of the Nazis as anal characters. He might well have quit while he was ahead. Having created in Greck a character who was even more typical of the anal personality than Bressen was, the novelist apparently felt inspired to fill the void in chapter 7, immediately after Greck's demise, with the figure of Captain Filskeit, a person who is so absurdly anal as to be a cardboard caricature. Filskeit glances around his office and approvingly notices that, "everything was in order." He flies into a rage when someone is guilty of "sloppiness," hates dirty jokes, and spurns smoking, drinking, and women (102–3). Obviously—*too* obviously—a product of the authoritarian tradition, he considered it "a matter of pride . . . to carry out all orders to the letter" (104–5). Even the captain's bestial facial features reveal his brutality in comic-book fashion. Fifteen years later, in *End of a Mission*, Böll would poke fun at the tendency of journalists to attribute crude features to criminal types as a matter of course. With the war fresh in his mind, however, as he wrote *And Where Were You, Adam?* Böll did not seem to have the sangfroid to delineate all of his Nazi characters as skillfully as he did Bressen and Greck. The very extremism Böll himself so often decried is evident in his portrayal of Captain Filskeit, an anal partisan of racial purity whom we would love to hate but cannot, because he seems unreal.

It could be argued that Böll's depiction of the Nazis as anally oriented persons who tried to cover their moral filth with a pristine facade is an oversimplification of the complex phenomenon of the growth of fascism in Germany. However, an examination of Böll's entire oeuvre reveals that he was well aware of the varied causes of the Nazis' rise to power. In his essays, lectures, and interviews he commented on such elements as authoritarianism, the economic situation, the fanatical lust for power, anti-Semitism, and nationalism, and he discussed their role in the Fascist takeover. Furthermore, these problems come to the forefront in a number of Böll's fictional works, such as *Billiards at Half-past Nine* and *The Clown*—scatological allusions are few and far between in both of these novels. There can be no doubt, though, that the anal character traits had a certain fascination for Böll, and in such works as *And Where Were You, Adam?* and (as we shall see in the next chapter) *Group Portrait with Lady* he turned the spotlight on this leitmotiv.

Böll saw anality as part of a mindset that lowered the Germans' resistance to Nazism. Consequently (if we may be permitted to use an unsavory metaphor reminiscent of the children who relieved themselves in the soup kettle in Günter Grass's *Tin Drum*),[19] even when Böll concocted a scene blending all of the nonscatological ingredients described above, he could not resist adding just a soupçon of anality to the Nazi stew. A case in point is a passage near the beginning of *The Clown*, in which Hans Schnier describes how Nazism affected his childhood. Hans's parents and his scowling teacher, Brühl, are the stern authority figures to whose discipline he must submit; economic problems are implied by the references to the exploitative nature of the Schnier coal-mining empire; the fanatical lust for power is personified by Hans's ruthless Hitler Youth leader, Herbert Kalick; and anti-Semitism and excessive nationalism are clearly stated in the goal of Brühl and Frau Schnier "to drive the Jewish Yankees from our sacred German soil." Serious matters are being discussed here, and just as a most shocking moment arrives for Hans—the point at which his mother tells him that his beloved sister Henrietta has volunteered for antiaircraft duty instead of going on a school outing as he had supposed—Frau Schnier's response contains a throwaway line that is quintessential Böll: "Outing? Nonsense. She has gone to Bonn to volunteer for the Flak. Don't peel your apple too thick. Look, son, watch me."[20] And there we have it again, the anal personality, this time (as in the case of Greck's mother) appearing in the form of parsimoniousness. Frau Schnier's remark about the apple is not the anticlimactic non sequitur that it appears to be, for the second half of her reply to her son is, in Böll's eyes, the logical concomitant of the first. Both types of meanness, heartless chauvinism and stinginess, are symptomatic of an estrangement from what is best in human nature. By shifting her attention from her daughter's perilous situation to her son's apple-peeling techniques without batting an eyelash, Frau Schnier demonstrates a perversion of values. For such persons, the waste of a few paper-thin morsels of fruit may prove more provocative than the waste of human life.

It was not simply a scatological problem that attracted Böll's attention, then, but an existential one: the tension in his works springs from the struggle between what is authentic in life and what is unnatural, contrived, or managed, between genuine human values and artificial ones. In his essay "To a Bishop, a General, and a Cabinet Minister Born 1917," Böll described a wartime meeting with the principal of the school from which he had graduated; reminiscent of Greck's scheme of values, the man's eyes immediately went to Böll's sleeve to see if the young soldier was wearing the "Crimea patch": "I never forgot his disappointed glance at my sleeve; it explained a lot about him that I had never understood before: that curse of Hindenburg that lies so heavily on decent patriotic German professors, and the mentality for which a thing doesn't exist unless it is *documented*." Böll's response to this "mentality" resounds in his essay "In Defense of 'Rubble Literature'": "It is our task to remind the world that a human being exists for more than to be bureaucratized."[21] Clearly, this was Böll's credo as a writer. Because he refused to put persons in pigeonholes (Filskeit is a rare exception), Böll included among his characters card-carrying Nazis who eventually are capable of reformation (Bleibl in *The Safety Net*) and persons such as Schnier's teacher Brühl, who, although he is acclaimed as "a man with a 'courageous political past' because he never joined the Party," is a de facto Nazi.[22] "There have always been Nazis in Germany," observed Böll in a 1976 interview with René Wintzen, adding, "Probably there will always be some."[23] This statement applies not just to Germany, of course, but to all nations, for in his works Böll dealt with a problem that is universal and timeless. Viewed as just one part of the quest for inner veracity, the determination of what is truly dirty and clean is, as Böll himself stated, "a permanently relevant theme."[24] The dilemma of humanity's alienation from the ground of being takes many forms, but for Böll its most dramatic manifestation, as he indicated in the Wintzen interview, was "a horde of men in brown jackets, brown pants, brown caps, real shit colors, who marched boisterously through the city, not as a suppressed minority but as a ruling majority."[25]

ECHOES OF *And Where Were You, Adam?* may be found in Jakov Lind's World War II story, "Soul of Wood." Although in some cases Lind utilizes scatological imagery in order to convey the depravity of war and the sick nature of its participants just as Böll did, his use of excremental references serves many other purposes as well. One might say that "Soul of Wood" presents a rogues' gallery of anal attitudes, containing characters who, combined, cover a wide range of scatological experiences.

The excremental images and references used by Lind in this story appear to be arranged in four distinct sections, each contributing to plot and/or character development. The first scatological allusion in the story helps to establish the nature of the relationship between the one-legged Hermann Wohlbrecht, the main character in the tale, and Anton ("Toni") Barth, the Jewish paralytic for whom Wohlbrecht has cared since the boy's infancy and whom he is now attempting to hide from the Nazis. As Wohlbrecht carefully readies his charge for the escape to the mountains, he buckles a urine receptacle onto him; when the trip has been completed, Wohlbrecht removes the container and empties it. We later learn that this action, which appears to be automatic on Wohlbrecht's part, became so as a result of years of tending to the boy's needs when he worked as a servant for Toni's parents. In a fit of pique, Wohlbrecht complains to the Nazi Professor Mückenpelz of the hardships he experienced in that role: "It was pretty tough. Day in day out upstairs and downstairs, emptying the chamberpot, emptying the pee bottle. Feeding him. Wiping his mouth and everything else. Making the bed. Reading him stories. Shopping. Taking out the slop jar. Upstairs, downstairs. And every minute: Hermann, the child is calling you" (62).[26] Thus Lind establishes the parent–child relationship between Wohlbrecht and Toni.

Although Wohlbrecht's tone here is a dissatisfied one, the reader has already seen extensive proof of the tenderness the protagonist feels for "his" Toni. The details of Toni's care that Lind has chosen to present to the reader—feeding, storytelling, and the cleaning up of excrement—establish Wohlbrecht as more of a parent to Toni than the boy's own parents, who apparently spent most of their time agonizing about their predicament while Wohlbrecht did the dirty work. It is not surprising that Wohlbrecht should develop proprietary feelings toward the child whose excrement he has cleaned up for years; adoptive parents share these emotions, as do many governesses and full-time babysitters.[27] Such persons often voice the view that it is not just giving birth to a child that makes it "yours"; rather, it is the daily, routine, conscien-

tious performance of chores—drudgery revolving around dirty diapers and runny noses more than dimpled smiles and lace-covered
booties—that binds one irrevocably to a child. (Commitment to such
malodorous duties is, after all, what makes Busch's "Good Grandmother" good.) In a very human way, Wohlbrecht's devotion and possessiveness toward Toni combine with his instincts of self-preservation
to bring about his ultimate downfall.

"Inmates are strictly forbidden to smoke, spit, whistle, sing, make
noise, swear, or urinate except in the proper place. Heil Hitler" (50–
51). With this injunction against assorted natural functions, Lind begins the section in which his second type of scatological allusion appears, the portion of the story in which Wohlbrecht is confined to the
Saint Veith insane asylum. Not strictly a mental institution, Saint
Veith is a center for the extermination of Jews and various other persons who are troublemakers in the eyes of the Nazis. Here Wohlbrecht
meets Professor Mückenpelz ("Mosquitoskin"), the director of the institution, and Dr. Wimper, who to some degree resemble Böll's Bressen
and Greck, respectively. The similarities of Wimper to Greck are particularly noticeable: both are anal personalities who dislike the dirt
with which the war brings them in contact; both espouse certain of the
Nazi beliefs without being as ardently militant as Bressen or Mückenpelz; and both detest the inconvenient disruptions that the war brings
to their lives. Wimper is particularly disgruntled about the nature of
his daily duties; he is not bothered so much by the number of people
he is expected to exterminate as he is by the endless forms his hated
superior insists that he fill out. Lind writes of Wimper, "He hated that
Mückenpelz, that Prussian shithead, like Satan himself. It's an outrage, the things that man does. First that crap about his schedules that
nobody can make head or tail of, and now his shitty reports" (56). Repeatedly, Wimper refers to the "shitty reports" as the bane of his existence and longs for the day when he will get revenge on Mückenpelz;
he envisions this moment of reckoning in a song he improvises when
he and Wohlbrecht are drunk: "Heil Hitler to you, Mückenprick, / A
needle in your ass I'll stick" (69).[28] The Saint Veith events draw to a
close as the Russian forces approach the asylum. Finishing his duties
with typically compulsive anality, Wimper exterminates fifteen Jews
in as many minutes, washes his hands, and hastens to his quarters to
finish packing.

The third type of scatological imagery with which Lind presents the
reader is a sort of Baal-like vulgarity, a contrast to the personal fastidiousness of the Nazi administrators of Saint Veith. Although the most

striking scene of this type immediately follows the Russian attack on Saint Veith, there are foreshadowings of scatologically uncouth behavior earlier in the story. Lind uses spitting as a leitmotiv for unpleasant or inadequate characters, such as Wohlbrecht's cowardly brother-in-law, Alois, who upon his arrival to help Wohlbrecht hide Toni, "washed his hands, brought up phlegm from deep down (breathing came hard to him), and spat vigorously at the only tree in the yard" (15). Similarly, the gendarme whom they encounter on the way to the hiding place sucks on his teeth during the early part of their conversation (because the use of toothpicks is not allowed when one is on duty), then later triumphantly spits out the morsel of food that he has located (19). The results of Gershon Legman's extensive studies of "dirty" jokes would back up the effectiveness of this sort of imagery in designating unsavory characters. Legman observes that people who can tolerate the most explicit sexual tales, or even those involving urine or feces, become upset when stories deal with mucus or vomit; perhaps, Legman conjectures, this is because of the connotations of illness—in the case of mucuslike discharges, not only tuberculosis but also venereal disease may come to mind.[29]

In an attempt to convey the Nazi-soldier-as-savage motif, Lind presents the reader with a vignette crammed full of nonstop, distasteful scatological imagery. Fleeing the asylum and trying to beat Mückenpelz and Wimper to the now valuable Jew hidden on the mountain, Wohlbrecht hitches a ride with two soldiers, Gschwandfänger and Bischof; the former takes pleasure in spitting on the heads of the retreating infantrymen, and the latter "farted so loud it was painful" (74). The response of these two bestial characters to Wohlbrecht's pathetic tale of the hiding of Toni and his request for their aid in retrieving what he believes is Toni's corpse is indicative of their degree of refinement: "Gschwandfänger had to belch, that Hungarian sausage was still heavy on his stomach, and Bischof took a mouthful from the thermos flask, spat against the windshield, and began to wipe it off. He wished he could give this cripple a boot in the ass, throw him out of the car, and punish him by taking his wooden leg away. He'd look good dancing on one leg. The idea appealed to him so much that he let out another wind—he could do it at will—that made the windows rattle." After repeated pleas by Wohlbrecht, Bischof snaps, "Lick my ass," and Gschwandfänger, out of pity attempting to be somewhat more polite, says, "Look, . . . we don't give a shit about your Jew!" (75). The latter proceeds to explain that they will not need to impress their conquerors with their supposed efforts to help a Jew, because they are good soldiers who only did their duty and "beat the shit out of the Commies" (76). Finally, the grown-up, armed, and brutalized Max and Moritz drop Wohlbrecht off with a farewell of "Go shove it up" from Bischof, and they appropriately vanish "in a cloud of diesel fumes" of extremely black humor (77).

At the completion of his journey across the river and up the mountain, Wohlbrecht leaves the absurdly earthy atmosphere of the army truck and enters an otherworldly zone peopled by spirits and even a witch. The mountain air imparts to him a sort of moral adrenalin and singleness of purpose: he must find "his" Toni, no matter what the cost. As he hastens through the night, an angel asks him, "Wohlbrecht, aren't you afraid?" and Wohlbrecht replies, "Shit." (The answer in the original German, "Ich scheiß drauf"[30]—literally, "I shit on fear"—conveys more precisely the emphatic nature of the protagonist's retort.) In this final section of the story, we find Wohlbrecht using speech that expresses anal hostility, but it is not the careless antagonism of the soldiers, which desecrates whatever it touches. It is a heroic hostility born of desperate times and indicative of the insight that very little in life is worthy of being considered sacred. When the angel warns Wohlbrecht that if he persists in his quest Wimper, Mückenpelz, and the soldiers may destroy him, he responds in a scatological crescendo of emotion: "I shit on Wimper and Mückenpelz and all the soldiers in the world. On war and peace and corpses and even on the Americans. On my aching leg and even on Hochrieder. Nobody's going to touch my Toni. Even his skeleton belongs to me" (78).[31]

Unfortunately, this passage is Wohlbrecht's swan song. Despite his Herculean efforts, ominous notes are present in the pervasive smell of the urine of the witch's cats and the oppressive atmosphere of her annually aired-out home.[32] Even with the witch's assistance, Wohlbrecht barely manages to beat Wimper, Mückenpelz, and Gschwandfänger to Toni and is soon overpowered by the other three. There is a momentary triumph when the resurrected deer man Toni (anything is possible in the rarefied mountain atmosphere) vomits on Gschwandfänger's uniform as the trio tries to force-feed him salami and black bread. In response, the soldier calls Toni a "swine," and Wimper chimes in, "Lousy Jewish pig" (78). (The epithets in the original German have stronger connotations of excrement or filth: *Scheißkerl*, the equivalent of the English "shithead," and *Drecksau, jüdische*, or "filthy Jewish pig.")[33] Predictably, Wohlbrecht cannot abide sharing his Toni with this despicable threesome. He revolts, and like all rebels he must be exterminated. Handing Mückenpelz his gun, Gschwandfänger orders the professor, whom he calls an old *Mückenscheißer* ("Mosquito-shitter"),[34] to shoot. This linking of mosquitoes and excrement lends a sense of debasement that underlines the tragically ignoble circumstances of Wohlbrecht's death. Lind's reference in the story's last paragraph to Wohlbrecht's eventual resurrection, however, implies that the sort of buoyant spirit expressed by Wohlbrecht in his reply to the angel cannot be totally destroyed.

HERMANN WOHLBRECHT'S climactic speech on the mountaintop revealed a disillusionment that had been expressed in very similar terms by George Grosz in 1933: "three cheers for 'scientific' communism. . . . three cheers for class hate!!!! three cheers for 'unscientific' fascism with its race hate!!!! Shit on them both."[35] The bizarre and tragic occurrences that accompanied the rise of the Nazis to power affected different artists and writers in different ways. Actual events in Germany were more horrible than anything the most outlandish artistic or literary imagination could fantasize. Grosz, accustomed to caricaturing reality, now found reality too distorted to lend itself to depiction in his previous style. Beth Irwin Lewis comments of this period in Grosz's life: "The enormity of what he was trying to portray and his own impotence to do anything about it robbed these drawings [in *Interregnum*, Grosz's last major portfolio] of the incisiveness and brilliance of his revolutionary post-war drawings. . . . Under the impact of totalitarianism, Grosz's pen faltered and finally became silent. When he illustrated books and articles in America, his drawings were illustrations, nothing more.[36]

The same phenomenon may be responsible for Böll's description of Captain Filskeit. Eyewitness accounts of the boundless sadism and the cold compliance with orders—regardless of their human implications—practiced by the officials at the Nazi death camps virtually defy comprehension. Figures such as Filskeit very possibly did exist. Terrence Des Pres has summarized the problem that such real-life monsters present for the writer by his comment, "Extremity makes bad art." In his study of the experience of survival in the concentration camps, Des Pres discusses the horrifying development of life's imitating fictional representations of hell. "How much is metaphor," he asks, "how much plain fact? Or is there any longer a difference?" We may find echoes of both Greck and Filskeit in Des Pres's assertion that the camps present us with "realized archetypes of eternal victimhood and of evil forever triumphant." In the case of Greck, Böll wisely applied the literary technique of irony to show us that the camp inmates were not the only ones destroyed by the Nazis, that the officers themselves were the victims of their own sick thought patterns. Filskeit, however, because of his one-sidedness—no matter how closely he resembled real war criminals—was a poor candidate for depiction in a novel that is generally characterized by psychological realism. As Des Pres comments, "Archetypes have actualized in events so exaggerated, so melodramatic and patently symbolic, that no serious novelist, except perhaps in parody, would now attempt to treat them as art."[37]

One response to the dilemma of life's being more grotesque than fiction has been the development of documentary theater since World War II. The playwrights who employ this format re-create on the stage actual historical events, selecting *which* details to present on the basis of their dramatic effectiveness. Peter Weiss, who used this technique effectively in *The Investigation* as well as in other works, explained, "This critical selection and the principle according to which the clippings from reality are arranged result in the quality of the documentary drama."[38] *The Investigation* is based on the actual court record of the trial of twenty-one persons who took part in perpetrating the horrors of the Auschwitz concentration camp. Weiss tells his readers in the notes at the start of the play that they will be presented with a distillation of the evidence from the trial: "This condensation should contain nothing but facts. . . . The nine witnesses sum up what hundreds expressed."[39]

In choosing the evidence with which he will confront his audience, Weiss has included a number of incidents and details that are explicitly or implicitly scatological in nature. These data tell us much about the Nazis and their victims. For one thing, they present us with an uncompromising portrayal of the sadistic practices of the individuals in charge of the death camp. Not only did the authorities deny the prisoners the use of toilet paper, but a special latrine detail attempted to speed up the natural processes of elimination by means of physical abuse:

> The latrine detail saw to it
> That nobody sat there too long
> They clubbed the prisoners right and left
> To drive them out
> Many of the prisoners
> simply couldn't get done that quick
> Part of their rectum stuck out from the strain [38]

In addition to limiting the amount of time spent on the toilet, the Nazis went so far as to determine the time of day when inmates could relieve themselves:

> You had to relieve yourself in the morning
> After that you couldn't
> Anybody caught trying
> was locked up [39]

The camp administrators' mistreatment of the prisoners reveals not only their own brutality but also the extent to which they attempted to dehumanize the persons in their charge. An incident that took place during the unloading of new arrivals at the camp's railroad station illustrates dramatically the leaders' sadism and their view of their prisoners as being worth no more than discardable excrement: a Nazi named Baretzki beat a woman who had just given birth and kicked her infant to death, referring to it as "garbage" and "shit" (25). The use of such terms in regard to a newborn human being reveals to the audience the depth of the degradation suffered by those who were interned at Auschwitz. From the moment of their arrival at the camp, the captives were treated like filth. The soup they were served was essentially garbage, consisting of table scraps and sometimes even pieces of paper or rags (41). In violation of all standard medical practices, they were treated with unsterilized instruments (91). The prisoners had to undergo such humiliating experiences that eventually, like the soldiers in *All Quiet on the Western Front*, they felt totally estranged from life-as-usual:

> When they made us lie down on the tables
> in the reception room
> and inspected our rectums
> and our sexual organs
> for concealed valuables
> every last remnant
> of our usual life
> vanished [40]

As their civilized lives became only a memory, the prisoners discovered that they were living an existence in which the traditional distinction between a person's "higher" and "lower" natures had vanished. For them, the dual roles of publicly conducting oneself with dignity and finesse and privately performing the excretory functions shared by lower forms of life no longer coexisted as a two-track system. Privacy and cleanliness disappeared; *unten* obliterated *oben*. As they found themselves awash in excrement, the quest for personal fastidiousness became utterly futile. For starters, their only source of water was located next to the latrine; in order to be able to wash, they had to hold their bowls under a "thin trickle of water" that dripped into "vats full of excrement" (39). The bowls themselves served as symbols of the impossibility of decent hygiene:

> The bowls we were given
> served three different functions
> to wash in
> to get our supper in
> and to relieve ourselves in at night [39]

Des Pres describes such scatological abuses as "one of the worst aspects of the camp ordeal. When cleanliness becomes impossible and human beings are forced to live in their own excretions, their pain becomes intense to the point of agony. The shock of physical defilement causes spiritual concussion, and, simply to judge from the reports of those who have suffered it, subjection to filth seems often to cause greater anguish than hunger or fear of death."[40] In his chapter entitled "Excremental Assault," Des Pres gropes to find an explanation for this phenomenon; at one point he raises the possibility that the prisoners' anguish was caused by the violation of the rules of hygiene they had been taught as children—but he soon rejects this solution as too facile. A mere lapse in manners or even the disruption of ingrained habits could not cause such psychic pain, Des Pres concludes. The key to the trauma, as he sees it, lies in the fact that toilet training is more than an externally imposed code of behavior; it is "the ritual organization of an inherent biological process." Thus, although many taboos tumbled in the death camps, scatological abuses such as those detailed by Weiss brought particularly intense pain because more than a violation of "cultural imposition" was involved. "What human beings will or will not tolerate depends, up to a point, on training of all kinds," writes Des Pres, adding, "Beyond that, however, there are things absolutely unacceptable because something . . . in our deepest nature revolts."[41] What Des Pres is implying is that the severity of the Nazis' excremental abuses struck at the prisoners' *internalization* of the concepts of defilement and purity. It is embarrassing and distressing to be forced to behave contrary to one's upbringing and the expectations of society; however, when one has no choice but to act in opposition to one's own innermost perceptions of what is best, then one is devastated. The situation with which Weiss confronts his audience, therefore, goes beyond the uneasiness experienced by Remarque's Paul on the train. It goes beyond the pathos of Greck's tears. *The Investigation* portrays the nadir of human suffering.

Weiss expresses the extremity of the prisoners' plight in the metaphor of the "ass of the world." A former camp doctor, asked by a prosecutor how he could have tolerated the murder of innocent persons, replied:

> There was nothing I could do about it
> My first day there
> the army doctor said to me
> We're in the asshole of the world here
> and we have to behave accordingly [199]

Richard L. Rubenstein discusses this metaphor in *After Auschwitz: Radical Theology and Contemporary Judaism.* After pointing out that anal characteristics have often been associated with the devil (as has been demonstrated earlier in this study with regard to Martin Luther), Rubenstein observes "that in German folk-culture the Devil is either a Jew or the Lord of the Jews, who are supposed to exude fecal odor. The *anus mundi* was the habitat of the Devil. If ever men successfully created such a habitat on earth, it was at Auschwitz."[42] Rubenstein then refers to the Nazis' need to turn the Jews into excrement: "Only at the *anus mundi* could the Jew as deicide, betrayer, and incarnate Devil be turned into the feces of the world. Rudolph Hoess, the Nazi commandant at Auschwitz, was one of the many Nazis to note and complain of the hideous fecal stench of the camp. . . . The SS wallowed in human stench to destroy what they regarded as the ultimate in human evil. As had so frequently occurred before, those who saw themselves as overwhelming a radical evil felt compelled to fight evil with evil."[43] Weiss graphically depicts the result of this effort to transform human beings to excrement, as one of the witnesses describes the corpses at Auschwitz:

> The heaps of people were befouled
> with vomit
> excrement urine and menstrual blood [256]

One of the most striking dramatic contrasts in *The Investigation* is that between the unspeakably filthy, dehumanized plight of the captives and the fastidiousness of the camp administrators, who attempted to block the camp's excremental ambience from their minds by concentrating on the clean, the noble, the beautiful. There are numerous examples in the drama of the pains that many of the Nazis took to keep themselves clean, especially after a killing had taken place. A particularly vivid instance of obsessive cleanliness is the behavior of SS Corporal Stark:

> We knew exactly how Stark would behave
> when he came back from a killing
> Everything in the room
> had to be in order and absolutely clean
> and we had to chase the flies out
> with handkerchiefs
> If he spotted a fly
> he would go into a rage
> Even before he took off his cap
> he would wash his hands in a basin
> his flunkey always had ready for him
> on a stool next to the door
> When he had washed his hands
> he pointed at the dirty water
> and the flunkey had to run out
> for more
> Then he handed us his jacket to be cleaned
> and washed his hands and face again [145]

It is clear from Stark's elaborate toilette that he is desperately trying to avoid contamination from the "filth" that has just been destroyed. His washing may also, however, be an indication of at least some personal guilt, à la Lady Macbeth. The distorted state of mind of this young officer is indicated by the fact that on occasion he would discuss Goethe's humanism with the same individuals whom he later helped to exterminate.

Weiss presents evidence in *The Investigation* that those in charge of the concentration camps in no way abandoned their warped thinking after the war. Even during their trials the accused show no remorse for their deeds; instead, they maintain that the charges against them simply constitute a campaign to defile them. They, however, will tell only "the absolute truth" (96). (In the original German, the phrase used is *die reine Wahrheit*;[44] *reine* does mean "absolute," but its primary meaning is "clean," an irony that cannot be translated into idiomatic English.) Similarly perverse is the fact that, after the war, the accused Dr. Capesius, who had participated in Cyclon B gassings, became the owner of a beauty parlor, the advertising slogan of which was "Be beautiful / with beauty treatments by Capesius" (234).

The presence in *The Investigation* of characters who emphasize cleanliness, often to a fanatic degree, while simultaneously propagating the most extreme scatological abuses leads us to suspect we are dealing with yet another literary depiction of the Nazi as the anal personality. Lind's Wimper and Böll's Greck both share the compulsive hand-washing habit of SS Corporal Stark. Even Remarque's Himmelstoß may be seen as an early foreshadowing of the type. Clearly, at least some modern German authors who attempt to depict the psychopathology of those who perpetrate war have considered it necessary to include the anal personality in their casts of characters. In doing so, we may ask, were they achieving psychological realism or creating a mythical stereotype?

The suggestion has been made that the Nazis were, in fact, anally fixated. Rubenstein interprets Nazi aggression as an attempt to return to the uninhibited soiling of pre-toilet-training days. He notes, "While the Nazis could not without incontinence give free rein to their own anal obsessions, they could and did turn the Jews, whom their folk-culture regarded as the satanic murderers of the dead God, into feces."[45] Dundes, as was mentioned earlier, carries this hypothesis further by suggesting that the holocaust sprang from the anal fixations of not just one group of demented leaders but of Germans in general. Jakov Lind would seem to share the view that the Nazis were seeking to purge the world of Jews because of the latters' supposed "filth"; Lind observes, "Eichmann said he never hated the Jews. Hitler probably did. But it was not a question of hatred, it was a matter of law enforcement. They didn't come to kill the Jews, this was just an unfortunate logical consequence of a laudable task—to clean up a mess, to straighten out what looked uneven, to put order into chaos. It was not done with Asian-Oriental emotionalism, it was carried out with Lutheran cold-bloodedness, with the Lutheran compulsion to remove anything 'dirty.'"[46]

Many psychologists, including Freud, have considered sadism one way in which anality may manifest itself. English and Pearson, for example, describe a young patient who responded to his mother's strict demands "by being overclean and by being destructive and cruel."[47] Rubenstein ties this theory in with the brutality displayed by those Germans who were in charge of the death camps, tracing their bitterness and hostility back to their "unconscious resentment" of their own strict toilet training:

> The Germans have always been exceptionally proud of their orderliness and cleanliness in the home as well as in the wider community. They seem to have lacked the understanding that the most rigidly disciplined of men are often the

most inwardly rebellious and resentful. Such men often make excellent disciplinarians with others, because they want to make sure that none escapes the bitter training which has been inflicted on them. Undoubtedly this discipline, with all its self-perpetuating harshness, begins with toilet training.[48]

A more complex interpretation of the excremental mistreatment of the prisoners is found in the views of Heinrich Böll. There is abundant evidence in Böll's works of his theory that anal biases contributed to the predisposition of some Germans to accept Nazi ideas and behavior. He did not limit his explanation of the scatological abuses of the concentration camps to an anal interest in purging and/or messing, however. In the course of being interviewed by Karin Struck, the novelist described deprivation of personal hygiene as "a controlling device." Although he agreed with the interviewer that Hitler displayed "a washing compulsion," Böll's emphasis was on the withholding of the means of cleanliness as a power play that reduces captives to a helpless state: "if, over a period of three days, you deny a person the opportunity to wash, to shave, or to attend to his appearance in any way, then you have debased him psychologically."[49] In light of Ernest Jones's assertion that the quest for power is "intimately connected with the anal-erotic impulse,"[50] Böll's remarks to Struck may represent yet another elaboration on the anal personality theory; however, the novelist should be credited with reaching beyond the normal literary depiction of anality in terms of cleanliness–filth motifs to probe the Nazis' motivation more fully.

Des Pres, whose views are based on the actual accounts of eyewitnesses, takes an approach akin to Böll's. Calling the scatological humiliation of the death camp prisoners a "special kind of evil" that "is a natural outcome of power when it becomes absolute," Des Pres explains: "The death of the soul was aimed at. It was to be accomplished by terror and privation, but first of all by a relentless assault on the survivor's sense of purity and worth. Excremental attack, the physical inducement of disgust and self-loathing, was a principal weapon."[51] Reacting to *The Investigation*, Manfred Durzak received a similar impression, that of "the mechanics of economic exploitation and of the ruthless expansion of power . . . which—in the extreme case of the concentration camp—could depersonalize the individual to such a degree that he would lose the last vestiges of humanity and sink beneath the level of existence of an animal."[52] Des Pres follows Durzak's line of thinking as he explores the relationship between the Nazis' manipulations of the prisoners' cleanliness needs and the formers' psychological defense mechanisms: "And here is a final, vastly significant reason why in the camps the prisoners were so degraded. This made it easier for the SS to do their job. It made mass murder less terrible to the murderers, because the victims appeared less than human. They *looked* inferior." When captives have been reduced to the level of vermin or garbage, their exterminators can rationalize "that so much rotten tissue has been removed from life's body."[53]

Des Pres's theories come the closest of all the above-mentioned hypotheses to the findings of Gilbert, the prison psychologist at Nuremberg. Gilbert does not present us with any profiles of the Nazis as anal personalities. He does not even find much evidence of compulsive behavior, so often linked with anality by psychologists. A so-called cultural pseudocompulsiveness, defined by Gilbert as the "tendency to carry to a nonadaptive extreme the repetition of group behavior rituals," was noted in the Nazis as a group.[54] Rigid behavior rituals for the purpose of "undoing" anxiety (such as Stark's ablutions) were not generally observed in individuals, however. Anticipating views such as those of Dundes, Gilbert comments, "German national character has, indeed, also been described as compulsive in nature. But . . . we must distinguish between true psychopathology and the cultural epiphenomenon. . . . we must not infer from the apparent maladaptive functioning of the group the psychopathology of its members."[55]

Sadism, though it certainly was included in the psychological makeup of some of the leaders examined by Gilbert, was not the determining factor in the attitudes of many of the Nazi chieftains toward the Jews. Gilbert found socioeconomic factors to be the origin of a great deal of the prejudice. Some Nazis did express regretful feelings with regard to their crimes, leading the prison psychologist to remark that "human empathy was not dead, but only perverted, in the Nazi microcosm."[56] The twisted views of the leaders were facilitated by the sort of defense mechanisms described by Des Pres, including "rationalization of ulterior motives" and "sublimation of aggressive tendencies." Consequently, many of the leaders "washed their hands (and minds) of any guilt feelings."[57] Despite Gilbert's use of a metaphor that would win the approval of a number of the writers of modern German war literature, the psychologist finds psychopathic characteristics only in those who directly supervised the death camps. The other Nazis, he concludes, were normal persons whose distorted thinking allowed them to be caught up in a drama of social pathology.[58]

Are Wimper, Greck, and Stark, then, simply figments of overactive literary imaginations? Not entirely. *The Investigation* is, after all, based on actual court records. Other evidence would seem to indicate that persons with anal personalities or traits (who of course exist in virtually any civilized society) were attracted to the Nazi cause. Rudolf Hoess, chief of Auschwitz, is a case in point. Joachim Fest depicts this notorious Nazi as a person who had been fixated on extreme cleanliness, dutifulness, and orderliness since childhood. Viewing Hoess as conforming all too eagerly to the authoritarian regimen of the death camp, Fest remarks that "the only philosophy of life he had with which to confront the monstrous conditions was that of the recruit who takes a naïve and foolish pride in a well-made bed and the look of satisfaction on an NCO's face." For Hoess, observes Fest, the use of gas as a means of killing was appealing because it was "as rational as it was bloodless and hygienic." When Fest mentions the "ambitious, cold hunger for organisation typical of a man of his stamp," it is likely that the "stamp" to which the author is referring is that of the anal personality.[59] Hoess's colleague at Auschwitz, Josef Mengele, also has been described in terms of his "exaggerated immaculateness" and "passion for cleanliness." One survivor has likened the camp to a dog pound in which Mengele ordered the keepers (the inmate doctors) to "wash up the excrement" so that the dogs (prisoners) would remain healthy for his research on eugenics; another former inmate remarked that Mengele was "Clean, clean, clean!"[60]

Similarly, in *A Little Yes and a Big No* George Grosz described his Professor Mueller (see chapter 1, herein) as "a stickler for discipline and military promptness."[61] According to an anecdote expunged from the English version of Grosz's autobiography, Mueller, upon discovering that the young artist had dared to take a break from his studies to eat a roll, briskly snapped, "Go shit. Make use of time."[62] When the students in Mueller's class painted the head of a model, "every hair of the eyebrow had to be counted. . . . Our crayons, numbering one to five, had to be sharply pointed—truly a symbol of order and discipline in the absolute Prussian sense." Grosz commented, "If I appear to be devoting an unusual amount of space to Professor Mueller, it is because there are a great many like him even today. . . . One can never make a rebel out of a conservative. Professor Mueller, who might well have been a product of my imagination and a symbol—which he was not— was just such a conservative."[63] After World War II, Mueller was dismissed from his post at the Dresden Academy because of his Nazi past. Students contended that his misdeeds had included the removal of Grosz's art works from the academy walls. (Undismayed, Grosz sent "CARE packages" of cigarettes to his former professor, whose earthy, scatological language he had found so amusing.)[64]

For persons such as Mueller, the Nazi propaganda regarding racial purity must have had enormous appeal. Prepared by the old idea of the purification of the *Volksgeist* and filled with the not surprising longing to clean up the dirty, decadent society depicted by artists such as Grosz, at least some individuals with marked anal fixations very likely reacted favorably as the Nazis purged libraries and galleries, censored music and drama, and eliminated "inferior" human beings. Anally oriented persons were probably moved to become more active and visible in a society whose leaders were bandying about such terms as *Säuberung* ("cleansing" or "purging"), *Judenreinmachen* ("Jew purification"), and *Rassenhygiene* ("eugenics"). When these anally fixated individuals assumed supervisory positions in the death camps, the survivors remembered them.

Paul Fussell has observed that persons writing war memoirs or war fiction based on their own recollections tend to select for inclusion in their works those situations that are particularly ironic.[65] The role played by individuals with anal traits in the horrors of the Third Reich made an indelible impression on those who observed it because of its inherent irony. Out of leaders who prized order came utter chaos. The survivors who watched this contradictory phenomenon retained it in their memories. It had not surprised them that their captors demonstrated brutality, but it struck them as totally out of character when some of these morally impure villains, the very instigators of their excremental humiliation, displayed penchants for cleanliness![66] The paradox was preserved in oral history, in courtroom records, and in memoirs, and thus it presented itself as raw material for postwar writers. *The Investigation*, for example, consists of Weiss's veneer of artistic arrangement imposed on the layer of order with which the survivors structured their own memories.

Certainly, the image of the anally oriented Nazi appealed to German authors because of its dramatic value. Writers frequently exaggerate for effect, and the runaway anality that had been observed in some of the Nazis who supervised the death camps, what Böll called "a superhygienification, propagation to the point of anankasm, to the point of a washing compulsion,"[67] together with its concomitant sadistic brutality, provided authors with the types of excesses that produce deeply stirring literature. Thus the references to anality in the descriptions of Nazi figures in postwar German writings serve not just a psychological or philosophical purpose but also a literary one: in addition to acting as aids to characterization, they provide the type of vivid thematic antithesis that distinguishes literature from a journalistic reporting of fact. Because it enhances the dramatic and ironic impact of their works, German authors have chosen to put this construct on the actuality of the Nazi experience, to impose the framework of the anal personality on persons who, in most cases, were far more complex. But the literary stereotype, though historically tenuous, contains at least a kernel of metaphoric truth. The postwar writers understood that, as Fest implies in his chapter on Hoess, the grim reaper of the concentration camps often appeared in a perverse disguise: "This radical evil appears most clearly when viewed in its least obvious aspect." It was because the Nazi ideology presented itself as an "appeal to idealism" that it had such insidious power.[68] Weiss grasped this irony when he included in *The Investigation* the sentiments that were printed in capital letters on the roof of the death camp kitchen:

> THERE IS ONE WAY TO FREEDOM
> ITS MILESTONES ARE
> OBEDIENCE DILIGENCE CLEANLINESS
> HONESTY TRUTHFULNESS
> AND LOVE OF COUNTRY [122]

7

"as beautiful as snow": A Reversal of Values

I would have liked to hear Henrietta's voice so much," muses Hans Schnier, the protagonist of Heinrich Böll's novel *The Clown*, recalling his deceased sister, "even if she had only said 'nothing' or for that matter 'Oh shit.' From her lips it had not sounded vulgar at all. That time she said it to Schnitzler, when he spoke of her mystical gift, it had sounded as beautiful as snow."[1] This aesthetic turnabout, startling though it may seem, is the metaphorical cornerstone of the writings of Heinrich Böll. Continuing his reminiscences, Schnier describes Schnitzler, the type of pompous character whom Böll often presents as a contrast to straightforward, natural figures such as Henrietta: the "plump, well-groomed" Schnitzler "was always raving about the noble European spirit, about Germanic consciousness," and had written a novel, "French Love Affair," the diction of which is illustrated by the quotation, "the names of French wines ring out like crystal goblets which lovers raise and touch in mutual adoration." A comparison of Schnitzler's pretentious phraseology with Henrietta's uninhibited "shit" reveals the aesthetic polarities with which Böll's writings are suffused. Lest the reader misconstrue Henrietta's language as vulgar, Böll informs us through Schnitzler that, although the ever-sublimating Schnitzler had asserted that "a mystical gift could very well go hand in hand with the 'compulsion to hurl dirty words,'" in fact the use of the word *shit* in Henrietta's case "was not the least compulsive and she did not 'hurl' the word at all, she simply said it."[2]

The values that Böll assigns to language and the way in which it is

139

spoken are not merely aesthetic, however; language and one's mode of expression are also indicators of moral fiber. Using the sort of mirror-writing technique that Büchner employed in *Woyzeck*, Böll provides a counterpoint to the Henrietta–Schnitzler passage later in the novel. When the despairing Schnier attempts to telephone his brother Leo, a student at a Catholic seminary, he cannot get past the bureaucrat who answers the phone. Asking that Leo be informed that his brother's soul is in danger, Hans receives the following response from the businesslike old man on the other end of the line: "'Soul,' he said coldly, 'brother, danger.' He might just as well have said: Muck, manure, milkman."[3] In the mouths of the inhumane characters in Böll's writings, the most noble sentiments sound mundane and at times even vulgar; the taking-in-vain of the names of the saints and the Holy Family by the cruel prostitutes and nursing nuns at the end of *Group Portrait with Lady* illustrates this point clearly. On the other hand, the matter-of-fact, almost clinical use of scatological diction by morally pure characters is a sign of their naturalness.

In view of the Nazis' corruption of such terms as *purification* (of art, culture, race, etc.) and *hygiene*, it is not surprising that dirt, refuse, and excrement gained an unusually high level of respectability in postwar German literature. This is especially true of the writings of Böll. When Böll delivered his *Frankfurt Lectures* during the 1963–64 fall semester at the University of Frankfurt, he began by stating that his goal was "to deal with an aesthetics of the humane." Later in these lectures, Böll emphasized the significant role that society's discards play in his aesthetics: "The humaneness of a country can be deduced from what lands in its garbage: those everyday items, things that still are usable, poesie; whatever is discarded and is deemed worthy of annihilation." Böll then applied his thoughts to his own profession, that of the writer: "Evidently literature can choose as its subject matter only those things that society declares to be garbage, that it scorns."[4] Finally, Böll discussed the role of humor in his aesthetics, and again he stressed the rejects of society:

> Humor requires a certain minimal optimism and at the same time sadness (which possibly makes it suspect to those who do not possess it); because the word *humores* signifies liquid and also juices and all the body fluids, such as bile, tears, saliva, as well as urine, it creates a bond with the material side of existence and bestows upon the latter a humane quality. Crying and laughing are distinguishing characteristics of *Homo sapiens*. It seems to me that there is only one humane application possible for humor: to determine the nobility of those things that society considers to be trash.[5]

Böll's belief that humane humor demonstrates the nobility of that which society discards as useless underlies all of his works. From Böll's earliest to his later publications, the reader continually encounters a much more positive representation of society's losers than of its winners. One of the best examples of Böll's noble (and humorous) depiction of "trash" is his novel *Group Portrait with Lady* (*Gruppenbild mit Dame*). Böll achieved his goal so noticeably in this work that some of the more fastidious, conservative critics have been terribly offended by it. Consequently, the reviews of this novel were often quite negative, as is illustrated by the following statement by Reinhard Baumgart: "Around a disorderly, almost slovenly main character Böll has fashioned a novel for which *undisciplined* or *uncouth* would not be inaccurate adjectives."[6]

Undoubtedly Böll's frequent, uninhibited use of excremental allusions in *Group Portrait with Lady* is the cause for much of the concern over this novel. What shocks many scholars particularly is the apparent interest in the processes of elimination displayed by the main character, Leni Gruyten Pfeiffer. Manfred Durzak, for example, cannot tolerate the thought that Leni combines her excremental interests with a love of the poetry of Hölderlin: "The excremental sphere and Hölderlin's poetry are poles apart."[7] Durzak's objections to the characterization of Leni could perhaps be justified if she exhibited some kind of vulgar enjoyment of excrement. This, however, is not the case at all. It will be demonstrated later in this chapter that Leni accepts excrement as a natural part of human life. She does not deliberately look for opportunities to use scatological terms; on the other hand, neither does she share the neurotic aversion to dirt or excrement that Böll perceived in some Germans. It is precisely this natural, uncomplicated attitude towards excrement that enables Leni to remain free from fears and guilt feelings. Just as she accepts all parts and functions of the human body as natural and good, she also accepts all human beings as equal and cannot detect any difference between, for example, a Jew and a non-Jew. Thus, in contrast to the Nazis, Leni is not driven by fears of being contaminated by certain "filthy" people. Leni's appreciation of Hölderlin, then, is not at all inconsistent with the unprejudiced humaneness she represents.

Leni's interest in her own waste products can be traced back to her preschool days. This fact was reported to Böll's "author" with some unease by Marja van Doorn, a former maid in the home of Leni's parents: "Even as a child, Leni was fascinated by the excremental processes to which she was subject and on which—unfortunately in vain!—she used to demand information by asking: 'Come on now, tell me! What's all this stuff coming out of me?'" (36)[8] It seems that Leni was destined to clash with the repressed society that produced her; neither her mother nor Marja could provide the answer to the girl's daring question. Marja genuinely likes Leni, but the maid, trained within the system, is well aware that the polite society of the day considers open, frank discussions of bodily functions unseemly. Thus Marja finds Leni's simple, straightforward questions an indication of a "passionate" interest in excrement, and she is too rattled to be able to respond. Leni's mother, traditionally feminine in her delicacy and primness, is even less capable of answering her daughter's supposedly shocking questions. Although the "author" suspects that this fragile, ineffective woman might have had the potential to become a left-wing radical, "Needless to say, she never 'touched' Zola—as she had been taught not to, and one can imagine her horror when eight years later her daughter Leni asked about her (Leni's) *bowel movements*. For her, Zola and excrement were probably almost identical concepts" (78).

Leni finally receives the answer to her question during her two years (from age twelve to fourteen) as a student in a girls' boarding school run by Catholic nuns. Here Leni has the good fortune to encounter another uninhibited and enlightened individual, Sister Rahel. This nun, a converted Jewess, has been assigned a "duty that was regarded by all the other nuns as disgusting, as being beyond the call of duty, but that was carried out by Sister Rahel with nothing short of enthusiasm, with devoted attention to detail: the inspection of the products of youthful digestion in solid and liquid form" (47). Rahel, whose role most of the other nuns consider to be "halfway between toilet attendant and cleaning woman" (48), is the first person whom Leni has ever encountered who answers her questions truthfully and openly. Except for her relationship with Rahel, Leni's upbringing has been and continues to be primarily in the hands of ascetic nuns and equally puritanical male religion teachers who are horrified by any behavior that might be construed as an expression of sensuality. Thus, when Leni eagerly anticipates her First Communion with the remark, "Please, please give me this Bread of Life! Why must I wait so long?" she is rebuked for her vulgarity and banned from participation in the sacrament for two more years; her religion instructor, Erich Brings, "found Leni's spontaneous expression of sensuality 'criminal'" (42). Similarly, when the girls at the boarding school receive their so-called instruction in human sexuality, they are told a great deal of sublimated nonsense. Using "culinary symbolism" and revealing "not so much as a hint of accurate biological details," the instructor, Mr. Horn, "compared the result of sexual intercourse, which he called a 'necessary reproductive process,' with 'strawberries and whipped cream'" (44). Ironically, this kind of indirect representation of one of life's most natural acts is ultimately more obscene than an honest, direct answer, and thus Leni blushes for the first time in her life. Here again, one's use of words reveals one's character: the teacher's inability to face biological functions straightforwardly is betrayed by his saccharine dessert-cart circumlocution.

In contrast to the girl's other tutors, Rahel teaches Leni the open and unashamed acceptance of human corporeality. Leni learns from Rahel that human wastes need not be feared and that in fact the end products of the digestive process can serve a very useful function. The examination of feces and urine, according to Rahel, provides an excellent method of determining the physical and psychological condition of the person who produced the excrement. Sister Rahel has become such an expert examiner of human waste that she can make an analysis with just one glance and actually is able to predict the girls' scholastic potential from the appearance of their excrement. Rahel's first examination of Leni's stools enraptures the nun, and she explains to Leni, "My girl, you're one of Fortune's favorites—like me." Leni intensifies Rahel's initial joy by achieving the very rare ability to pass her stools cleanly, without any need of toilet paper. This "ideal state" had earlier been described by Rahel as she lectured the girls on ways of cleaning themselves after a bowel movement, stating "that for a healthy and—she would stress—intelligent person it was possible to perform this bodily function without so much as a scrap of paper" (50). With Leni's achievement of the "ideal state," a bond for life has been formed between the two women.

Rahel is a perfect example of Böll's theory that the most noble persons are often society's discards. This highly intelligent, extremely well-educated nun (she was a trained biologist, medical doctor, and philosopher) had been demoted from her teaching status when the authorities in Rome suspected her of "mystical materialism" (51)—a term that may not be a bad description of Böll's own philosophy. Instead of leaving the order and returning to a secular existence, as the Church had hoped she would do, Rahel shocks everyone by accepting "the demotion as a promotion" (51) and is ultimately very happy in her new position of *Toilettenfrau*. The celibate, life-fearing Church was afraid of the impact that the life-affirming Rahel would have upon her pupils. Ironically, by being demoted to the lowest possible position, Rahel was able to become even closer to the girls because her status was now no higher than that of the girls themselves and the distance between teacher and pupil was thus removed. Furthermore, because the other nuns considered Rahel's duties to be disgusting, she was left to herself to pursue her scatological-philosophical research.

Sister Rahel's scatological activities provide an effective, humorous contrast to the stifling, impotent atmosphere at the boarding school. Even though no one wanted to carry out the despicable task, someone was needed to watch the stools of the girls for signs of diarrhea and other diseases. In addition, the ascetic nuns also wished to have a spy make sure that the girls engaged in no unclean behavior. Thus, when Rahel was appointed stool inspector, she was required to be on the lookout not only for symptoms of illness but also for "noticeable lack of cleanliness in terms of the digestive process as well as breaches of accepted standards of morality" (49). No one had anticipated that Rahel would refuse the dirty task of reporting any violations by the girls and would instead devote herself enthusiastically and good-naturedly to the examination of feces and urine. It is this very zest for her research, as well as her own lack of shame for the job she is per-forming—not a kinship with the evasive Mr. Horn—that is reflected in the fact that Rahel does not "hesitate to apply the term 'classical ar-chitecture' to the various shapes of bowel movements" (57).

One might question whether Böll's very detailed treatment of the scatological expertise of Sister Rahel is not somewhat exaggerated; it must be remembered, however, that Rahel serves as a representative of the relaxed, life-loving persons whom Böll hoped would one day predominate in his native country, and thus her thoroughness in the study of excrement is a reaction against those whom Böll considered excessively fastidious. Victor Lange has pointed out that Böll's fre-quent use of excremental allusions throughout *Group Portrait with Lady* is directed primarily against such hypocritical cleanliness: "If fecal matter is involved so conspicuously, so pointedly, in this biogra-phy of Leni, . . . then it is probably in order to call into question all sleazy, impotent propositions regarding hygiene, all smug supposi-tions of cleanliness."[9] Böll's great concern regarding the continued em-phasis on cleanliness in postwar Germany is clearly expressed in his "Letter to a Young Non-Catholic," in which his reference to the con-stant television commercials for whiter and whiter wash becomes a chastening reminder of earlier attitudes toward filth: "Perhaps you re-member that word was spread about that the ethnic groups that the Nazis set out to exterminate—Poles, Jews, Russians—were *dirty*." Böll envisioned as the end result of the German drive for cleanliness "Clean leadership, clean morality—and then the 'clean' bomb is placed in these clean hands."[10]

Because of Böll's awareness that the pursuit of cleanliness may reach fanatical and thus harmful proportions, he had a particular affinity for supposedly "filthy" figures such as Rahel or Leni, who are in fact far more human and noble than those people who feel offended by them. For example, Rahel, the "eager little nun, with a mania for mysticism and a mania for biology, suspected of scatology, accused of biologism and materialistic mysticism" (52), is depicted by the novelist as a more endearing and morally worthy character than the mother superior of the boarding school, who "considered it beneath the dignity of a lady to vouchsafe so much as glance at her own excrement" and who leaves her order to work with a Nazi women's organization (49). Eschewing the false pride of the mother superior, Rahel continues to tell the girls at the school the truth about all the biological functions of the human body. In no way, however, is Rahel licentious in her teachings. When she discovers that Margret Zeist often sneaks away from the school during the night and has sexual relations with local boys, Rahel breaks into tears and forces Margret to promise that she will never take Leni along. Similarly, Rahel never encourages the girls to engage in the examination of feces or urine themselves. In fact, she dissuades her girls by telling them "that, when one had acquired some personal experience, a glance at the excrement ought really to confirm what one was aware of anyway on rising: the degree of well-being; and that it was almost superfluous—after sufficient experience—to look at them, unless one was not certain of one's condition and needed a glance at them for further confirmation" (54). Because two witnesses, Margret Zeist and B. H. T., have confirmed these words to the "author," they can be accepted as important proof of Rahel's lack of prurience.

Rahel does, however, make use of the results of her research whenever she deems it appropriate. In one instance, her expertise helps to save the life of a young man, the secondhand bookseller B. H. T., for "her private (forbidden) experiments with urine" turn up the knowledge of how he can keep the level of albumen in his urine elevated in order to avoid military service (52–53). Because Heinrich Böll, like many of his characters, occasionally could not resist the temptation to needle his opposition a bit longer than perhaps is necessary, he had his "author" point out that Rahel kept detailed records of her scatological observations, and these approximately 28,800 analyses of excrement represent "an astounding compendium that would probably fetch any price as a scatalogical [sic] and urinological document." Unfortunately, our time cannot profit from this treasure: "Presumably it has been destroyed as trash!" (48).

Rahel's fate is consistent with other peoples' opinion of her. As the Nazi persecution of the Jews intensifies, Rahel's former Jewishness is used as the appropriate excuse for removing her from all duties and confining her to a tiny broom closet in the attic. In this abode intended for cleaning utensils, Rahel is allowed to die a lingering death from lack of food, as well as from loneliness. The nuns, of course, later claimed that they were doing a very brave deed by hiding Rahel instead of turning her over to the Nazis.

The final victory, however, belongs to the "excremental" Rahel. In a very clever and humorous way, Böll capitalizes on changing Catholic attitudes toward miracles. To the embarrassment of the enlightened postwar Catholic Church in Germany, roses grow from Rahel's grave each December (recalling the hymn "Es ist ein' Ros' entsprungen" and thus linking the outcast Rahel with Christ's nativity). The Church, which now accepts scientific explanations for what it previously considered to be supernatural phenomena, is confronted with an obvious miracle, which it cannot acknowledge. Rahel's body is exhumed several times and reinterred each time in a different place. When this does not stop the miracle, her remains are cremated and the urn is placed in the monastery's chapel, only to have roses appear in it; the ashes then are buried, "and again: roses" (355). Finally the only recourse left for the Church is to declare that a thermal spring has been discovered that is causing an old rosebush to bloom. (Viewed in terms of poetic justice rather than scientific fact, it is not surprising that the remains of a person who devoted herself to the study of excrement should prove to be extraordinary, fertilizer!)

Even though Rahel's activities were forcibly brought to an end in 1938, her ideas live on in her disciple Leni, who, as was seen earlier, is instinctively "a person who was extremely dependent on secretion and hence digestion, totally unsuited for sublimating anything" (208–9). In his depiction of Leni, Böll presents the reader with a character with a perfectly integrated personality: sublimation is alien to her nature. Rather than seeing sublimation as a noble method for overcoming one's baser nature, Böll viewed it as a way of getting out of touch with the core of one's being. In this regard he was like the Zen masters who, according to Thomas Merton, "frequently took their examples from the monastery latrine, just to make sure that the student should know how to 'accept' every aspect of ordinary life and not be blocked by the mania of dividing things into holy and unholy, noble and ignoble valuable and valueless. When one attains to pure consciousness, every-thing has infinite value."[11] Leni's wholesome attitude regarding the oneness of life sets her apart from the society of her day, which, in Böll's opinion, is composed largely of persons who think in dualities, idealizing the spiritual while disparaging the physical.

Terrence Des Pres, in analyzing the characteristics of the death camp survivors, found them to be very much like Leni. The advance-ment of Western civilization has been based upon sublimation, ac-cording to Des Pres, resulting in the creation of positive symbolism re-garding cleanliness and negative symbolism in connection with dirt. This life has been negated "in favor of another life, higher, purer, else-where." In the eyes of those conditioned to think in terms of "Oben and Unten," the "value of life has been reduced to zero, to excrement."[12] As was noted in chapter 6, however, the extremities of war tend to wipe out the *oben–unten* duality. A process of "radical de-sublimation" takes place. With the traditional values destroyed, a new perspective on life is necessary if one is to survive; and, Des Pres tells us, survivors are people who "do not live by the rules." Beyond the mind–body split they discover a "far deeper stratum of the human psyche, one that is life-affirming and life-sustaining." These persons have an almost primi-tive "biological wisdom," which enables them to share with others their simple joy in the concrete; because they are not ashamed to ad-mit their corporeality, they possess the comforting realization that "in life's own needs the spirit can have a home."[13] There can be no doubt that Leni is just such a survivor. A slight variation on Des Pres's image of finding a spiritual "home" in the acceptance of bodily functions may be observed in the fact that anatomical illustrations are part of the de-cor *chez* Leni, for she decorates her apartment with color photographs of the organs of the human body: "Less frequently observed organs, such as the human intestines, also adorn Leni's walls, nor are the hu-man sexual organs, with an accurate description of all their functions, absent as enlarged tabulated wall decorations" (25). Such an un-ashamed affirmation of the human body is of course seen as an affront and as vulgar by the "refined" elements within society.

An incident from Leni's youth, recalled by Lotte Hoyser, reveals that Leni's lack of inhibitions goes back many years. The year is 1940 and the place Margret's apartment, where someone has discovered that the toilet is stopped up. After Leni's brother Heinrich and her cousin Erhard Schweigert fail to solve the problem by the use of vari-ous implements, and while Lotte Hoyser and Margret are overcome with disgust, Leni saves the day in a direct, effective manner: "She simply plunged her hand down, her right hand, and I can still see her lovely white arm covered with yellow muck to above the elbow, then she grabbed the apple and threw it in the garbage pail—and all that horrible mess instantly gurgled away out of sight, and then Leni washed herself thoroughly, mind you, and over and over again" (98–99).

After having cleaned herself carefully, Leni adds a startling remark to her toilet adventure: "Our poets never flinched from cleaning out a john" (99). Manfred Durzak has compared Leni's plumbing aplomb and her unexpected observation to Böll's own "unconventional" but nevertheless effective way of coming to grips with the facts of German history. It appears, however, that Durzak (who refers to what Böll calls the *Klo* as "the sanitary installation") is offended by Leni's statement: "One may find fault not only with the taste of this imagery but also with its insipid meliorism, which in this case is linked to the task of the poet."[14] If one views this metaphor in terms of Böll's concept of humor as expressed in the *Frankfurt Lectures*, however, and if one keeps Böll's misgivings in regard to excessive cleanliness in mind, Durzak's objection is no longer valid. Lotte Hoyser, whom Leni's remark impressed as "electrifying" (99), probably also questioned, if not the "taste," at least the incongruity of mentioning toilet cleaners and poets in the same breath. Such a reaction, however, belies an understanding of what Böll explained as "the paradox that Leni was sensual precisely because she was not altogether sensual" (209). For Leni, the admirer of Kafka, the unearthly horses are harnessed to the earthly vehicle (404). Biological functions and poetry, the body and the soul, are inherently intertwined.

In her radio interview with Böll, Karin Struck claimed to have been "astonished" by this episode, just as Lotte Hoyser was; Struck's critical appraisal of the scene was, however, much more favorable than Manfred Durzak's—perhaps because she was burdened with fewer preconceptions. If one approaches such texts not so much as "a Germanist or some kind of literary connoisseur but rather as a totally naive reader," advises Struck, then one can have "a very positive experience" that can affect one's view of reality. Struck also was amazed by the novelist's originality in his use of the motifs of dirt and cleanliness, and the interviewer succeeded in getting Böll to admit somewhat grudgingly, after initial caveats about precursors in this iconography, that the bathroom scene under discussion has a certain literary novelty. Warming to the topic, Böll added impishly that he would not deny that it "perhaps is a rather good passage."[15]

Leni's action in the toilet-cleaning scene, as well as her statement about poets, represents the novelist's humorously expressed, yet very seriously intended hope that an overly clean, repressed society would turn toward a natural acceptance of life. Böll's prescription for the ailing human race was for it to become, like Leni, less cerebral and more corporeal, so that a freer, more humane society might be achieved. Thus characterization became an important technique for the author-as-therapist. To some extent, Böll's works, and particularly *Group Portrait with Lady* with its large cast of characters, may be viewed as allegorical representations of the inner workings of the German psyche. Seen from this perspective, the personae of the novels and stories represent various stages on a continuum of mental (and spiritual) health. Whereas Leni, as stated above, epitomizes the perfectly integrated personality, other figures, such as Schoolmaster Horn, are not fully developed characters but actors in a modern morality play who might well wear name tags reading "Uptight about Bodily Functions" or "Compulsively Clean." Just as persons completing psychotherapy often use the metaphor "I wanted to clear all that garbage out of my mind," so Böll felt that the Germans must do some mental and spiritual housecleaning—becoming clean in a wholesome, not a fanatic sense—if past errors are not to be repeated. In a number of Böll's works he depicted the Nazi era as a time when a normal interest in cleanliness and order escalated into neurotic if not psychotic proportions in some Germans; when these abnormally intense anxieties about tidiness were coupled with the aggressiveness and megalomania of the Third Reich, a purge of supposedly "filthy" non-Aryans resulted. Furthermore, Böll perceived the remnants of this mindset to be lingering in many Germans long after the war, with the compulsive tendencies becoming apparent in, for example, the work addiction of the *Wirtschaftswunder* ("Action will be taken") or the phobias about foreign workers or terrorists (*The Safety Net*). By depicting neurotic mental patterns in terms of concrete characters and situations, Böll hoped to effect a postwar healing process, liberating the Germans from the impediments to the wholeness of mind and spirit that is evident in Leni.

The characters at the extreme ends of Böll's continuum, such as the morally snow-white Leni and the wicked Nazis, bring to mind fairytale figures, and indeed Leni's disgorging of the apple from the toilet recalls the Brothers Grimm's tale of "Schneewittchen," in which the poison apple becomes lodged in the heroine's throat. Bruno Bettelheim states, "Snow White's partner is the prince, who 'carries her off' in her coffin—which causes her to cough up or spit out the poisonous apple and come to life, ready for marriage. Her tragedy began with oral incorporative desires: the queen's wish to eat Snow White's internal organs. Snow White's spitting out of the suffocating apple—the bad object she had incorporated—marks her final freedom from primitive orality, which stands for all her immature fixations."[16] By transferring the obstructing apple from the throat to the toilet, Böll has moved the psychological ramifications of the symbol from the oral to the anal. According to Böll, anal fixations are a key symptom of the emotional rigidity that led to the Nazi cruelty of World War II and that tends to suffocate the inclination toward a relaxed acceptance of life in the German consciousness even today. Through the toilet-cleaning scene, Böll tells his readers that only by ridding themselves of their mental blocks—perhaps with the guidance of poets—can the Germans "come to life" and achieve a true maturity.

In view of Böll's interpretation of Germany's problems in the twentieth century, the metaphor of a toilet that must be cleaned is both hopeful and understated.[17] Leni's successful completion of her task, furthermore, underlines Böll's basic optimism that the job can be done. In answer to Durzak as well as to Baumgart, who, as we may recall, considers Leni to be "disorderly, almost slovenly," the following comment by Böll should be remembered: "It is no accident that the practice of absolutely every art makes one dirty."[18] Leni personifies Böll's deep conviction that to live life and to be a true human being means that it is both necessary and desirable to immerse oneself in *all* of life, even if it involves getting dirty.

The brief toilet-cleaning scene also plays a crucial role in the understanding of Leni's brother Heinrich and her cousin Erhard. Although these two young men see Nazism as the filth it actually was, they lack the determination and ruggedness necessary to survive the ordeal. The sensitive, intellectual Heinrich is so disgusted by the insanity that has overcome Germany that he sees no sense in continuing to live. Although his father could easily have kept him out of military service, Heinrich deliberately enlists, his motivation being expressed clearly in a statement he made during an argument with his father: "Dirt, dirt, dirt—that's what I want to be too, just dirt" (67). Leni's daring cleaning of the toilet in the presence of her brother and cousin, followed by her comment, "Our poets never flinched from cleaning out a john," was very likely also intended as a form of encouragement to these two young men. In fact, the reader learns much later in the novel that the shocking statement about poets was made "referring to H. and E." (336). The two youths, however, who may be viewed as symbols of the impotence of much of Germany's bright but impractical intelligentsia, do not possess Leni's instinctual ability to survive.

The refined, idealistic, and well-educated Heinrich, who in his hunger for culture "had devoured the whole Western world," came to realize under the Nazi regime that his high-minded vision amounted to just a "little pile of shit, . . . and he was confronted with that indescribable crap" (89). The young Gruyten's cynicism is revealed in his letters home—referred to by the "author" as "early examples of concrete poetry" (71)—which consist of excerpts from military regulations (perhaps Heinrich's way of indicating that the indescribable "crap" speaks for itself). One of these letters lists detailed instructions for the disposal of manure and suggestions that it be sold or exchanged in the way that will be most advantageous economically; one rule, which reflects the obduracy of the Nazi "dirt," is that "Any balance under 'Manure Revenue' in the 'S' ledger is to remain to the credit of the troop unit concerned even when the latter is transferred to another barracks or another garrison" (322). The cerebral Heinrich cannot cope with this inescapable, cut-and-dried crassness. Out of despair over the collapse of his vision of civilization, he engages in self-destructive actions and apparently convinces Erhard to join him. The two men deliberately sell an antiaircraft gun to the Danes, whereupon they are executed by the Nazis. Lotte Hoyser reports that Heinrich's last words were "Shit on Germany" (90).

Leni exhibits an ability to cope with life that her brother and cousin lack. Her swift, fearless response to the crisis with the clogged toilet characterizes her entire life style. She never thinks much about her actions; rather, she responds according to her instincts and the needs of the moment. This occasionally causes her to make a mistake, such as marrying Alois Pfeiffer, but usually her body guides her correctly. Certainly a clear indication of Leni's ability to go with the grain of life is her relaxed attitude toward dirt. Because of her calm adaptability, she succeeds in situations in which others stand helplessly by.[19] In fact, Leni's lack of anxiety over the excretory functions at times is very helpful in bringing her happiness. Thus, while working at Pelzer's flower shop, she and the Russian prisoner of war, Boris Koltowski, discover that a well-timed trip to the toilet, "which was not segregated as to sex" (232), is about their only opportunity for a minute of privacy in which to assure each other of their mutual love. It is in front of this excremental place that Leni whispers the simplest, yet most important words to Boris: "I love you" (234).[20]

Although Leni's lack of inhibitions regarding excrement and bodily functions was seen by Böll as a desirable mental state, and even though this approach to life may at times bring her luck, the reader should take care not to place more emphasis on Leni's positive scatological attitudes than the novelist intended. Leni's goodness does not arise from her lack of anxiety toward offal; rather, she accepts the human body and its waste products because she is good. R.H. Blyth comments on a similar outlook when discussing the following haiku by the seventeenth-century Japanese poet Bashô:

> Fleas, lice,
> The horse pissing
> Near my pillow.

According to Blyth, Bashô—stranded in uncomfortable accommodations during a rainstorm—is neither philosophically displaying indifference to his fate nor expressing "an impossible love of lice and dirt and sleeplessness" by poeticizing his situation. Blyth detects here the unruffled tone of a person who simply accepts life as a whole, embracing what is natural without disgust.[21] Bashô's equanimity in the presence of filth springs from a tranquil soul, as Leni's does; it is a *sign* of a mind at peace, not a *means* of achieving enlightenment or salvation.

As was asserted at the beginning of this chapter, the aesthetic and moral reversal of perceiving positive values in scatological elements is Böll's metaphorical cornerstone; it does not constitute his entire symbolic structure, however. In Böll's works, particularly in *Group Portrait with Lady*, one finds that scatology with connotations of worth is part of an overall network of contrasts that provide the bases of dramatic tension: dirty and clean, sloppy and neat, generous and parsimonious, relaxed and stiff, underachieving and overachieving, and many more. In *Group Portrait with Lady*, Böll utilizes all of these polarities to advance his contention that society's discards are really its most worthwhile members. Because there are so many characters in the novel, however, and because human beings, whose personalities are reflected in their word usage and in their attitudes toward "filth," are complex, Böll's system of contrasts becomes at times very involved. Although the positive values assigned to both excrement and dirt in general predominate, one also finds the corollary of this theme—examples of cleanliness or orderliness portrayed in negative terms, such as the detailed Nazi military regulations concerning ablutions that constitute Heinrich's letter of 14 January 1940 (69–70). Furthermore, one also finds in *Group Portrait with Lady* instances of what one might designate "bad dirt," and, once in a rare while, the "good clean" appears.

Leni, who, as we have seen earlier, was appalled by the overly fastidious natures of her inhibited teachers, finds equally loathsome the tendency of anal personality types to acquire and retain money and material possessions (the "bad clean," as exemplified by acquisitiveness and stinginess). During the war, Leni avoids going to her father's office, offering the explanation "that the 'sight of those stacks of freshly printed money' make her sick to her stomach" (151). The ultimate example of this motif is the scene that takes place near the end of the novel when the "author" visits the Hoyser, Inc., office complex. Although the scene opens with an example of dirt with negative connotations—the view from the Hoyser conference room is of the Rhine "at the precise geographical point where the still majestic river enters upon its very, very filthiest state" (363), a condition obviously brought about by uncaring tycoons such as the Hoysers—the predominant imagery in the passage is that of a despicable degree of orderliness and avarice. This high-rise kingdom with its hermetically sealed windows and push-button apparatus is kept humming smoothly by a secretary described by the "author" as a "blond, medium-bosomed efficiency-machine." When she discovers that the "author" does not have business cards, the automatonlike Trude jots down his address "with a look of open disgust, her expression implying that she was being forced to handle a type of excrement whose stench was of a particularly revolting nature" (368). Otto Hoyser and his two grandsons, Kurt and Werner, are obsessed with profits and status symbols, and the brothers cannot understand why the "author" refuses their offer to replace his jacket when it is ripped by their grandfather during an emotional outburst. According to the "author," Kurt and Werner fail to show "the remotest understanding of the fact that a person is more attached to an old object than to a new one, and that there are some things in this world that cannot be assessed from the insurance angle" (369). Here again we see favorite Böll themes: the insistence that human beings should resist being reduced to facts and figures and the assertion that society's "trash" can have value.

Using terms similar to those of Baumgart, the brothers refer to "Aunt Leni's sloppy ways" (371), and in a total perversion of logic—at least from Böll's point of view—Werner describes Leni as "inhuman" because of her indifference to "a wholesome striving after profit and property," which is, after all, "part of human nature" (377). Several of Leni's decisions have particularly disgusted the Hoysers: she has resigned from her job; she sublets rooms to foreigners, including garbage collectors; she is perfectly happy with her son Lev's job as a garbage collector; and she has a Turkish lover. Their main objection to Leni, however, is her indifference to the acquisition of wealth. The snobbish, excessively meticulous Hoysers in their airtight offices reflect Böll's view that the more one attempts to control life, the more one pollutes it. A gleaming facade often hides inner filth.

Recalling some of the imagery with which he conveyed the horrors of war in *And Where Were You, Adam?* Böll uses scatology in a similarly negative manner in *Group Portrait with Lady*. Thus Leni's eyes and instincts cause her to reject Nazism. A brief exposure to the sublimated brown of the Nazi uniforms suffices for her: "she did not like the brown uniforms at all—the Storm Troopers' uniform was particularly distasteful to her, and those who feel able to some degree to put themselves in her place in terms of her scatalogical [*sic*] interests and of her scatalogical training at the hands of Sister Rahel will know, or at least suspect, why she found this brown so exceedingly unpleasant" (59). (As we saw in chapter 6, some years after writing *Group Portrait with Lady* Böll disclosed in an interview that this repulsion by the brown Nazi uniform mirrored his own feelings precisely.)

Throughout the novel, it is suggested that Leni's instincts regarding what is and is not dirty are accurate. Böll depicts the Nazi period as one characterized by a deep moral filth, which particularly comes to light during the closing months of the war. In one instance, the "author" recalls that, in anticipation of the end of the war, some Nazis were trying to pass themselves off as humanitarians in their treatment of the persons whom they planned to exterminate. As evidence, Böll quotes from actual Nazi directives, which state, among other things, "that it is irresponsible to keep the workers locked up for many hours in railway cars so that they are not even able to relieve themselves. Opportunity must as a matter of course be given at intervals to allow these people to fetch drinking water, wash, and relieve themselves" (262). The irrelevance and hypocrisy of such "humanitarian" concern is then pointed out by the "author" in appropriately caustic terms: "Now it is important to realize that the conquest of continents or worlds is by no means easy, that those people had their problems too, and that they tried to solve them with German thoroughness and to document them with German meticulousness. Whatever you do, don't improvise! Nature's calls remain Nature's calls, and it simply won't do for people destined for execution to turn up on delivery as corpses!" (263).

Also very revealing is Ilse Kremer's report of the terrible final attack by the Allies on 2 March 1945. Ilse spent this day hiding in the basement of a brewery with several other persons, including a man belonging to the SA. Although the attack was traumatic for everyone present, the one who totally fell apart was the fellow in the brown uniform, who "simply shit in his pants till they were full, he was trembling all over as if he had the shakes—and he peed all down his pants too and then ran outside, just ran outside yelling" (271). The SA member's reaction reveals the cowardice that was hidden beneath the Nazis' mask of strength. Here again, as in the case of Greck in *And Where Were You, Adam?* an inwardly defiled person is outwardly showered with urine and excrement.

The most extreme example of the "bad dirt" of war in *Group Portrait with Lady* is the description that Boris's friend Bogakov gives the "author" of his experiences as a prisoner of war. Not only did the prisoners sleep in urinals, but they were served soup made "of rotten potatoes mixed with every conceivable kind of kitchen garbage flavored with rat droppings—sometimes a hundred men would die in one day."[22] Bogakov survived these conditions, as well as the often fatal diarrhea that plagued the prisoners on their marches, because of his stamina, his avoidance of the polluted food, and his being, like Leni and Rahel, "favored by Fortune" (311).

Just as dirt is not invariably assigned a positive value in Böll's writings, so cleanliness does occasionally have redeeming virtues. In fact, the novelist once stated "that, naturally, cleanliness, or washing oneself, also has a beautiful, elemental, and very human side."[23] An idyllic tableau of cleanliness appears near the end of *Group Portrait with Lady*, as the "author" luxuriates in Schirtenstein's massive bathtub. Marja van Doorn has mended the tear in his jacket, and Schirtenstein has loaned him a shirt which, although it is not a perfect fit, is "thoroughly acceptable" (385). While the "author" is in this beatific state of spotlessness and tidiness, he partakes of the ultimate pleasure: he hears Leni singing in her apartment next door.

Because scenes such as this are not very common in Böll's works, his readers might conclude that he undervalued the hygienic. Nothing could be farther from the truth. In his radio interview with Karin Struck, the novelist seemed determined to clear up any misconceptions regarding his view of cleanliness. "Naturally," he stated, "the ability to keep oneself clean is a good thing." Böll's tone with the interviewer was unusually emphatic as he pointed out that for many—no, for *most* people—cleanliness "is very important, psychologically as well as in regard to their self-image; we do not want to downplay or scoff at that, Ms. Struck." Recalling his days as a prisoner of war, Böll described the rare opportunity for a good scrub then as "a real festival" and "a high mass."[24] (These terms recall the writer's 1959 essay, "In Defense of Washtubs," in which he referred to laundry day in the town of his ancestors as "a special feast day.")[25] It was Böll's conclusion that only when cleanliness is carried to an extreme, as embodied in the nightmarish plethora of detergents and sprays dreamed up by industrialists and advertisers who prey on the public's needs and fears, does it cease to be the sort of blessing experienced by the "author" as he bathes.[26]

Two other passages in *Group Portrait with Lady* are worthy of mention because of their relatively positive portrayals of cleanliness; both, however, are tinged with overtones of hypocritical societal attitudes and thus lack the unadulterated joyousness of the scene in Schirtenstein's bathroom. The first is the pivotal incident designated by the "author" as the "coffee incident" (207), which takes place in the wreathmaking workshop where Leni is employed during the later portion of the war. She offers a new employee, the Russian prisoner of war Boris, a cup of her own enviable mixture of coffee, and the jealous Nazi Kremp, one of several Fascist types employed in the shop, uses his artificial leg to dash the cup from Boris's hand. Leni's calm, deliberate response to this attack causes everyone to watch her in breathless fascination:

> What does she do? She picks up the cup, it had fallen on the peat moss lying around there so it wasn't broken, she picks it up, walks to the faucet, rinses it carefully—there was a kind of provocation in the care she took over this—and I believe that from that moment on she acted with deliberate provocation. Damn it all, you know how quickly you can rinse out a cup like that, and thoroughly too, but she rinsed it as if it was a sacred chalice—then she did something entirely gratuitous—dried the cup, carefully too, with a clean handkerchief, walked over to her coffeepot, poured the second cup from it—they were those two-cup pots, you know—and carried it over to the Russian, as cool as you please, without so much as a glance at Kremp. Not in silence, either. No, she even said: "There you are." [203]

Recalling the incident, one of the other employees, Grundtsch, assesses its significance: "No one could find any other explanation for what she did other than pure innocent humanity, the very thing that was forbidden to be shown to subhumans, and yet, you know: even a fellow like that Kremp could see that Boris *was* human. . . . Through Leni's brave deed Boris was simply made a human being, proclaimed a human being—and that was that, in spite of all the bad times ahead" (205–6).

Another employee, Mrs. Hölthohne, is of course correct in observing that the coffee incident reveals Leni's "courage," "warmth," and "humanity" (205). It would be an oversimplification, however, to say only that Leni's fastidious washing and drying of the cup is an example of the "good clean" because it is Leni who is doing the cleaning. The scene also illustrates Leni's deftness and determination in combating the proponents of racial purity in terms that they can clearly understand. Because neither she nor Boris is in fact a fanatic about cleanliness, she would not need to do more than give the cup a quick rinse. However, the response that she has chosen (which contrasts in its subtlety to her employer Pelzer's spitting in the direction of Kremp's prosthesis)—her incredibly careful cleansing of the cup as if it were a sacred chalice and the subsequent drying of it with a clean handkerchief—becomes a form of sign language, the meaning of which those who overvalue fastidiousness cannot mistake. In her attempt to dignify Boris and declare his membership in the human race, Leni is, one might say, rubbing the noses of the Nazi types in their own mystique of purity.[27]

The contrast in the "coffee incident" scene between the outwardly immaculate but morally impure Nazi types and Leni, a virtuous, humane person who does not turn away from filth, whether in the form of a stopped-up toilet or an "inferior" human being, brings to mind the words of Jesus from Matt. 23:25–26: "Woe unto you, scribes and Pharisees, hypocrites! for ye make clean the outside of the cup and of the platter, but within they are full of extortion and excess. Thou blind Pharisee, cleanse first that which is within the cup and platter, that the outside of them may be clean also." If *Group Portrait with Lady* may be seen to some extent as a sermon in which Böll advances his theologically or ethically based "aesthetic of the humane," its text would surely have to be the seventh chapter of the Gospel according to Mark, which begins with a number of scribes and Pharisees finding fault with some of Jesus' disciples because the latter ate bread with unwashed hands; Mark then describes some of the cleanliness rituals of the Pharisees, including the washing of cups. Later in this chapter we find Mark's account of the formulation by Jesus of the New Testament ethics that so influenced Martin Luther and that was to become a dominant motif of Catholic author Böll:

And he saith unto them, Are ye so without understanding also? Do ye not perceive, that whatsoever thing from without entereth into the man, it cannot defile him; Because it entereth not into his heart, but into the belly, and goeth out into the draught, purging all meats? And he said, That which cometh out of the man, that defileth the man. For from within, out of the heart of men, proceed evil thoughts, adulteries, fornications, murders, thefts, covetousness, wickedness, deceit, lasciviousness, an evil eye, blasphemy, pride, foolishness: All these evil things come from within, and defile the man. [Mark 7:18–23]

The similarity of this passage to Böll's thinking becomes even more apparent when one considers that the sense of defilement expressed in these lines is conveyed in the German (Luther) Bible by the use of the adjective *gemein,* the exact word used by Böll in *The Clown* to point out what Henrietta's use of the word "shit" is *not.*[28]

Cleanliness also receives good marks from Böll in the section of *Group Portrait* that deals with Leni's son Lev. A psychologist's examination of the young man reveals that he has inherited his mother's "pure innocent humanity." In fact, at the age of fourteen, he exhibited "a heightened love of order, a compulsion to tidiness," and was often seen sweeping the apartment and the street outside. As a child, his favorite toy was a broom (Rahel's demise in the broom closet is recalled here). The psychologist's interpretation of these tendencies is "that this is one way of demonstrating and practicing cleanliness . . . vis-à-vis an environment that consistently abuses and defiles him" (412). Lev, like his mother, is pure in heart and sensual and nonacquisitive by nature, and in the cases of both persons society overlooks the unearthly horses and sees only the "filthy," earthly vehicle. The psychologist reaches a conclusion about the young garbage collector that takes cognizance of this dilemma: "The fact that garbage collection is his occupational desire and aim proves that he has instinctively sought the appropriate polarization: an occupation that serves the purposes of cleanliness but is regarded as dirty" (417).

Although a great deal of Böll's intertwining of the motifs described above is playful, his message is clearly a serious one: the terms *clean* and *dirty* do not automatically have good and bad connotations respectively. A solid set of values, a loving nature, and a warm acceptance of all of life are the touchstones that should be used to determine what is and is not genuinely clean. Blessed are the pure in heart for they can recognize purity when they see it. It is because of Böll's ethics that a single object or action can be assigned varying values throughout his works. A clean handkerchief, for example, represents an immaculate rectitude if it is the one Leni uses to dignify Boris; it has negative connotations if it is one of the unused ones tossed in the laundry by Hans Schnier's father. The latter are sterile status symbols, spotless because the elder Schnier lacks the humanity to weep or even have a runny nose.[29] Similarly, a person who is dirty or shabbily dressed because of hard manual labor, adverse circumstances, or even simple unpretentiousness should not be scorned, according to Böll, and in fact evokes one's respect; on the other hand, wealthy individuals who dress in tattered hippie garb and go unwashed because it is chic at the moment are viewed by the author as basing their actions on external criteria of acceptability rather than on their own best instincts and values.[30]

Clinging to what is fashionable, to outward appearances, to playing by the rules, until one has lost contact with the inner core of being was viewed by Böll as the downfall of many of his fellow Germans and perhaps of all human beings. As we saw earlier in the quotations from Mark, this antilegalistic approach goes back to the teachings of Christ. In work after work Böll reminded his readers of the goodness of the life God has given them, a goodness that embraces rather than transcends war, pain, ugliness, and yes, even dirt. The paradox that the novelist wanted his readers to ponder is that those who follow their instincts are often more civilized than those who slavishly obey the dictates of society. Leni, Böll's fairytale princess, recognizes the inherent worth and dignity of the commonplace and therefore has the royal touch. Saved by her garbage collector friends from an untimely eviction at the end of the novel, she defeats the antiseptic business world and, in true Cinderella fashion, is free to live happily ever after. Her good-natured acceptance of what others consider dirty is a sign that Leni is, as Sister Rahel had predicted, Fortune's favorite.

8

The Excremental Wheel of Fortune

Dirt is my destiny," declares Ossias Würz in Jakov Lind's novel *A Better World*.[1] Würz's statement is not a reflection of Leni Pfeiffer's good-natured acceptance of the excremental side of existence; nor is it a mirroring of the outlook of the war fiction discussed earlier—namely, that human beings at their worst end by wallowing in excrement. War, after all, is temporary. What Lind and a number of other modern German authors are trying to express is an even greater pessimism. Human beings, they suggest, are *always* enslaved by their physical limitations. The war will never be over. From birth to death, we are trapped like squirrels on a treadmill in a cycle of eating, evacuating wastes, and eating again, on and on ad infinitum. Human destiny is simply this.

Although the formula probably never has been stated so succinctly as in a 1976 *Stern* photo feature (fig. 30),[2] the metaphor of the alimentary-intestinal cycle also is used to express a nihilistic *Weltanschauung* in some of the poems of Gottfried Benn—particularly his earlier verses. As a medical doctor, the young Benn witnessed a great deal of squalor and human suffering, and he felt deep despair as a result of his observations. Because the poet/physician chose to express his negative view of life in verses that blend surrealistic imagery with concrete medical terminology, it is not surprising that scatological references often appear in his writings. Benn's excremental metaphors reflect the same loathing of the human body that can be found in Martin Luther's *Table Talk*. Luther, however, looked forward to the salvation of the soul; Benn could not share this optimism. Nor did his daily encounters with the corporeal lead him to Böll's "mystical materialism"; rather, they led to

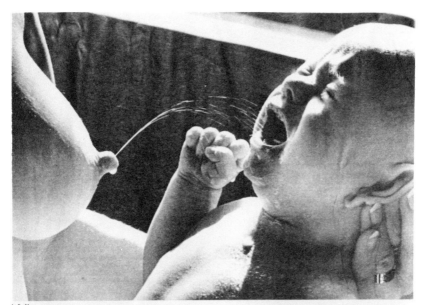

Wie gewonnen...

...so zerronnen

30. Photo feature: "Wie gewonnen . . . so zerronnen" (*Stern*). Photographs
© by Erik Petersen (above) and © by Clive Limpkin (below).

a profound pessimism regarding any hope of transcending one's bodily limitations.

One of the most bilious of Benn's poems is the three-part "The Doctor" (1:11–13).[3] In the first section of the poem Benn sums up the effect his profession has had on his outlook, saying "Ich lebe vor dem Leib"; the catchy succinctness of this declaration might be translated most appropriately in contemporary colloquial English as "The body is where I'm at." Just as his office was filled with persons suffering from conditions indicative of their vulnerability and also of their vices, so Benn's verses are suffused with images of physical and moral degeneracy. Although the entire poem stresses the body's frailty and proneness to deterioration, part 2 dwells particularly on intestinal and sexual disorders, linking them in a dismaying description of human decline:

> At age seventeen crab lice,
> to and fro between foul mouths,
> intestinal disorders and nourishment,
> women and Infusoria,
> at age forty the bladder begins to leak.

These lines provide a clear example of the melding of sex and scatology, of excrement and aliment, that is typical of the works we shall be considering in this chapter. The line "to and fro between foul mouths" is particularly effective because of its multiple connotations. In the original German, the reference to "foul mouths" is conveyed by "übeln Schnauzen." Because *Schnauzen* suggests animal muzzles, the term adds a note of bestiality; taken in the context of the entire poem, however, one cannot help but conjecture that the mouths in question are not simply facial but may also include any of the openings in the genital area. The adjective *übel* conjures up images of both sickness and evil and thus intensifies Benn's description of human weakness. These frail creatures, according to the poet, are characterized by the to-and-fro movement of aliment to excrement in which all bodily openings are virtually interchangeable and equally foul. Whether they ingest food, evacuate wastes, or serve as the sites of sexual activity, these "mouths" are reminders of mortality: as Benn writes in part 3, "earth drops through the holes."

The sense of being earthbound is reinforced when Benn asks in part 2, "You speak of the soul—What is your soul?" Instead of supplying an esoteric answer, the poet simply places before us an old woman who "craps in her bed" each night and a dotard whose thighs are cemented together as a result of his incontinence. Because these elders are no longer in control of their digestive processes, "the slop you hand them slumps into their intestines." Dismal as their last years may be, Benn finds no reason to portray human beings' start in life in a more upbeat fashion. This section of the poem ends with several lines (introduced by an appropriate "Ecch!") that inform the reader that the earth, which under more majestic circumstances erupts with volcanic fire, created human life by spitting up "a snoutful of blood" that ends in a "declining arc."

Excretory eruptions of this sort, followed by a sense of waning, appear often in the works of those authors who use the alimentary-intestinal cycle as a leitmotiv. Benn employs this type of imagery again in part 1 of "Finish" (2:389), in which he describes vomit that overflows and is then sucked up again. In "Appendix," a poem about an appendectomy, two of the more dramatic moments center around eruptions, first of blood, then of pus: "Is that pus that starts to squirt? / Has the intestine perhaps been hurt?" When the spurtings subside, the surgeon reports, "I cannot find anything in the filth!" (2:365).

The excrement-centered life cycle appears once again in the second stanza of Benn's poem "Room of the Women in Labor" (1:16). In "The Doctor," part 2, the reader was confronted with the image of an old woman dying in a mess of her own feces; the other end of the cycle, birth, is treated similarly in "Room of the Women in Labor." The scene is a scream-filled clinic or maternity hospital for impoverished women. A callous doctor, hardly a proponent of romanticized views of the beauty of childbirth, urges a woman in labor to bear down as if she were having a bowel movement: "Excrement, too, comes from the pushing!" After the woman follows his instructions, "Finally it comes: bluish and thin. / Urine and feces anoint its skin." The frail, oxygen-starved baby begins its life, anointed not with frankincense and myrrh but with excrement; in Benn's view, he or she will leave this life in precisely the same state.[4]

The dismal world that Benn portrays—in "Brothel" (2:409) he calls it "the anal world"—is one in which head and behind are interchangeable and in which the disorganization of one's internal organs reflects the senselessness of external events. In "Meat," one male corpse says to another,

> Hey you, kindly wash the excrement out of my armpit!
> And, furthermore, the right auricle isn't
> supposed to peer out of the anus!
> That sure looks like hemorrhoids! [1:36]

Later, a dead youth remarks, "The brain rots just as the ass does!" (1:37). In such a world, it would not be surprising if one wished to follow the example of the person in "Meat" who committed suicide, leaving behind a "crap-life" (1:37).

ALTHOUGH HIS TONE is not as bitter as Benn's, Erich Kästner is equally lacking in optimism for the future of the human race. Kästner places the blame on human beings' own stupidity and their futile attempts at "civilization." In "The Evolution of Humankind," the poet writes: "The earth is a cultivated star / with much flushing of water" (223).⁵ One of the achievements of civilized beings is that "They process the leftovers / of their digestive systems into wadding." Despite this and many other advancements, however, Kästner proclaims that human beings are "still the same old apes" (224).

In "The Tongue of Culture Reaches Far," Kästner again rejects the notion that civilization is on a steady continuum of evolutionary progress. Using a bizarrely humorous metaphor, Kästner suggests that "culture" stick out its tongue as far as possible in order to lick all locales with its influence, because, after all, there are still "Eskimos without—I beg your pardon!—toilets" (92). Scoring the absurdity of civilized "achievements," Kästner ends this poem with a pair of rebellious exclamations that he has wryly phrased in a discreet fashion in the hope that he will not offend refined society:

> The street sweeper must hold the *Abitur*,
> required to be well-read in smut and dirt.
> One muses sometimes: Culture—
> it can lick my . . . ! It can kiss your . . . !
> It does so in a way that's most expert. [93]

It is the stupidity of the civilized world that bothers Kästner most of all. In "The World Is Round," he muses:

> Ah, if the world would only be formed square
> and all the dummies fell in the latrine!
> Then—no more people anywhere.
> Then life would be serene. [62]

The view that the nature of things is cyclical and improvement is not in sight is voiced by Kästner in the poem's opening stanza:

> The world is round. That's why she will abide.
> There is no front and no behind.

Who views the world from her backside
in fact her face will find! [61]

One senses echoes here of the centuries-old notion that the devil has a
face on his posterior. Poets like Benn and Kästner find no more hope
for salvation in the temporal world than Martin Luther did, although
their devils may take different forms. Concludes Kästner, "The world
remains round, / and you remain an idiot" (62).

A BLEAK FATE in which human beings, dominated by instinctual
drives, achieve no more than sexual encounters, eating, and the evacuation of wastes is depicted in Iwan Goll's drama, *Methusalem; or, The
Eternal Bourgeois*.[6] "Nothing new. The world's getting so old," declares
the main character, the archetypal bourgeois businessman Methusalem, in the play's opening line (82). It is not accidental that this character is named after the oldest man who ever lived, according to the
Bible; throughout the drama, Goll stresses the pessimistic point that
human nature never alters, regardless of changes in time, place, or political or economic conditions. No matter where one travels, according
to one character, "One can never escape oneself!" and "if you eat too
many sardines, you'll belch" (106).

There is no escape, according to Goll, and physical life goes on even
after all traditional spiritual values have been destroyed. All that remains is the sexual drive and the alimentary-intestinal cycle, and
Methusalem is extremely knowledgeable in both areas. His expertise
enables him to come up with a thorough recycling plan for the business he would like to found with his prospective son-in-law, Max Kingdumbcombe: "We buy up all the cattle in Europe: the hides for our
shoe factory, the tripes for army sausages, the meat can be sold as a
waste product" (100). Thus Goll portrays his twentieth-century version of eternity in terms of the persistence of the physical, material
world. He acknowledges in the introduction to the drama that this is
not a pleasant or invigorating insight: "Drama should be without beginning or end, like everything else here on earth. But sometime it has
an end—why? No, life goes on, everyone knows that. The drama stops
because you have tired, grown old in a single hour, and because truth,
the most potent poison for the human heart, may only be swallowed in
very small doses" (80).

All of the characters in *Methusalem*, from the sexually oriented
Student to the fat-bellied burghers, are dominated by their physical
needs. There are "No more 'heroes,'" writes Goll in his introduction,

"just people, no more characters, just naked instincts. Quite naked" (79). Methusalem's leitmotiv throughout the drama is his constant devouring of steaming bowls of goulash—at one point interrupted by a request for his "salts" (laxative) (83). The tycoon's long-suffering wife Amalia devotes most of her time to keeping her husband's digestive tract filled with his favorite concoction, and she is quite disgruntled when he dies without first gobbling down the latest potful of freshly prepared goulash before it gets cold (111). The Methusalems' friends, the Messrs. and Mmes. Enteritis, Bellé, and Kingdumbcombe, are, as their names suggest, personifications of the wealthy bourgeois types whose god is their bellies. Their seemingly illogical conversations, written in the free association format that Goll enjoys using, abound in scatological double entendres:

> Mrs. Kingdumbcombe: O, does anybody know of a good laxative?
> Mr. Enteritis [*to Mr. Bellé*]: Now listen: first you buy a body belt.
> Mrs. Enteritis [*sticking her oar in*]: No, first take some cold Kruschen salts and boil them in water . . .
> Mr. Enteritis: If there's no gas get the plumber in.
> Mrs. Enteritis: Then you'll have to wash your feet. [97]

Goll often uses the technique of the scatological anticlimax to illustrate the futility of lofty ideals and aspirations. Thus, in the midst of a discussion of the death of postal assistant Pee-wee, who had been a lover of art, Methusalem calls for his laxative (82–83). Similarly, when the Student, who wavers between poetic valentines, practicality, and raw sexuality, wishes to engage in premarital relations with Methusalem's daughter, Ida, in the park, he is scatologically thwarted—in a manner reminiscent of the works of Busch:

> Bloody bad luck, I just had to fling her down
> When along comes an old dame, giving her poodle a piddle—
> Ambrosian hour for ever ruined! [95]

Even the costumes in the drama reflect this technique. Amalia wears elegant clothes and precious jewels, but her finery is always covered by a filthy kitchen apron (81, 98). The Methusalems' prim, robotlike son Felix receives an anticlimactic rebuff after he finally summons up some emotion—and vulgar terminology—in an angry speech to the Student:

> Felix: You swine, you Jew, you enemy of the people, you jackal, you mangy cur [*groping for words*] you, you dung-heap, you syph sore, you, you . . .

Student [*hands in his pockets, laughs*]: Mr. Methusalem, your fly's undone!
[105]

Such jolting juxtapositions are common in the works of the Dadaists, with whom Goll often crossed paths. What separates Goll from most of the German Dadaists, however, is his degree of pessimism. Grosz and his comrades, for a time at least, saw hope for social change through communism. Methusalem is indeed a Grosz caricature of a bourgeois tycoon come to life; the significant difference between Grosz and Goll, however, is that Grosz always depicts the working class sympathetically, whereas Goll in his hopelessness finds the masses and revolutionaries subjects for satire as well.

There are several aborted revolutions in *Methusalem*. The first is "The Revolution of the Beasts," a revolt of the various stuffed animals in Methusalem's home. The normal processes of nature and traditional logic are turned upside down and inside out in this topsy-turvy scene, in which the Monkey envisions an "animal republic" (87), complete with human fertilizer for the animals' fields. It is also the Monkey who sounds the battle cry:

> I call on you to start the animal revolution!
> We are chosen by God to cleanse this earth of that human filth
> Which pollutes the rivers,
> Burns the forests,
> Soils the skies,
> And stinks on earth like no other being! [85]

In keeping with the perverse logic of the scene, the Dog suggests that the others should not place too much credence in the Monkey's views, because "The monkey is descended from man!" In contrast to the decadent humans, the animals are characterized by the Monkey as "We moderns, we sensitive intellectuals!" (86).

The Monkey extolls "the spirit! the spirit! The Ideal!" but his supposedly idealistic goals smack more of *unten* than *oben*:

> The right to sniff at all trees, bushes, lamp-posts
> And walls without consideration of synthetic morality,
> The right to mate in the middle of the street
> Without fear of nagging old maids,
> The right to piss on monuments, kiosks and fountains
> Even during ceremonial occasions. [86]

Because the human beings, to judge from their behavior in the play, have already seized these rights for themselves and are in complete control, the animal revolution is doomed to failure. Methusalem, who has been asleep during the uprising, awakens, and the beasts resort to their lifeless positions.

The second unsuccessful revolt in the drama is the first strike of the workers in Methusalem's shoe factory. Urged on by the Student, they shout for, among other goals, "Shit / Petrol / Freedom!" When the mob becomes too unruly, Methusalem pushes a button and a safe opens; six armed policemen pop out and disperse the crowd. Goll's stage directions give the scene a dramatic conclusion and the audience time for reflection:

> While things are quieting down two gold-braided lackeys bring in a lavishly-carved commode, help Methusalem to unbutton his trousers and pull them down and seat him on the afore-mentioned stool. The mob is completely mastered. The policemen stand stiff and respectful. Methusalem smiles and farts. Curtain. There can be an interval here. [92]

In Goll's view, no revolt can amount to more than a standoff. In the Student's most impassioned speech (which includes a parody of *Faust*), he asserts,

> I am the deed!
> I am the Revolt, the spirit, the salt,
> That will decompose your stagnant waters,
> All your mouldering civilizations!
> Consume in fire all your laws like old newspaper,
> Knock the false dentures out of your morals,
> And as for your fat bourgeois bellies . . . [108–9]

Goll does not allow the Student to gain the ascendency over Methusalem, however, because he sees both figures as opposite sides of the same coin. Methusalem answers,

> Don't waste your time, my student dreamer,
> Ruined wreckage of the garrets,
> Revolutionary of the empty belly,
> Filled with pipe dreams from cheap tobacco;
> I'll take you on. [109]

Whether human beings are governed by empty stomachs or full ones is inconsequential, according to Goll. Both are victims of their corporeal natures, and therefore dreams are impossible. As the Bear had remarked earlier, "Revolution has nothing to do with Idealism!" (87). The play's last scene finds the subdued Student sitting in the park with his shotgun bride, the Methusalems' once ethereal daughter Ida, who holds their child, Godfrey, in her arms; their conversation begins:

> Ida: It's peed on my dress again.
> Student: Did you buy the frankfurts?

Ida asks the Student when the revolution will end, and he replies, "When the others don't have a mansion left." This prompts Ida to inquire, "And when we have one?" The answer: "The new Revolution starts." Thus the only hope for improvement that Ida can muster is, "If only Godfrey would stop peeing!" (112).[7]

Long before this last scene, Felix has shot and killed the Student. The rebel's soul flies off in the form of his winter coat, but his body stands up and remarks, "Behold my departing soul! Say hello to your sister for me, will you?" (107). Similarly, although Methusalem has been shot and killed by the Student during a workers' uprising, the "Eternal Bourgeois" jauntily strides up to the young couple at the end of the last scene, announces the introduction of a new rubber heel, and utters the play's closing line: "Filthy weather, thank goodness. But I must be off now to my goulash" (112). The alimentary-intestinal cycle endures long after the death of idealism. *Methusalem*, then, illustrates still another overturned maxim: one can kill the soul but not the body.

THE EXCREMENT-CENTERED life cycle from which one cannot escape is also an important metaphor in Günter Grass's novella *Cat and Mouse*. At the very beginning of the work the reader is made aware of the continual buildup of rust and sea gull droppings on a partially sunken Polish minesweeper. Throughout the rest of the book this setting reappears many times. Its significance in regard to Joachim Mahlke, the main character, has been pointed out by Emil Ottinger: "This hard, slowly accumulating crust is described over and over again. It parallels the way in which Joachim Mahlke becomes encumbered by his appearance, his development, his leitmotivs, the influences of his environment, until he perishes in the rust-encrusted shipwreck."[8] A more detailed examination of this process sheds additional light upon its meaning. When the sea gull droppings are first mentioned in *Cat and Mouse*, the reader not only is given a detailed description of their accumulation but learns that they were not left on the ship undisturbed. Instead, Pilenz, the narrator, recalls that he and his friends, when in their early teens, used to scrape the droppings off with their fingernails and toenails. In fact, one learns that these children "chewed the stony, shell-like mess into a foaming slime" (10).[9]

Once the chewed-up excrement was spat overboard, it was frequently caught in flight and consumed again by the sea gulls. Thus Grass has created a continuing cycle that begins and ends with the dropping of feces by the gulls.

The meaning of this excremental cycle, as far as Pilenz and his friends are concerned, has again been explained by Emil Ottinger: "Students in their early teens, brilliantly described in their common regression into infantilism, which was triggered by their adventure—digging around with their fingernails and toenails and eating droppings and spitting phlegm: a playful ritualization of the oral phase and ejaculation through the mouth."[10] It is also their childlike suggestibility that enables the youths to find all sorts of connotations in the taste of the droppings: "The stuff tasted like nothing at all or like plaster or like fish meal or like everything imaginable: happiness, girls, God in His heaven" (10).

The novella contains several other examples of similarly infantile excremental behavior. There are Pilenz's supposedly sophisticated female cousins from Berlin, who eagerly "amid whispering and tittering" (57) urinate on the ice so that Mahlke can more easily dig a hole through it. Later Pilenz tells of the vulgar graffiti that covered the walls of the Reich Labor Service latrine (146). Finally, in regard to Mahlke's desire to make a speech at his former Gymnasium as holder of the Knight's Cross, Pilenz says that Mahlke "wanted to address the stench of three hundred schoolboys, farting high and farting low" (161).

As a result of their infantilism, the adolescents depicted by Grass accept with glee the excremental cycle that imprisons them. They participate fully in excremental activities and show little, if any, desire to escape into a more refined existence. The one exception among this group is Joachim Mahlke. He is the one individual who from the very beginning refuses to participate in the scatological behavior of the others. Thus Pilenz recalls: "Only Mahlke had long nails, though they were yellow from all his diving, and he kept them long by neither biting them nor scratching at the gull droppings" (10). Similarly, Mahlke does not urinate on the ice as the others do, nor does he participate in vulgar jokes at school or write obscenities on the walls of latrines.

The fact that Mahlke is different from the other boys is also expressed through a physical characteristic, his huge Adam's apple. This conspicuous feature on the one hand attracts the attention of the other youths and on the other hand causes them to make fun of him and even to torture him, such as when the cat is allowed to attack it as if it were a mouse. Thus the Adam's apple is symbolic of Mahlke's position among his peers: to a certain degree he is admired, but at the same time he remains an outsider and is resented. Johanna Behrendt finds a deeper symbolism in this physical feature, tying it in with the tug-of-war between physical urges and spiritual longings that takes place in Mahlke's psyche.[11]

The protagonist's attempts to overcome his elementary human drives and find a higher purpose in life are, however, doomed. Despite his early successes in avoiding the infantile behavior of his peers, Mahlke eventually succumbs. The failure of his search occurs symbolically as early as chapter 3, for here Mahlke is drawn into the excremental cycle. The setting is again the minesweeper, surrounded by the flying gulls. The boys are sitting around in the nude, masturbating in the presence of a girl, Tulla Pokriefke, who eagerly observes the process and enjoys stirring the spilled semen with her big toe. Again Mahlke does not participate. Instead, he is diving, but this time he has no luck. Precisely at this moment when he returns with empty hands, Tulla challenges him to prove he is the equal of the other boys. Because Mahlke did not bring anything back from his dive, he has nothing with which he can divert the others' attention from Tulla's challenge; finally he gives in and satisfies the girl's infantile curiosity. Just as Mahlke had previously outdone the others in a variety of physical achievements, his erect sexual organ "looked much more grown-up, dangerous, and worthy to be worshipped" (44). Even though Mahlke is again admired by the others for his precociousness, his decline has already begun, because he has given in to the infantile desires of the others. As he ejaculates his sperm into the ocean, both the infantile youths and the sea gulls react: "we laughed for joy as the gulls swooped down, screaming for more" (45).

Earlier, the gulls had rejected the results of a similar but less natural eruption, Mahlke's squirting of foam from an old fire extinguisher into the sea ("a big mess of whipped cream turned sour" [13]). The fact that the gulls now devour the protagonist's life-generating sperm just as they had devoured their own droppings after they had been chewed and spat out by the boys places him within the same excremental cycle as the others. Erhard Friedrichsmeyer has remarked that "the unnaturalness of Mahlke's onanism, in the sense that the natural act serves propagation, appears in revoltingly sharp focus when we read that the sea gulls swallow Mahlke's sperm. The vessel for it is not a woman, but a scavenger bird." Friedrichsmeyer then sees this excremental circle as "a brutally deranged cycle of creation. Human life turns up as an excrement, instead of a human form."[12]

Although Friedrichsmeyer correctly identifies the significance of the sea gulls in regard to Mahlke, he goes too far when he sees this character as "the redeemer that fails."[13] As Robert Spaethling had pointed out, "to speak of Mahlke as a redeemer who fails goes beyond the interpretative possibilities of the novella. Mahlke seeks 'Erlösung' [salvation] for himself."[14] It is more plausible to see the protagonist as Johanna Behrendt does, as a youth in search of a higher meaning in life. The masturbation scene at the minesweeper then simply demonstrates that all such yearning is in vain.

Despite Mahlke's long and intensive striving to find some kind of lofty purpose in life and to free himself from humanity's base elementary drives, he does not succeed. As the novella proceeds, one learns that "the encrusted gull droppings . . . had multiplied" (74), and simultaneously Mahlke's search becomes more and more absurd until all his efforts are concentrated upon the attainment of a Knight's Cross for himself. As soon as Mahlke's sole goal in life becomes a tangible one, a development that occurs in the middle chapter of the book (chapter 7), it is clear that his entire search has been a dismal failure. Instead of a noble, elevating aim, his goal is the meaningless but "coveted lozenge" (64) of Nazi Germany. Thus his eyes have now become fixed on the same target that the rest of the infantile world is pursuing.

Mahlke's capitulation is also demonstrated by his increasing enslavement to excrement toward the end of *Cat and Mouse*. When Pilenz encounters Mahlke in chapter 10, the latter has been drafted into the Labor Service, and Pilenz immediately notices a mark of his friend's imprisonment: the cap he is wearing is "saturated with the color of dried excrement; the crown was creased in the middle in the manner of a civilian hat, but the bulges were closer together, so close as to produce the plastic furrow which explains why the Labor Service head covering was commonly referred to as 'an ass with a handle'" (135). Particularly striking in this stigmatization of Mahlke is the description of the hat as "saturated with the color of dried excrement." The phrase brings to mind the drying, accumulating gull droppings and thus links this scene with the metaphor of the excremental life cycle.

Mahlke's life is further complicated by scatological elements in chapter 11. In this chapter Pilenz, who has now also been drafted into the Labor Service, arrives at the same compound where his friend had served a year earlier. At first it appears that Mahlke may be victorious after all, for here in the latrine Pilenz finds Mahlke's name carved into the wood, with a reference to the Virgin Mary beneath it (145–46).

Briefly Mahlke and his allegiance to the Virgin conquer "all the more or less wittily formulated obscenities which, carved or scribbled from top to bottom of the latrine wall, gave tongues to wooden boards." Pilenz can find no peace in this latrine as long as his friend's words are there: "For while I relieved myself, while the maggot-ridden dross of my age group accumulated behind me and under me, you gave me and my eyes no peace: loudly and in breathless repetition, a painstakingly incised text called attention to Mahlke, whatever I might decide to whistle in opposition" (146). From Pilenz's recollections of the latrine it is clear that Mahlke is still pursuing his search for a higher purpose and for redemption from the elemental human drives. Mahlke's "painstakingly incised text" is indicative of the protagonist's continuous striving for what is *oben*, with the contrasting *unten* of what is perverse and infantile conjured up by the vulgar graffiti and the "maggotridden dross," which is piling up here like the gull droppings on the minesweeper. Although Mahlke's words almost make a believer out of Pilenz at this point, the latter finally turns against Mahlke as he had done earlier when he or one of his companions released the cat on Mahlke's "mouse." Pilenz takes an ax and eradicates both Mahlke's name and his religious phrase from the latrine.

Although Pilenz does not discover it until somewhat later, Mahlke actually surrendered to the baser human drives almost a year before Pilenz removed his name and message from the latrine. A few men who had served in the camp when Mahlke was there tell Pilenz and the other draftees incredible stories about Mahlke. One of the men recalls that Mahlke had been asked by one of the chief officers to build a rabbit hutch at the latter's house; when the ascetic protagonist at first refused, he was degraded to latrine duty. Mahlke's need for recognition made his demotion unbearable, and so he gave in. He never finished the rabbit hutch, however; instead, he was seduced by the officer's wife, who kept sending for him until her ignorant husband walked in on them. Thus Mahlke's determination to be victorious over the needs of the body was finally destroyed; having abandoned his faithfulness to the Virgin and succumbed to the elementary sexual drive, Mahlke once and for all betrayed his spiritual nature and was assimilated by the rest of society (148–49).

The final debilitating stroke comes when Mahlke attempts to lecture at his former Gymnasium after having earned the Knight's Cross through his bravery in battle. Principal Klohse (one must not overlook the "Klo" in his name) refuses to give Mahlke permission to speak before the "farting" boys as other Knight's Cross bearers have done, because he cannot forget that Mahlke had once stolen the medal from one of those speakers (162–63). After even this small measure of recognition is denied him, the protagonist disappears into the hulk of the minesweeper, where the only reminder of his striving for nobility is the dung-dropping gulls (187).

Although Mahlke's disappearance remains a mystery, the possibility exists that he has committed suicide in a most unusual and excremental fashion. As he and Pilenz headed for the beach, Mahlke devoured a huge quantity of "unripe gooseberries" (176), which caused him to experience intense stomach cramps. Because Mahlke claimed he was too ill to swim out to the minesweeper, Pilenz begrudgingly went off to rent a rowboat. Even though Mahlke no longer seemed sick by the time he and Pilenz reached the minesweeper in their boat, it is likely that Mahlke deliberately gorged on the berries so that he would be unable to dive into the body of the sunken ship and find his way to the above-water radio room, which he had previously used as a secret hideaway. The unripe fruits, which can irritate both stomach and intestines and can result in diarrhea (as German children are often warned by their parents), may well have resulted in Mahlke's death. It thus seems possible that Mahlke, like Leni Pfeiffer's brother Heinrich, finally decided: "Dirt, dirt, dirt—that's what I want to be too, just dirt."

In *Cat and Mouse* Grass has powerfully demonstrated his view that, in a climate such as that of Nazi Germany, all attempts to achieve a spiritual victory over the base nature of life must end in hopeless disillusionment. In such an infantile world human beings are forever doomed to remain imprisoned in an absurd excremental life cycle. An analysis of the scatological material in this novella proves conclusively the absurdity of the claims of the federal state of Hesse in its 1962 "Petition to Have the Novella *Cat and Mouse* Included in the Index of Works that Are Liable to Corrupt the Young." The authorities claimed: "The work contains numerous descriptions of obscene acts that are apt to corrupt children and adolescents. . . . The objectionable passages, which present such scenes in graphic detail, have been interspersed throughout the narrative without any clear purpose. The manner in which these descriptions are presented leads one to conclude that they were inserted merely because of their appeal to prurient interests."[15] Fortunately, after several prominent scholars (among them Fritz Martini and Walter Jens) defended *Cat and Mouse*, the state of Hesse withdrew its request. Viewed in terms of the tradition of scatology in German art and literature prior to the publications of Grass's novella, the excremental allusions in *Cat and Mouse* should be seen not as an effort to appeal to prurient interests but as an author's skillful reworking of a familiar set of images in order to portray candidly his concept of the human predicament.

In Günter Grass's novel *The Flounder* (*Der Butt*) the novelist no longer presents the reader with a central character who attempts to stand aloof from the scatological degradation that surrounds him. Whereas Joachim Mahlke of *Cat and Mouse* fights a losing but nevertheless valiant battle against excrement, in *The Flounder* Grass depicts a world in which human beings are directly equated with their waste products. Although Grass takes us on a trip through human history from the Stone Age to the present, a close reading of this lengthy novel will leave no doubt in the reader's mind that Grass finds any notion of progress or evolution as represented by the Hegelian dialectic absolutely preposterous. *The Flounder* asserts that we are totally imprisoned by our excremental existence and all we can do about it is either to sit down alone and bewail this unfortunate state or to accept it with laughter, the latter being Grass's preferred alternative.

The devastating message of this novel is stated most succinctly in the poem "Empty and alone," which begins with the following lines:

> Pants down, hands joined as though in prayer,
> my eyes right on target:
> third tile from the top, sixth from the right.
> Diarrhea.
> I hear myself.
> Two thousand five hundred years of history,
> early insight and last thoughts
> lick and cancel each other out. [239][16]

The gruesome image of sitting on the john while thousands of years of history come pouring out of one's body in the form of diarrhea is anticipated at the very beginning of the novel, when the narrator describes himself as a person "clogged with so much past who finally sees a chance of relieving his constipation" (19). One may view the narrator, then, as an anally retentive person who has kept locked within himself mountains of historical facts that eventually must gush forth. Grass's view of his narrator (and perhaps of all Germans) is reminiscent of Norman O. Brown's vision of Luther as someone whose ideas were the product of his constipation. Indeed, it was quite common at the time of the Reformation for Protestants and Catholics to attack each other's writings by depicting the opponent's works as issuing from his anus.

The last stanza of "Empty and alone" makes it absolutely clear that all of society and every being from the highest, God, to the smallest— "the I"—is seen as excrement by Grass:

> So much emptiness
> is in itself a pleasure: in the crapper
> with my own specific ass.
> God state society family party . . .
> Out, the whole lot of you.
> What smells is me!
> If only I could weep. [240]

The revolting message that excrement is all that is ever really produced through thought, word, or deed is the most important leitmotiv of this novel. *The Flounder* literally overflows with direct or indirect references to the production of more and more excrement. Even God's creations are depicted as nothing more than a pile of excrement, as is clearly expressed in the following lines: "Why not a poem about a pile of shit that God dropped and named Calcutta. . . . If God had shat a pile of concrete, the result would have been Frankfurt" (186). If all of God's creations amount to nothing more than "piles of shit," then it can hardly be expected that human beings, who are themselves the result of that creative process, will produce anything better. This fact is amply demonstrated throughout *The Flounder*.

From the perspective of today's militant women, whom Grass satirizes in the novel, the excremental state of affairs is entirely the fault of men, because the latter have been in control of human history from neolithic times until the present. This idea is clearly expressed in the crucial eighth part or month of the novel. Here four assertive lesbians set out to prove their equality to the male sex by daring to stage their own Father's Day activities near Berlin. On this day, which ironically coincides with Ascension Day, only men are allowed to go on excursions, which consist of ritualistic eating and drinking; the outings always end at a point where the men "piss against trees" (470). In an animalistic way, then, the men go through the excremental life cycle of eating or drinking, digesting, and defecating. The four lesbians dare to invade the men's territory and to hold an equivalent outing. During their role playing as men, one of them, Frankie, reaches a devastating conclusion with which the others quickly agree: "Since the end of the Stone Age, when the future started with copper, bronze, and iron, we men have done nothing but build shit!" (480). This bleak insight echoes the views expressed in the poem "Empty and alone."

Grass strikes a particularly pessimistic note by portraying the women who attack the male producers of excrement as being in no way better themselves. Thus the four lesbians can only respond to what they observe on Father's Day by imitating the scatological acts of the men in a classic display of penis envy. These four, whose jealousy of men is already evident in their transvestic behavior, such as the wish to be called by the masculine names of Billy, Siggie, Frankie, and Maxie, copy the masculine ritual of eating and drinking beer. Finally, when they can no longer hold the beer in, Maxie begins the most ludicrous part of the imitation: "instead of relieving her bladder in the usual squatting position, she unbuttoned the fly of her jeans, spread her legs, took out a pink pecker with a deftness suggesting long practice, brought it into a horizontal position, and began, in time-honored male manner, to urinate against a pale mottled pine tree" (464–65). Although the four view this ridiculous act of urinating through an artificial penis as a liberating, self-assertive deed and boast, "No more penis envy" (465), the fact of the matter is that their charade proves just the opposite—a deep, obsessive desire to be masculine.

The failure of the four lesbians in their attempt to display a free and independent spirit anticipates the downfall of the entire women's emancipation movement at the end of the novel. Even though the "Flounder" claims in front of his tribunal of women that he is terribly sorry for his grave mistake of having encouraged men to take command of historical developments, and even though he expresses the desire that women from now on take charge of human affairs, one cannot overlook the important fact that he gives his tribunal the ironic title of "Womenal"—in fact, he speaks of the "Last Womenal" (516). This is a deliberate insinuation by the Flounder that the Last Judgment will be the moment when all human beings end up in a urinal. The consistent references to the tribunal as a Womenal throughout the last part of the novel leave little doubt as to Grass's opinion of what lies ahead for human beings when women control the world.

The dismal excremental imagery in *The Flounder* would seem to point to only one appropriate response for all human beings: total resignation (an idea that appears to be supported by the poem "Empty and alone"). Yet the narrator of the novel suggests quite the opposite alternative: human beings should openly acknowledge their excremental nature and laugh about it, for isn't it really quite funny? This surprising attitude, which is surely the direct result of a strong inclination toward black humor and is very reminiscent of the outlook of Wilhelm Busch, accounts for the two longest scatological scenes in the novel: "Fat Gret's Ass" and "Inspection of Feces." It is quite clear, then, that the narrator succeeds in overcoming his own inhibitions. As he releases the many facts that he had obsessively hoarded within himself, he is able to return to a natural and humorous acceptance of excrement.

"Fat Gret's Ass" is certainly one of the most grotesque and shocking scatological scenes ever written. Grass seems to return here to the German "Schwänke" of the sixteenth century, which displayed the same unabashed joy in playing and shocking with excremental material. The narrator not only openly endorses sodomy and coprophagy but raises "ass licking" to the level of religious worship, thus equating what many people would consider life's greatest taboo and the rites that they hold sacred: "And if you sexual sociologists, deep in worry blubber from counting flies' legs, had been asked in as witnesses when . . . I came at her from behind but first, to make it all soft and as wet as wept on, licked her asshole and environs like a goat (hungry for salt), which was easy to do when Fat Gret offered her double treasure for worship, you would have seen the archetype of Christian charity, our partner-oriented fervor" (203–4). When the narrator dubs this type of contact "the archetype of Christian charity," all previous bounds of aesthetic propriety appear to have been shattered by humanity's excremental and bestial nature.

The combination of clearly blasphemous elements with a scattering of such undeniably humorous references as "her double treasure" and "counting flies' legs" is obviously intended to have a dual effect. The strongly puritanical and obsessively clean readers will be totally disgusted, and at the same time more liberated readers who share the German inclination toward scatological joking will not be able to refrain from laughing. To those (such as the narrator's wife Ilsebill) whose views and upbringing place them somewhere between the two extremes, those persons who, while reading this passage, may find a hint of a smile flickering across their lips even as they are trying to suppress it, the narrator encourages, "All right, laugh. Get that stuffy look off your face. Have a heart. It's funny, isn't it? Let me tell you about white beans and nuns' farts. How they argued about bread and wine and wine and bread, the right order in which to take the Eucharist; a quarrelsome century. Margret, Fat Gret, laughed herself healthy over it" (205). This encouragement to laugh oneself healthy as Fat Gret had done suggests the presence of a positive alternative in *The Flounder:* one will be able to survive the insanity of life if one's sense of humor overrides one's disgust.

Grass's playfulness is also evident in the first chapter of the fourth month, "Inspection of Feces," but in this instance he states his views with a blunt directness. The reader finds the narrator scolding Ilsebill, who represents the queasiness of modern civilization with the mere mention of excrement, for her refusal to examine her feces for a swallowed tooth with a gold crown. The narrator deplores her attitude, "For our fecal matter should be important to us and not repel us. It's not a foreign body. It has our warmth. Nowadays it's being described again in books, shown in films, and painted in still lifes. It had been forgotten, that's all" (235–36). The narrator goes on to describe in great detail how neolithic people used to evacuate their waste products in the presence of friends and how this group act was a joyful social event: "What today is said to stink and is crudely amalgamated with latrines and slit trenches . . . was natural to us, because we identified with our feces. In smelling our turds, we smelled ourselves" (237). It is precisely because the narrator of *The Flounder* never loses his sense of humor and is able to return to a natural and primitive acceptance of excrement that he is not destroyed by the despairing thought of his own excremental nature and existence. These adaptive techniques allow him to continue to exist in the eternal "pisspot" of life, a symbol that Grass acknowledges having borrowed from the Grimm fairy tale "The Fisherman and His Wife" (20).

ONE COULD HARDLY imagine a more pessimistic work than Jakov Lind's novel *A Better World*. Lind depicts a world in which all attempts at improvement are ridiculous because humanity is totally governed by the elementary corporeal functions: the food consumption–defecation cycle and the animalistic sexual drive. Whenever the characters in this novel take a look at themselves or philosophize, they reach most depressing conclusions. Thus Roman Wacholder states at the very beginning of the work: "The human being is the connecting pipe between the feeding bowl and the garbage pail" (10). Wacholder's main antagonist, Ossias Würz, has an equally dismal vision of human life. As he examines himself, he compares his body to a rotting continent: "The stomach is a river in the jungle, hot, muddy, poisoned by insects and crocodiles and small fish with sharp teeth. The bladder is its origin. The spring. . . . This swampy, uninhabitable, godforsaken continent is called Ossias Würz. He rots away in the sludge, in the stagnant water" (109). Both of these representations of the human race recall the cycle of eating and waste evacuation that is a theme in the works of Benn, Kästner, Goll, and Grass. The metaphorical depiction of the bladder as the source or origin also places excrement or urine at the beginning of the cycle. Thus life is depicted here once more as imprisonment in an excremental cycle.

What little plot there is in *A Better World* results from the characters' absurd attempts to escape from the horrible truth of this excremental fate. Würz, especially, is overcome by an irrational fear of filth and is characterized by Lind as a grotesque exaggeration of the anal obsession with cleanliness. In order to achieve his conviction (reminiscent of the kitchen motto in *The Investigation*) that "Cleanliness and order is freedom" (18), Würz has built a six-meter-high wall around his house to protect himself and his family from all the filth and germs that are ready to pounce upon them from the outside. Inside his fortress of cleanliness Würz wages his incessant and ludicrous battle against filth. He and his wife Rita are constantly cleaning and disinfecting. Even the ceilings, which they have divided systematically into numbered areas of ten square centimeters each, are not spared from this fanatical scrubbing (43). Würz's absurd obsession is vividly demonstrated even in his mode of dress: "He withdrew into his closet. A few minutes later he stepped out of the closet dressed in a white coverall and white shoes and gloves, on his head a white crash helmet and on his face a white gas mask; he went to workroom number two in the basement in order to fetch paint and paintbrush. For the painting of the walls in room fourteen . . ." (47–48).

Despite his frantic activity, Würz cannot escape from excrement, because he cannot escape from himself. No matter how much he has cleaned, he is always overcome by "disgust" (45) whenever he looks at himself in the mirror. In fact, the only method he has of confirming his existence is his observation of his own excremental smell: "The spiritual inventory taking could begin now. He repeated the words: Here I am, Ossias Würz, fifty-five years old, a man in his middle years, no beauty queen—when suddenly he recalled the rectal exam. Quickly he stuck his right index finger into his rectum, smelled it, was satisfied with the smell, and could now continue. I am the son of my father, the son of my mother, the grandson of my paternal and maternal grandparents. I am the husband of my wife, the stepfather of my sons, unemployed, living at number 9 Melchior Street. Here" (35). Finally, Würz's filth phobia enslaves him completely. He now sees dirt everywhere and feels that the only solution is the destruction of everything, including himself. At an earlier stage of his paranoia, his attitude was remarkably similar to that of an anal-erotic patient who told psychoanalyst Karl Abraham, "Everything that is not me is dirt."[17] Now Würz's cry for help reveals that his fears have taken him a step farther. "Help! Existence is a dirty existence. Everything that is, is dirty. Only what is not is clean. Nothingness, even nothingness is dirty. My house is something and it is nothing, and both are full of filth. Perhaps filth is clean— can dirt be clean? Impossible, impossible. Dirt is. Dirt is dirt. My destiny. Dirt is my destiny. My destiny is dirty and therefore, therefore they must exterminate me, now, immediately and instantly" (110).

Wacholder's behavior and view of himself are in every regard as depressing and neurotic as those of Würz. Instead of living behind a huge stone wall, Wacholder dwells in a pile of paper on a dilapidated sunken ship, a home that reminds one of Mahlke's abode on the minesweeper. Wacholder's choice of domicile reflects his low opinion of himself. As he tries to sleep in his ramshackle abode among the weeds, he cannot find peace; he keeps dreaming of his carnality and awakens, screaming, "I am the animal" (8).

Wacholder is obsessed with disgust with his own sexuality and is convinced that he once murdered a prostitute with his immense sexual organ (here again Joachim Mahlke comes to mind). In his recollection of his supposed crime, Wacholder continually links sex with offal. He remembers the prostitute as being filthy and excremental but also sensually appealing—an ambivalence that may spring from unresolved psychological conflicts, as discussed in chapter 1: "Away with the skirt, away with the garter belt. It's opening-up time now. Stinks like a toilet. . . . It's extremely juicy. Once more yes? No! I say yes. No! Yes! Yes! Yes! . . . so beautifully warm—yuck, does it stink" (65). English and Pearson would contend that the link Wacholder makes between sex and the processes of elimination is as much an anal fixation as is Würz's obsession with the removal of every trace of filth from his life. It is their view that the sense of disgust that often arises during childhood cleanliness training "in later life causes people to be very ashamed of their body and to be ashamed of sexual functioning especially. In other words, some of the emotion that is engendered . . . over bowel and bladder functioning spreads out and encompasses sexuality, since the organs of sexual functioning and excretion are the same."[18]

In Wacholder's mind there is no room for nobility in life. Love, beauty, and concern for others are totally foreign to him. Instead, as demonstrated above, he links all his experiences to excrement and thus to death. Just as sexual intercourse represents an excremental deed to him, so he sees his entire country as a dung heap: "There were the occupational forces and they are gone now too and we are where we've always been. On the manure pile" (68). Wacholder's sole purpose in life has become his determination to entice Würz from his fortress of cleanliness. He apparently wants to drag everyone into his "manure pile." It is noteworthy that Wacholder justifies all his efforts against Würz by claiming that he is really helping his best friend. In what appears to be a perverse subconscious expression of his own violation of the prostitute, Wacholder maintains that he must help the clogged or constipated Würz: "He locked himself up—he is being freed. What is locked up comes out. What is inside doesn't remain within. Otherwise the human being would not be a pipe, as life is. For life too is a pipe . . . especially human life. It flows and flows but it can also get clogged up. Würz is clogged up, I mean to say he has clogged up life. I didn't want it that way and I could not prevent it. He didn't deserve it. No one is guilty. The war. Well, what can one do?" (12).

These last lines by Wacholder are very significant. According to Lind (not only here but in his autobiography as well), since World War II the world has become constipated due to humanity's moral filth. The atrocities of the war have made life permanently meaningless. *A Better World* illustrates Lind's pessimism through the portrayal of a world populated by insane, absurd creatures who are totally submerged in their own filth and guilt. There is no hope for this world except to destroy itself. Thus Wacholder goes out on his birthday and buries himself alive, dying "only so that the others had something to laugh about. but the others did not laugh" (165).

THE WHEEL OF FORTUNE as depicted in F. W. Murnau's silent film classic, *Der letzte Mann* (known in English as *The Last Laugh*),[19] takes the form of the revolving door at the Hotel Atlantic, through which the film's main character enters one morning as a stately, highly respected chief porter and leaves the same evening as a wizened restroom attendant. Prior to his inevitable meeting with fate, the porter is an important part of a pristine world that functions with crisp, Teutonic efficiency. On a rainy evening, people with umbrellas scurry in and out of the hotel like swarms of parasol ants; the porter staggers under the weight of a large trunk like a worker ant carrying a huge bread crumb on his back. Even the working-class neighborhood where the porter lives resembles an anthill or beehive full of industrious activity: lack of money does not keep the residents from airing out their bedding and beating their carpets thoroughly and regularly. On the porter's fire escape, it is his all-important uniform that is aired and brushed early each morning whereas the other neighbors have nothing more significant than bed linen to freshen. Thus the porter's status in his neighborhood is established; the audience's awareness of his lofty position is reinforced when, as he leaves for work, a woman flails her arms wildly in the air to keep the dust from her carpet beating from settling on her distinguished neighbor's spotless uniform. The porter's erect, majestic bearing and the meticulous way in which he grooms himself for a day at his job show the audience not only that he accepts the values of his society but that he is the epitome of them, as a general might personify the qualities of an orderly, well-disciplined military life style.

Fate has no respect for uniforms, however, and the germ of the porter's destruction is contained within the enormous, stately body that helped him to achieve his position of prominence. He makes an irrevocable mistake: he grows old. The hotel's mechanically efficient business manager, a figure reminiscent of Methusalem's robot/son, Felix, notices that the porter has found it necessary to sit down and rest for a moment after carrying a heavy trunk; the manager jots down this unforgivable sign of human frailty in his notebook and loses no time in summoning the porter to his office to inform him—by handing him a letter—that, in view of his long years of service, he is being given a new post that will correspond more appropriately to his age. Having presented the porter with the devastating news of his demotion to lavatory attendant in this characteristically antiseptic way, the manager then strides into his own restroom to wash the stains of guilt from his hands.

The literary-artistic motif that appears in this scene (and that we have discussed earlier), that of the basically decent person who is not a stranger to filth versus the inhibited, compulsively orderly, emotionally frigid anal personality, is not clearly understood by all critics. Hence Siegfried Kracauer describes the porter's demotion as a "rather humane administrative measure."[20] Kracauer has ignored not only the manager's brisk notetaking and compulsive hand washing but also the callous way in which he turns his back on the porter; despite Murnau's most obvious symbols—the roaring fire in the manager's fireplace and the cigarette smoke that he blows in the porter's face—it does not dawn on Kracauer that this unfeeling automaton is the sort of demonic person who thinks nothing of dispatching an elderly man to the nether regions, and who is anything but humane.

As the former porter is led off to his new post, the audience is not yet aware what the exact nature of the old man's duties will be, because that information was not contained in the portion of the letter flashed on the screen. We simply see him as he descends a long flight of stairs into a dark lower region. By locating the lavatory in, one might

31. "The Far-sighted Members of the Commission Report" (Ernst Barlach).
Courtesy Ernst Barlach Nachlassvertretung GmbH.

say, the bowels of the earth, Murnau indicates the degree of contempt
in which the pristine, mechanized German society holds the performance of natural functions, and thus the setting emphasizes the abyss
into which the porter has sunk in the view of his contemporaries. In
addition to signifying the decline in the porter's fortunes, the underground location of the lavatory has other connotations: one might
think of the grave, hell, or the existence of vermin either in sewers or
in natural tunnels beneath the surface of the earth. The German cinema audience of 1924, furthermore, had the hideous experience of the
dysentery-ridden trenches of World War I fresh in their minds; Paul
Fussell has observed, "To be in the trenches was to experience an unreal, unforgettable enclosure and constraint, as well as a sense of being unoriented and lost."[21] These feelings surely parallel those of the
porter after his banishment to the restroom. The lavatory's remote location also suggests the human tendency to repress what we would

32. Lavatory scene, from *The Last Laugh*. Courtesy Museum of Modern Art/ Film Stills Archive, West 53rd St., New York City.

like to forget: the processes of elimination, poverty, old age, and death. In "The Far-sighted Members of the Commission Report" (fig. 31), Ernst Barlach portrayed the poor in a similar state of subterranean exile, their hands protruding from sewer grates as unconcerned officials stomp over them without so much as a downward glance.[22]

Literally having been treated like dirt, the once-swaggering porter slumps into a verminlike existence. Instead of escorting attractive women to their taxis, he now brushes dandruff from the shoulders of the hotel's prosperous customers and wipes the dirt from their shoes. These spoiled magnates are in such a mannequinlike state of paralysis that the old man must turn on the faucets for them and hand them towels that are only inches away from their fingertips. Their preening at the restroom mirror recalls the porter's own elaborate toilette in his more fortunate days. Now, like the porter's fate, the semispherical shape of the enormous umbrella emblazoned with the words "Hotel Atlantic" with which he once sheltered his head has been overturned: the protection and security of a respectable job withdrawn from him, he slouches in a chair at the far end of the lavatory, holding a bowl that also bears the hotel's imprint (fig. 32).[23] The old man cannot bring himself to eat from this receptacle, which contains a thin liquid from which fumes rise. Its form closely resembles that of a chamber pot.

Unable to eat in the ambience of the lavatory, the porter's degradation is carried a step further as he is shown crawling on all fours to clean the floor. It is at this point that his humiliation is discovered by an aunt, who, thinking he still holds his highly respected position, has decided to surprise him with a hot lunch from home. Directed by the new porter to the top of the stairs leading to the underground restroom, her horror at seeing her unkempt, defrocked relative peering dismally from the lavatory door registers itself in a monumental scream. This scene was considered so crucial by the film's script writer, Carl Mayer, that he urged cameraman Karl Freund to devise a new technique to record the reaction in the old man's eyes to the aunt's shock. Freund complied by inventing the method of putting the camera on a platform with wheels; however, because the restroom was located so far underground, the innovative technique had to be modified in this case by mounting the camera on a crank-operated fire ladder.[24]

The horrified aunt rushes with the tragic news to the porter's adoring niece (who, although she has just been married the day before, is already bedecked in housecleaning apparel, broom in hand). The fall in the fortunes of the head of the household causes the family's morale to crumble completely. The first indication the porter has of this upon his return home is the pile of unwashed dishes on his table, a reflection of the previously fastidious family's emotional disarray. Haltingly he ascends to the newlyweds' apartment. In one of the film's most pathetic moments, the old man's shaking hand reaches for the doorbell and then falls away. Spotlighted in the center of the frame, we see a close-up of the implement that he cannot bear to pull: it is a wooden handle supended at the end of a long cord—a replica of the device used to flush an old-fashioned toilet. When his trembling hand finally does pull the cord, the porter soon finds himself flushed away by his family with as little affection as they would demonstrate for a pile of excrement.[25] He retreats to the only place in which he now belongs, the hotel lavatory, where we first see his bowed form illuminated by the flashlight of his only remaining friend, the night watchman; later, he is completely enveloped in darkness.

Siegfried Kracauer sees the tragic state of affairs described above as the result of a breakdown in the authoritarian system, for "the film implies that authority, and authority alone, fuses the disparate social spheres into a whole." Kracauer observes that the porter's neighbors revere his uniform "as a symbol of supreme authority and are happy to be allowed to revere it. Thus the film advances, however ironically, the authoritarian credo that the magic spell of authority protects society from decomposition."[26] Kracauer is of course correct on one level. The film contains elements of naturalism and can be interpreted in part in terms of social strata and authority figures. *The Last Laugh* is also an expressionistic work, however, and as such it explores emotions and the subconscious. Authoritarianism may help to bind society together, according to some viewpoints, but it is mechanisms such as sublimation and rationalization that prevent the human psyche from falling apart. The porter's decline is compounded by the fact that he not only is demoted but is demoted to the toilet. No longer a demigod rising above his family and neighbors, he is now just one of the rest of them—a human being. Among the greatest potential threats to our sense of dignity and worth are these: we defecate, we grow old, we die. The cycle takes us from dust to dust; praise be to the person who makes us think that we can overcome our physical limitations, and woe to the one who, by succumbing, proves that we cannot!

Terrence Des Pres refers to *dignity* as a term that is becoming passé, that "has grown suspect and is seldom used in analytic discourse." The word still had profound meaning for the film audiences of the twenties, however, and as defined by Des Pres it may still be highly significant: although it can refer to "the ways power cloaks itself in pomp and ritual and pride," the word in its most basic sense designates "one of the constituents of humanness, one of the irreducible elements of selfhood."[27] Dignity in both of these applications is relevant to the case of the porter, and its loss on the superficial level as well as on the basis of his self-image is the source of his tragedy. Karen Horney, writing about the universal applicability of the German phrase *Angst der Kreatur*, remarked that "factually all of us are helpless towards forces more powerful than ourselves, such as death, illness, old age."[28] Add to this list our difficulties in mastering fully the processes of elimination—particularly at the beginning and end of the life cycle—and one begins to realize the degree to which the constituents of the porter's view of himself as a worthwhile individual have escaped his control.

An excremental degradation has connotations that a demotion of a different sort would not have. Traditionally, in "dignified," polite society, the room used for the processes of elimination is as far as possible from the rooms in which more "civilized" activities occur. In the case of *The Last Laugh* the location of the restroom underground, with all its negative connotations, places the protagonist in an "Oben und Unten" situation in which he is clearly the underdog. Despite the fascination that excrement would seem to have for some German writers and artists, the fact remains that for persons such as the porter and the chic clientele of the Hotel Atlantic, literati who employ scatological imagery are engaging in the shocking paradox of mentioning the unmentionable. And, unlike Sister Rahel, who considered her assignment a promotion, most persons of any social class would rate the job of restroom attendant near or at the bottom of their lists of career goals. In his discussion of the experience of Jews in the Warsaw Ghetto who hid for days in the sewers, crawling on their hands and knees in the dank darkness, Des Pres comments that if their tale "were from a novel, how easily we might speak of rites of passage; of descent into hell; of journey through death's underworld. We would respond to the symbolism of darkness and light. . . . And we would not be misreading. For despite the horror, it all seems familiar, very much recalling archetypes we know from art and dreams. For the survivor, in any case, the immersion in excrement marks the nadir of his passage through extremity. No worse assault on moral being seems possible."[29]

Old age and death pose similar threats to our sense of worth as human beings. It is morale building to attain an advanced age if doing so elicits respect from our fellow beings and brings us a position of seniority in our profession, a seat of power from which we can control those under our supervision. When ageism enters the picture, however, one is viewed not as having "paid one's dues" but as having "one foot in the grave"; in the porter's case he soon shuffles off with *both* feet to his subterranean exile, stripped of the prerogatives that should reward long years of service.

Death, of course, is the ultimate insult if one cannot approach it with dignity. The creators of *The Last Laugh* intensified the normal fear of a humiliating demise by playing up the traditional link between death and excrement via decomposition. When the porter is demoted and must give up his uniform, his decay is implied, for his grandiose apparel has become his "second skin," and the sloughing off of this epidermis signals his decline.

Clearly, the experience of mortification was highly relevant for the film's postwar German audience, who had hoped for a victory in World War I—or at least for a hero's death for the fallen; instead, as was revealed so graphically in *All Quiet on the Western Front*, many of the soldiers came to an ugly, defecating end. When one has lost all the trappings of a normal, civilized existence, everything, as Des Pres asserts, "depends on the body."[30] But, for a person of the porter's years, the body is a precarious prop on which to lean; consequently, his exile to a place associated with the decomposition of waste matter implies a bleak prognosis for his survival. The porter's demotion, therefore, exemplifies (in a much more heartrending way than do the works of Wilhelm Busch) how one's dreams of pomp and glory can become an excremental nightmare.

The fact that Mayer's theme was too horribly real for comfort worried the film's producer, Erich Pommer. Just as World War II struck a number of writers and artists as a reality that went beyond one's wildest imaginings, so the years after World War I found many Germans in actual circumstances that were too painful to see on the screen. After ten meetings, Pommer convinced Carl Mayer to add an epilogue to *The Last Laugh*. "We added the happy ending," Pommer later commented, "because without it the film would have been too much like real life and would have been a commercial failure. After the war, many former businessmen, kings, etc. were occupying menial jobs. What is left if you take the uniform away from the general? Nothing. The head porter was the most important man in the hotel. This was the story of thousands and thousands of people in Germany to whom this had happened. But the audience did not catch on. The happy ending said: by chance, tomorrow you might go up again."[31]

Forced to give another spin of the excremental wheel of fortune, Mayer managed by means of skillful satire to make his capitulation something of a victory. First, he gave the audience what it wanted in the way of plot: the porter inherits a fortune from an American multimillionaire who dies in the restroom, the latter having specified in his will that his heir would be the person in whose arms he expires. Rising from his nadir of chamber-pot broth to the zenith of a sumptuous feast in the hotel dining room with his old friend the night watchman, the porter does not forget the lesson fate has taught him. After gorging himself on gourmet delights, he (inevitably) strides off to the restroom, where he kisses the new lavatory attendant on both cheeks, tips him lavishly, and makes sure another customer is equally generous. In an ending that is fitting for a male version of the Cinderella story, the porter, the night watchman, and a passing beggar ride off in an elegant horse-drawn carriage.

Although the average moviegoer of the twenties may have been pleased with this conclusion, the observant viewer cannot help but note that Mayer, through his use of scatological allusions, has put in question the porter's victory over the forces of degradation and decomposition. Though his former social status has been regained and indeed surpassed, he cannot escape his corporeality. The big black globs of caviar that are plopped on the watchman's plate are costly, but their appearance is reminiscent of the lavatory. The gluttonous table manners of the porter and his friend are as animalistic as the former's crawling on the restroom floor. The fat, brown, cylindrical cigars that the porter and his successor in the lavatory smoke, the coins that the new multimillionaire drops into everyone's hands, and the mounds of sickeningly rich food are part of an excremental iconography that is all brought together in a frame depicting a scatological trinity—*money* (a tip for the new attendant) left in the *bathroom* in a *dish*. Norman O. Brown has written of the intertwining of these themes in the human mind:

> it is inherent in the money complex to attribute to what is not food the virtue that belongs to food. In Freud's succinct formula, excrement becomes aliment; but it remains excrement, as Midas . . . discovered when he became hungry. . . . Ruskin perceives money-gain as the pursuit of the dream of sublimated anality. . . .
>
> The superfluity complex thus invades and corrupts the domain of human consumption; in technical psychoanalytical terms, the anal complex is displaced to, and fused with, the oral complex. . . . The resultant confusion is exhibited not only in the bottomless consumer demand for inedible goods which satisfy not, but also in the demand that food itself assume luxurious—i.e., superfluous—forms.[32]

The porter's "happy ending" constitutes final proof that human beings cannot transcend their bodily limitations; as the porter wallows in food and money, and another old man fumbles for towels in the restroom, the alimentary-intestinal tract is once again triumphant. Despite the efforts of the film's producer to repress the prevalence of the scatological side of life, it is the sensitive script writer Mayer who has in fact had the last laugh.

9

Conclusion

Much has been made of the fact that *The Last Laugh* succeeded as a silent film without a single caption (except for the director's note justifying the epilogue). Credit for this achievement may be given to Emil Jannings' acting ability and F. W. Murnau's gifted direction; Paul Rotha attributes the feat to camera skills, and Thomas Wiseman cites script writer Carl Mayer's innovations.[1] Of course, all of these elements played a part in the film's ability to narrate without subtitles. Siegfried Kracauer, however, offers still another explanation: "the interrelationship between the method of representation and the content to be represented is striking. It is not so much the technical ingenuity as the subject-matter . . . that causes the film-makers to introduce titleless narration."[2] *The Last Laugh* was able to tell, without a single written or spoken word, a stirring and affecting story, at least in part because of its inclusion of imagery that had strong connotations for the audience. Because of the traditional and varied use of scatological metaphors in German art and literature, which in turn reflects a cultural preoccupation with the cleanliness–filth conflict, excrement was naturally an emotionally charged subject for the German film audience. Hence the porter's demotion to the restroom was one of the most forceful and effective ways in which Carl Mayer could have portrayed the old man's decline. Because the average German filmgoer would automatically equate the slightest glimpse of the lavatory with dirt (which implies decomposition and, at least on the subconscious level, death), Mayer was able to render his theme dramatically by the power of suggestion without being overtly vulgar. *The Last Laugh* does not include a frame showing actual excrement, as does the television film of *A Man and his Dog;* it never even shows a toilet. Yet the audi-

191

ence surely empathized with the aunt's scream of horror when confronted with the porter's fate. Moviegoers seeing the film today are emotionally moved, too; but the predisposition of the German audience to Mayer's imagery, particularly in the difficult postwar atmosphere, must have lent the film a singular power at the time and place of its debut.

The literary and artistic legacy that aided the audience in comprehending the porter's tragedy included not only the works of Busch and Büchner but extended further back to Martin Luther and the Schwänke. Even the great Goethe, we have seen, could not resist inserting a scatological allusion in *Faust*. The tendency of modern German writers and artists to include scatological metaphors and expressions in their words is, then, not so much a shocking break with the past as a continuation and reworking of an established tradition. The themes, the images, and the terminology are not new, only their relative preponderance and explicitness—and, in some cases, the goals that the author has in mind when he uses them. Busch's clean, orderly Joseph, on his way to church in his top hat, and the impious, uninhibited dog who urinates on his sacred tome represent a dichotomy that reappears again and again in modern German literature, be it in the guise of Hercules and Augias or the Hoysers and Leni Pfeiffer. More than one German writer or artist has sensed in the *oben–unten* duality one of the basic conflicts of human nature.

Clearly, it has been the feeling of many modern German authors that scatological images would serve their purposes more effectively in certain cases than would other metaphors. For centuries, German as well as non-German writers have found scatological allusions to be forceful components of humor and satire; this would appear to be one of the most acceptable uses of literary scatology from a critical point of view and, as noted in chapter 1, Jae Num Lee has even suggested that nonsatirical uses of excrement in literature require an apology. There seems to be abundant evidence, however, to prove that, for many German authors and artists, scatology has served a vast array of more serious purposes, most of which require no apology whatsoever. Nowhere is this more apparent than in Thomas Mann's urbane novella *A Man and his Dog*. Although the Nobel laureate's tale is set apart by its genteel tone and its graceful style, it nevertheless has a kinship with other serious modern German literary works that contain scatological elements. The narrator's grappling for his identity through an examination of Bashan's and his own attitudes toward the excremental might well be considered a highly sophisticated, elegant version of

Ossias Würz's rectal exam. Here again, the themes and the metaphors are the same; only the "packaging"—Lind's intentionally explicit coarseness as opposed to Mann's mellifluous prose—contrasts strongly.

Mann's questions, "What am I? Who am I?" (which in the context of *A Man and his Dog* may be restated as "Am I a creature of nature or a product of civilization?"), have been answered with increasing frequency in modern German literature with a stress on the corporeal. The rejection of society and its values was most arrestingly revealed in the Dadaists' slogan, "Art is shit." Transmute the rebels' slogan to "War is shit," and one has the epitome of the attitude expressed in a number of works by twentieth-century German authors who found scatological imagery highly appropriate for conveying their views of the two world wars. As the ignoble events, military and otherwise, of the modern era convinced many persons that a civilized society was a false hope, some German writers and artists felt compelled to use excremental allusions to portray human beings as prisoners of their physical drives. This pessimistic viewpoint might best be summarized in still another variation of the Dadaists' slogan: Life is shit.

In the works of Heinrich Böll, an author who utilized scatology perhaps more than any other serious writer in Germany's literary history, one finds a convergence of virtually all of the possible uses of excremental motifs discussed in this study: there is gentle humor and sharp satire, earnest introspection and rebellious social criticism, as well as bitter (and bittersweet) portrayals of war and modern life in general. But there is still more. With his contention that the biological destiny decried by the pessimists in fact provides the cornerstone of a new, realistic approach to life based on total self-acceptance, Böll has given a positive twist to the iconography of dung, decay, and disenchantment. This final category is achieved by a simple shift of perspective: Böll's "mystical materialism" does not degrade human beings but rather dignifies the bodies with which they have been blessed.

It should be pointed out that the subdivisions of this study are to a certain extent arbitrary. Brecht's *Baal*, for example, might well have been discussed in chapter 8; it is only because Brecht is *slightly* more optimistic than the writers of the excremental life cycle (Baal transcends his physical limitations well enough to become a poet, and he has a certain joie de vivre) and because *Baal* so clearly typifies the revolt against the standards of the bourgeois establishment that it was included in chapter 5. Conversely, *Methusalem* might have been grouped with the discussion of Grosz, were it not for Goll's greater pessimism. Basically, of course, each writer and artist examined uses scatological elements in a unique way that defies classification—highlighting once again the hitherto unsuspected variety of ways in which the excremental has lent itself to literary and artistic purposes.

It should also be reiterated that this study by no means claims to be an exhaustive examination of scatology in modern German literature. The more one delves, the more one discovers, and it would certainly seem that a number of volumes could be written on the subject and its ramifications. Just as the variety of uses of excremental imagery should not be underestimated, neither should its ubiquitousness. On the other hand, the emphasis of this study on the frequent appearance of scatological elements in German literature should be construed by the reader neither as a "scatological approach to literature" nor as a "scatological interpretation" of the works discussed. Rather, an attempt has been made here simply to identify and analyze certain literary and artistic themes and metaphors that have often been overlooked and to ascertain their roles in the overall thematic or metaphorical structures of the works in which they appear. These excremental elements may be limited to a brief allusion or two in one work, whereas they may constitute a major leitmotiv in another; in any case, the concern of the writers of this study is to shed light on the significance of the references within their literary or artistic framework rather than to advance a stubbornly one-sided critical approach.

The fact that critics have seldom acknowledged nonsatirical usages of scatology in German literature does not imply that these more serious excremental motifs are always innovative. Germans do not have a monopoly on the use of scatological references in war literature.[3] Writers of other nationalities—T. S. Eliot and Samuel Beckett, for example—have also used excremental allusions to convey pessimistic outlooks or to comment on the dismal nature of modern life. Basically, what differentiates the German writers from those of other countries is the greater preponderance of scatological motifs in their works. Also, in the case of the nay-sayers discussed in chapter 8, one may find a distinctly northern European gloom: for them, life does not simply *resemble* excrement, life *is* excrement.

If there is one particular Germanic contribution to the realm of scatological literary imagery that is most unusual, it is Heinrich Böll's meticulous development of the theory that an open acceptance of the excremental is a sign of the healthy individual and society. Although Böll's "aesthetics of the humane" (see chapter 7) sounds deceptively simple, it presents a revolutionary challenge to the negative values that civilized society has attached to excrement. Despite their customary and not unsurprising role in literary and artistic works as indicators of filth, depravity, or human weakness, it should be noted that waste products have in actuality performed useful functions from a historical perspective. Manure is the world's oldest fertilizer, and it has been a source of fuel since ancient times. Offal has been used as an ingredient in cosmetics, and the ancient Romans even washed their clothes in urine.[4] For hundreds of years, excrement has been used to concoct medicinal remedies; urinalysis and the examination of stools are today and have been for centuries among the medical profession's most important diagnostic procedures; both are thus important indexes of one's state of health.

Böll certainly was sensitive to excrement's "redeeming social value," and the process of stool analysis even provided him with one of the major metaphors in *Group Portrait with Lady*.[5] For most persons today, however, the positive connotations of excrement have been overshadowed by the negativism of toilet training and civilized manners. Primitive human beings were not so jaundiced in their attitude toward excrement, as Theodor Rosebury has pointed out in *Life on Man:*

> Before abnegation changed man's early attitude toward his excretions into the one we have today, he felt awe and reverence toward them. He cherished them for real value tangibly demonstrated. The stuff was useful, and therefore the more magical. Feces renewed the life-giving virtues of the earth; urine did a better job of cleaning than plain water. . . . Today it is hard to reach back through our cultivated aversion and our affluence, when these materials have come to be prime symbols of worthlessness, to a time when aversion had not been thought of and anything useful was necessarily treasured.[6]

Difficult though it may be to reverse deeply ingrained cultural symbols (a Herculean task, like removing the manure from Elis, which may at times seem hardly worthwhile), Böll made the effort and reached back to more pragmatic primitive times, perhaps also to the uninhibited feelings of early childhood, in order to lay the foundation of his arresting aesthetic reversal.

German writers and artists had, of course, demonstrated an awareness of excrement's useful qualities prior to the publication of Böll's literary works. More than one writer had found, as Busch did, that a comfortable acceptance of bodily functions is an indication of a person's "naturalness"; others, such as Remarque, noted that excrement could provide an appropriate means of revenge. It may be recalled that Busch, in *The Birthday*, observed that a well-filled chamber pot could serve as a handy, lifesaving fire extinguisher. In Ernst Barlach's drama *The Dead Day,* a frankly scatological gnome proves his superiority over supposedly more highly developed and more intelligent human beings; the clever gnome has two excremental victories over the grasping Mother: once he frees himself from her by urinating on her, and later he asserts himself by ascending toward the ceiling after breaking wind.[7] These are scattered instances, however, and it was left to Böll to develop extensively in his fiction and to justify in his critical writings the notion of excrement as, in Rosebury's terms, useful and valuable.

Although Baal's hymn to the privy might also be considered a forerunner of Böll's theme, there is a significant difference. Through this vulgarly shocking affront Brecht was attempting to poke fun at civilized refinement. Böll reiterated many of the same views, but with serious undertones. The last two lines of the hymn (see chapter 5) show Brecht to be closer to the pessimism of the writers who dwell on the excremental life cycle than to the benign goodwill of Böll. Herbert Luthy, quoted in chapter 5, describes *Baal* as "not morbid at all" and as displaying "genuine spiritual depth" and "the piety of an uncompromising acceptance of the natural world because it is natural." He might better have applied these terms to Böll.

In fact, Böll created his own scatological paean in the essay entitled "To a Bishop, a General, and a Cabinet Minister Born 1917," in which he rhapsodized on the topic "The Favorite Word of Those Born in 1917." The word, which never actually appears in the essay, is clearly *shit.* Though Böll's praise of the term is written in as sharply satirical a style as Brecht's hymn, Böll's humor merely ornaments his serious intentions. For hundreds of thousands of German war dead, writes Böll, *shit* was "the last word spoken by them on this earth."[8] (As was seen in chapter 7, the term was included in the last sentence of *Group Portrait's* Heinrich Gruyten.) Although, according to Böll, millions of soldiers uttered this word countless times each day, *shit* is not just an obscenity used by war-weary military men but an important part of the German language in the widest possible sense: "That's right, a German word, and *not* 'Germany,' 'Fatherland,' 'God,' 'Nation,' 'Führer,' 'Mother,' or 'Father.'" Böll underlines the daring comparison of *shit* to *God* on two other occasions in the essay by paraphrasing the beginning of the Gospel according to John: "The word was in the beginning and in the end." Here again Böll stresses the dilemma portrayed in the toilet-cleaning scene in *Group Portrait:* German writers have not forgotten their humanity as represented by "the word," but the average German has. "Postwar literature has assured it a place and a certain historical duration," Böll writes, "but what has happened to the spoken word?" Sensing the need for a healing return to basic human emotions in postwar Germany, Böll suggests, "Perhaps the time has come when this German word of blessing may actually dispense a modicum of blessing." For the Catholic Böll, the earth is the Lord's— not the devil's, as the Lutheran outlook so often would have it. Böll urged his fellow Germans to accept as worthwhile even the dirtiest, most humble parts of God's creation, and thus the author's eye-catching juxtaposition of the words *shit* and *God* springs from his emphatically stated conviction: *"Germans are human beings too!"*[9]

To portray fictionally the uncommon, humane views that he preached in "To a Bishop, A General, and a Cabinet Minister Born 1917," Böll had to create an unusual heroine: Leni Pfeiffer is not like the classical heroines, who were goddesslike externally and noble spiritually as well, nor is she the morally crumbling modern anti-heroine. Radiating virtue even as she is immersed to the elbow in the toilet, and moreover *because* she is tackling such an unsavory task, Leni exemplifies Dejaneira's statement in Dürrenmatt's *Hercules* (see chapter 3): "You are a hero, and thus you will also remove the manure heroically." Böll's "aesthetics of the humane" led him to make a very special contribution not only to the development of scatological imagery but to twentieth-century literature in general and to modern definitions of human worth. Near the end of Böll's novel *The Clown*, Hans Schnier, another unpretentious, humane person trapped in the modern, stiflingly civilized world, admits his basic fondness for humanity, even though he seems surprised by his admission: "Strangely enough I like the kind to which I belong: people."[10] This is a remarkable attitude indeed amid the misanthropy rampant in contemporary fiction.

At this point the reader may feel as though he or she were about to go under for the third time in the cesspit of *And Where Were You, Adam?* Because we are, inevitably, products of contemporary society and its taboos, it is very likely that, despite our best efforts to be enlightened and unprejudiced, extensive explorations of scatology may leave us gasping for air. It is the hope of the writers of this study that their efforts to compile sizable amounts of data to support their contentions regarding the variety of usages of scatology in modern German literature have not left the reader with the impression that German writers and artists are hopelessly mired in the muck. Perhaps it is time to throw a few bouquets in the direction of the manure pile.

There is no question that modern German writers and artists are to be commended for their detailed explorations of a realm of imagery often ignored and for discovering in ostensibly coarse language very real poetic possibilities. Georg Büchner, for example, dazzles the reader with his skill at mixing vulgar terminology with exquisitely beautiful poetry in *Woyzeck*. Throughout this study, we have encountered touching, emotionally affecting moments wrung from scatological imagery: Paul's inarticulateness in the train, the old porter's trembling at the sight of a doorbell that conjures up tragic memories of the lavatory, Wohlbrecht's response to the angel. In "Soul of Wood," Jakov Lind has developed his characters so well, using an economy of style in which a few simple but telling touches reveal much to us about each figure, that we cannot help but identify with the very human Hermann Wohlbrecht. Wohlbrecht's basic decency causes the reader to admire him and to see him as a hero of sorts. In the emotionally sterile world that Lind portrays, Wohlbrecht's commitment to another human being, though tinged with selfishness and possessiveness, is commendable. Because of Lind's writing skill, Wohlbrecht's "Ich scheiß drauf" speech becomes as emotionally wrenching and even as inspiring for the modern reader as many of the great soliloquies of classical heroes. Lind has accomplished an astonishing tour de force in rendering poignant and uplifting a speech in which the character "shits" on just about everyone and everything.[11]

Paul Fussell, whose study *The Great War and Modern Memory* deals primarily with depictions of World War I in British literature, has found that war furnishes authors with "a number of generically rigid stage character-types, almost like those of Comedy of Humors: the hapless Private, the vainglorious Corporal, the sadistic Sergeant, the adolescent, snobbish Lieutenant, the fire-eating Major, the dotty Colonel."[12] To this list should be added the distinctly Germanic contribution to literary wartime characterization, the anally preoccupied Nazi. To contemporary American readers, raised on television reruns of "Hogan's Heroes" and grade-B Hollywood movies about World War II, the Nazi who washes his hands to cleanse his soul of guilt may be a cliché. One should bear in mind, however, that at the time the works discussed here first appeared they not only were original but also were striking evidence of a tough-minded, rigorous attempt at self-analysis on the part of the Germans. In fairness to the postwar authors, it must be pointed out that their works are not so one-sided as to stress anality as the *only* Nazi characteristic or to depict *all* Nazis as anal personalities. This study has of necessity limited itself primarily to scatological motifs, but the theme of Nazi anality is only a part of the complex literary reaction to the Third Reich.

Through their stirring use of excremental metaphors to convey the horrors of war, Remarque, Böll, Lind, and Weiss may perform the useful service of impressing on the mind of the modern reader the inevitably catastrophic consequences of a lack of truly—not superficially—civilized behavior. Böll's contribution to the understanding of the causes and aftermath of war is especially noteworthy because of the size and scope of his oeuvre and also because of his virtuosity in the use of scatological imagery. In addition to developing his innovative aesthetic reversal in *Group Portrait with Lady,* Böll demonstrated in *And Where Were You, Adam?* that he had also mastered the more traditional technique of using excrement to portray war at its ugliest. Greck's death scene, in particular, is memorable: in view of Böll's depiction of Greck as a sick anal personality, the excremental nature of his demise is strikingly fitting and undeniably sad.

It is a credit to modern German authors that they can move us—not in a sentimental way but genuinely and deeply—while using the terminology of the bathroom or depicting the conflicts surrounding the anal personality. These writers have succeeded not only in spite of their inclusion of scatology, although sometimes this is the case, but more often *because* of their skillful, sensitive treatment of excremental elements. Their desire to be honest and in touch with the basic realities of life, to create a "human art," has liberated them from hypocritical aesthetic standards—the truth has set them free.[13] The close perusal of art and literature that has been unchained from societal taboos may be unnerving, but we can hope that it is also an enlightening experience. It is the earnest desire of the writers of this study that those who have joined them in this lengthy encounter with an ostensibly distasteful subject will not find themselves, as Dürrenmatt might say, "encrapsulated," but that rather, like Kästner's street sweeper, they will have become "well-read in . . . dirt."

Notes

1. INTRODUCTION

1. In his Isenheim Altarpiece, Matthias Grünewald depicts the birth of Christ by showing the Holy Virgin holding the Christ child next to a bed, in front of which stands a chamber pot. The chamber pot acts as a very effective symbol for God's having become human.

2. Martin Luther, *Sämmtliche Schriften* (St. Louis: Lutherischer Concordia Verlag, 1887), vol. 22, col. 200; translated by Dieter and Jacqueline Rollfinke. Unless otherwise indicated, all translations in this volume are by Dieter and Jacqueline Rollfinke. Luther expert Jaroslav Pelikan comments, "The language Luther uses in his writings about sex and the human body is often quite explicit and offensive to pietist ears. But what truly offends pietists about Luther's language is not its coarseness but rather his recognition that the spiritual and mental aspects of human life are no more noble than are the physical and material ones. (Jaroslav Pelikan, "The Enduring Relevance of Martin Luther 500 Years After His Birth," *New York Times Magazine*, 18 Sept. 1983, p. 99).

3. Some writers deliberately use a scatological term in the title of a book or an article as a means of attracting readers. Curt Riess's *Theaterdämmerung oder Das Klo auf der Bühne* (Hamburg: Hoffmann & Campe, 1970) uses such a catchy and deceptive title. The author does not analyze the use of the toilet on the stage at all; instead, the title serves as a metaphor for Riess's opinion that contemporary German stage managers allow themselves such horrendous liberties in new adaptations of both classical and modern plays that the audience cannot wait for the chance to leave their seats and run to the toilet. In all fairness to Riess, it must be said that in a book of about 250 pages he manages to give one or two examples of the use of the toilet on the stage. That hardly seems to justify his title, however. It is ironic that Riess, who feels very offended by any thought of defecation on the stage, uses a scatological metaphor in the title of his book. Hans-Rudolf Müller-Schwefe, *Sprachgrenzen: Das sogenannte Obszöne, Blasphemische, und Revolutionäre bei Günter Grass und Heinrich Böll* (Munich: Pfeiffer, 1978) is also misleading in regard to what its title appears to promise. Müller-Schwefe mentions scatological elements only

once or twice in the entire book and even then in a most superficial way. The author claims to set out to examine the use of sexual obscenities and blasphemies in the works of Grass and Böll; in actuality, however, Müller-Schwefe treats the entire subject most gingerly, and his book never achieves a thorough analysis of its purported subject matter.

4. E.g., Karl H. Ruhleder, "A Pattern of Messianic Thought in Günter Grass' *Cat and Mouse*," *German Quarterly* 39 (1966): 599–612. Martha Banta, "American Apocalypses: Excrement and Ennui," *Studies in the Literary Imagination* 7, no. 1 (1974): 1–30.

5. Heinrich Vormweg, "Apokalypse mit Vogelscheuchen," *Deutsche Zeitung*, 31 Aug. 1963, as quoted in Gert Loschütz, ed., *Von Buch zu Buch: Günter Grass in der Kritik* (Neuwied: Luchterhand, 1968), p. 70.

6. Paul Englisch, *Das skatologische Element in Literatur, Kunst, und Volksleben* (Stuttgart: Julius Püttmann, 1928).

7. Jae Num Lee, *Swift and Scatological Satire* (Albuquerque: University of New Mexico Press, 1971), p 3.

8. John R. Clark, "Bowl Games: Satire in the Toilet," *Modern Language Studies* 4, no. 2 (1974): 43–58. Jost Hermand, *Stänker und Weismacher: Zur Dialektik eines Affekts*, Texte Metzler, no. 18 (Stuttgart: Metzler, 1971); quotation is on p. 36.

9. Another example of a scholar's discussion of scatology not so much as a literary technique but as a psychological revelation of the writer's *Weltanschauung* is Michael West, "Scatology and Eschatology: The Heroic Dimensions of Thoreau's Wordplay," *PMLA* 89 (1974): 1043–64.

10. Lee, *Swift*, p 29.

11. There has been a considerable increase in scatology in English and American literature during the past two decades. As examples one ought to consider such authors as Philip Roth, John Updike, or John Barth. (See Clark, "Bowl Games.") Even American television has acknowledged (primarily off-screen) the existence of the toilet in American homes on such shows as "All in the Family" and "The Cosby Show." Nevertheless, when a series debuting in the 1973–74 television season, "Lotsa Luck," dared to feature a toilet onscreen as an important prop, critics said of the show, "this one has scraped the bottom," "short on taste," "off-blue," and "one long toilet joke." The series soon was canceled. See Judy Fayard, review of "Lotsa Luck," *Time*, 29 Oct. 1973, p. 125, and Cleveland Amory, review of "Lotsa Luck," *TV Guide*, 13 Oct. 1973, p. 56.

12. Marielouise Jurreit, "Alles über Scheiße," *twen*, Dec. 1969, p. 140.

13. "Underground: Jahr des Schweins," *Der Spiegel*, 9 June 1969, p. 142.

14. Jurreit, "Alles über Scheiße," p. 121.

15. Ibid., p. 122.

16. "Underground," p. 150.

17. Dieter E. Zimmer, "Die Flüche des Präsidenten," *Die Zeit*, 28 June 1974, pp. 9, 10. Jakov Lind also writes of the significance of scatology in German profanity. In his autobiography, Lind says that during World War II he, a Jew, was

in the ironic situation of working in Germany on a German riverboat: "Bacher [the skipper], whose hands were constantly trembling, was a loud-mouthed, angry old man, who wouldn't let a sentence pass without the word *Scheisse*, in spite of the fact that his wife reminded him with a reproachful 'But, Eduard, is that necessary?'" When Lind staged a work slowdown, this was Bacher's reaction: "Lift your feet you *Scheisskerl*, you *Scheissholländer*, a little quicker you *Arschloch*, you *Holländischer Schweinehund*." Lind then relates these incidents to Germans in general: "Unlike the rest of the world, the Germans have no use for the expressive term 'fucking.' The word 'fucking' can only be used when it means just that. What is considered dirty and therefore insulting by the Anglo-Saxons means nothing to the Germans. For them, everything that has to do with the rear end, feces, and the anus is real filth. That's why the words *Arsch*, *Scheisse*, *Arschloch*, and 'Lick my arse' are 'real and serious insults'; they can only be used by people according to hierarchy. Insult is the privilege of the powerful. A director, a boss, an officer, a captain can call those underneath his rank any name he fancies; but saying to your superior 'Lick my arse' is equivalent to patricide" (Jakov Lind, *Counting My Steps: An Autobiography* [London: Macmillan, 1969], pp. 126–28).

18. Act 3, scene 17: When Götz is asked to surrender, he answers, "Tell your captain: I have, as always, dutiful respect for his imperial majesty. Tell him, however, he can lick my ass" (Johann Wolfgang Goethe, *Sämtliche Werke* [Munich: Deutscher Taschenbuch Verlag, 1962] 8:64).

The following is just one of the many examples of Luther's excremental treatment of the devil: "But just in case that [God's grace in forgiving our sins] doesn't satisfy you, you Devil, I've also dropped some excrement and peed; go and wipe your maw on that and chew yourself healthy on it" (taken from Luther, *Sämmtliche Schriften*, vol. 22, col. 770). For a detailed discussion of the excremental and Luther, including the conjecture that the Reformation leader's thought patterns were affected by his constipation, see Norman O. Brown, *Life Against Death: The Psychoanalytical Meaning of History* (Middletown, Conn.: Wesleyan University Press, 1959), pp. 202–33. John Osborne's play *Luther* (1961) also finds the origin of Luther's theological struggles in his bowel problems.

19. George Grosz, *A Little Yes and a Big No: The Autobiography of George Grosz*, trans. Lola S. Dorin (New York: Dial Press, 1946), p. 84.

20. Peter Farb, *Word Play: What Happens When People Talk* (New York: Knopf, 1974), p. 88. Gershon Legman, *Rationale of the Dirty Joke: An Analysis of Sexual Humor*, 1st ser. (Castle Books, 1968), p. 15. On the same page, Legman elaborates: "Germans and the Dutch . . . are obviously far more susceptible to scatology in humor than to any other theme. This is doubtless a reaction to excessively strict and early toilet-training, and general rigidity and compulsiveness in the Teutonic upbringing and character, and is an open release for the resultant 'cleanliness complex' in later life, common in all Anglo-Saxon cultures."

21. Farb, *Word Play*, p. 88. From the preceding discussion of profanity and dirty jokes, it must be clear that these areas present some very serious prob-

lems for translators, because certain jokes and curses would obviously be received very differently in various cultures.

22. Peter Rühmkorf, *Über das Volksvermögen: Exkurse in den literarischen Untergrund* (Reinbek bei Hamburg: Rowohlt, 1967), p. 41. All page references to children's rhymes are from this book. (We have taken some liberties with our translations in order to create similar rhyming verses in English, but we believe that the gist of the verses remains essentially the same.)

23. Alan Dundes, *Life Is Like a Chicken Coop Ladder: A Portrait of German Culture Through Folklore* (New York: Columbia University Press, 1984).

24. *Frau im Spiegel*, 6 Mar. 1980, p. 119.

25. The Servus ad (*Frau im Spiegel*, c. 1973), is a humorous reversal of the medieval tendency to depict the devil with his face on his posterior.

26. Figs. 3 and 4 are from *Frau im Spiegel*, c. 1973. The "Dukatenesel" is of course taken from the famous Grimms' fairy tale, "Tischlein deck dich, Esel streck dich, Knüppel aus dem Sack." We will see later that psychologists believe that in the anal personality an attraction to excrement becomes sublimated in the desire to save money.

27. *Stern*, 19 July 1979, p. 69.

28. "Deutsch wie es nicht im Wörterbuch steht," advertising brochure for Ernst Klett (Stuttgart, 1983), center section.

29. *Stern*, 7 Mar. 1974, p. 128.

30. *Stern*, 22 Sept. 1977, pp. 150–51.

31. Sigmund Freud, "Character and Anal Eroticism," in *The Standard Edition of the Complete Psychological Works of Sigmund Freud*, trans. under the general editorship of James Strachey (1959; rpt. London: Hogarth Press and the Institute of Psycho-Analysis, 1962), 9:169.

32. Erich Fromm, "Die psychoanalytische Charakterologie und ihre Bedeutung für die Sozialpsychologie," *Zeitschrift für Sozialforschung* 1, no. 3 (1932): 260.

33. Capt. John G. Bourke, in an amazing book that was originally published in 1891, demonstrates that the shame and disgust generally expressed by the "civilized" nations toward excrement were not at all shared by many primitive tribes. As an example he relates the following creation myth from Australia: "Mingarope having retired upon a natural occasion was highly pleased with the red color of her excrement, which she began to mould into the form of a man, and tickling it, it showed signs of life and began to laugh" (Capt. John G. Bourke, *Scatalogic Rites of all Nations: a Dissertation upon the Employment of Excrementitious Remedial Agents in Religion, Therapeutics, Divination, Witchcraft, Love-Philters, etc. in all Parts of the Globe* [New York: American Anthropological Society, 1934], p. 269; this reprint of the original book contains a short but interesting foreword by Sigmund Freud).

34. Fromm, "Die psychoanalytische Charakterologie," p. 261.

35. Ibid., p. 254.

36. Ernest Jones, *Papers on Psycho-analysis*, 3rd ed. (London: Baillière, Tindall, & Cox, 1923), p. 704. Hermand, *Stänker und Weismacher*, p. 20.

37. Theodor Rosebury, *Life on Man* (New York: Viking Press, 1969), p. 70. To-

day, manufacturers of washing machines, underwear, and laundry detergents are doing their best to capitalize on the German desire to be clean. In their ads they try to convince the German public that they are not clean enough and that their laundry should become whiter than white. Most notorious is the ad that appeared in *Der Spiegel*, 23 Feb. 1970, p. 193, which showed a German family with pigs' heads and implied that the Germans hardly ever change their underwear. Displaying a similar zeal for fastidiousness, an advertisement for Hakle Feucht-Toilettenpapier which appeared on pp. 104–5 of the 29 Sept. 1977 issue of *Stern* suggests that a person who has used the toilet should wipe herself or himself not once, not twice, but three times: "Here's the best way: dry–moist–dry." Such a threefold ritual might almost remind one of the three ordeals that many a fairytale hero or heroine faced before attaining a happy ending. In this case, however, the reward is not a princess or a pot of gold but rather "the marvelous feeling of emerging from the powder room absolutely clean."

38. Luther, *Sämmtliche Schriften*, vol. 22, col. 179.

39. "Am Bächle," *Freiburger Zeitung*, 3 Oct. 1977, p. 15. Heinrich Böll suggested a different explanation for the scatologically crude postures of some medieval gargoyles: the novelist believed that the figures, whose bare buttocks face the residences of bishops, reveal the resentment of the medieval artists toward their patrons in the hierarchy of the Catholic Church (Heinrich Böll, "Kunst und Religion," in *Werke: Essayistische Schriften und Reden I*, ed. Bernd Balzer [Cologne: Kiepenheuer & Witsch, (1978)], pp. 318–19).

40. Lind, *Counting My Steps*, p. 149. Böll, *Werke: Essayistische Schriften und Reden II*, p. 219.

41. Dundes, *Chicken Coop Ladder*, pp. 7, 80, 75, 105.

42. Ibid., pp. 119, 126.

43. Ibid., pp. 136, 141.

44. Ibid., p. 147.

45. Freud, "Character and Anal Eroticism," p. 170; and see Jones, *Papers*, p. 691, and O. Spurgeon English and Gerald H. J. Pearson, *Emotional Problems of Living: Avoiding the Neurotic Pattern* (New York: Norton, 1945), p. 65.

46. Otto Fenichel, *The Psychoanalytic Theory of Neurosis* (New York: Norton, 1945), p. 305. Seymour Fisher and Roger P. Greenberg, *The Scientific Credibility of Freud's Theories and Therapy* (New York: Basic Books, 1977), pp. 141, 164.

47. Fisher and Greenberg, *Scientific Credibility*, pp. 143–44, 163, 146.

48. Karen Horney, *The Neurotic Personality of Our Time* (New York: Norton, 1937), pp. 33, 21, vii–viii.

49. Gordon A. Craig, *The Germans* (New York: New American Library [Meridian Books], pp. 10, 22–23. G. M. Gilbert, *The Psychology of Dictatorship* (New York: Ronald Press, 1950), p. 12.

50. Emil Ludwig, "The German Mind," *Atlantic Monthly*, Feb. 1938, pp. 257, 258. Rudolf Walter Leonhardt, *This Germany: The Story Since the Third Reich*, trans. and adapted by Catherine Hutter (Greenwich, Conn.: New York Graphic Society Publishers, n.d.), pp. 98–99.

51. Gilbert, *Psychology of Dictatorship*, pp. 307, 305.

52. David Rodnick, *Postwar Germans: An Anthropologist's Account* (New Haven: Yale University Press, 1948), pp. 27, 20.

53. Immanuel Kant, *Anthropology from a Pragmatic Point of View*, trans. Mary J. Gregor (The Hague: Nijhoff, 1974), p. 180, and *Education*, trans. Annette Churton (Ann Arbor: University of Michigan Press, 1960), pp. 85–86, 2.

54. Dundes, *Chicken Coop Ladder*, p. 319. Benjamin Spock, *Baby and Child Care* (New York: Pocket Books, 1976), p. 287. English and Pearson, *Emotional Problems*, p. 45.

55. Spock, *Baby and Child Care*, p. 289. T. Berry Brazelton, *Toddlers and Parents: A Declaration of Independence* (New York: Dell [Delacorte Press], 1974), pp. 145, 110, 143.

56. Kant, *Education*, pp. 86–87. The original German may be found in vol. 9 of *Kants Werke: Akademie-Textausgabe* (1907; rpt. Berlin: Walter de Gruyter, 1968), pp. 481–82.

57. *Selected Papers of Karl Abraham*, trans. Douglas Bryan and Alix Strachey (New York: Basic Books, 1954), p. 388.

58. Brazelton, *Toddlers and Parents*, p. 142. Alan Watts, *Psychotherapy East and West* (New York: Random House [Vintage Books], 1975), p. 174.

59. Spock, *Baby and Child Care*, p. 286. Nathan H. Azrin and Richard M. Foxx, *Toilet Training in Less Than a Day* (New York: Simon & Schuster, 1974), p. 34.

60. John G. McKenzie, *Nervous Disorders and Religion: A Study of Souls in the Making* (London: Allen & Unwin, 1951), pp. 157, 160.

61. Abraham, *Selected Papers*, p. 373.

62. English and Pearson, *Emotional Problems*, p. 44.

63. Böll, "Schreiben und Lesen" (p. 259) and "Eine deutsche Erinnerung" (p. 562) in *Werke: Interviews I*.

64. Rodnick, *Postwar Germans*, p. 25, 24.

65. Brazelton, *Toddlers and Parents*, pp. 128–32.

66. Thomas Mann, "Germany and the Germans," *Yale Review* 35, no. 2 (Dec. 1945): 236, 231.

67. Craig, *Germany: 1866–1945* (New York: Oxford University Press, 1978), pp. 218–20.

68. Mann, "Germany and the Germans," pp. 236–37, 232, 241.

69. See Azrin and Foxx, *Toilet Training*, p. 34, for their theory that interaction between the child undergoing toilet training and a doll whom the child pretends to "train" is a most helpful form of playacting.

70. Horney, *Neurotic Personality*, p. 15.

71. D. T. Suzuki, Erich Fromm, and Richard De Martino, *Zen Buddhism and Psychoanalysis* (New York: Grove Press, 1960), p. 103.

72. Böll, "Schreiben und Lesen," in *Werke: Interviews I*, p. 259.

73. Ibid.

74. Taken from Freud's foreword to the reprint of Bourke's *Scatalogic Rites*, pp. vii–viii.

75. Heinrich Wölfflin, *The Sense of Form in Art*, trans. Alice Muehsam and

Norma Shatan (New York: Chelsea, 1958), pp. 222, 123. This work was originally published as *Italien und das deutsche Formgefühl* by F. Bruckman A. G. (Munich: 1931).

76. Christian Enzensberger, *Smut: An Anatomy of Dirt*, trans. Sandra Morris (London: Calder & Boyars, 1972), pp. 37–38.

77. Johann Wolfgang Goethe, *Gedenkausgabe der Werke, Briefe und Gespräche*, ed. Ernst Beutler (Zurich: Artemis, 1950), 5:521. Earlier in *Faust*, during the Walpurgisnacht scene, Goethe uses scatological terminology to illustrate the perversity of the dancing witches, who sing in chorus, "The witch is farting, the he-goat stinks" (ibid., p. 266).

78. Christian Dietrich Grabbe, *Werke und Briefe: Historisch-kritische Gesamtausgabe in sechs Bänden*, ed. Alfred Bergmann (Emsdetten: Lechte, 1960), 1:81.

2. WILHELM BUSCH

1. All page and volume references to the works of Wilhelm Busch are from Wilhelm Busch, *Werke: Historisch-kritische Gesamtausgabe*, ed. Friedrich Bohne, 4 vols. (Hamburg: Standard-Verlag, 1959).

2. Regarding Busch, Böll said in his lectures at the University of Frankfurt during the 1963–64 fall semester: "'One should not call any person a fool'; that is the gist of Jean Paul. In the works of Busch the opposite happens: the annihilation of the individual, the human being, the *Homo sapiens*, the humane. Unfortunately, German notions of humor right up until the present have been determined by Busch—not by Jean Paul, not by the ironic position of the romanticists. It is sardonic, gloating humor, which, rather than poking fun at nobility, simply refuses to acknowledge the existence of any human nobility whatsoever" (Böll, *Werke: Essayistische Schriften und Reden II*, pp. 88–89). It is noteworthy that Böll did not in any way attack Busch's use of scatological elements; in fact, we shall see later that Böll himself employed the excremental liberally. What concerned Böll is that Busch's humor appeared to him to be solely of the spiteful, malicious variety. Böll saw no compassion for humanity and not the sightest hint of optimism in Busch's works, and these are elements that Böll considered essential in a constructive approach to humor. We shall see in a later chapter that, because Böll's view of humor differed from Busch's, the ways in which he used scatology also differed markedly.

3. Peter Bonati, for example, in his examination of Busch's representation of evil, refers to an incident in *Julie* in which one character uses a scatological method to undermine another. Specifically, the druggist Mickefett slips a competitor for Julie's attentions a drink spiked with a laxative. Bonati's analysis of this incident is limited to one sentence, in which he describes it as just another example of Busch's oft-repeated theme of the strong assertiveness of the human will, a concept Busch evolved from such thinkers as Schopenhauer and Nietzsche: "Mickefett's behavior, his thinly veiled gloating, shows that he experiences his struggle for influence as a question of power and that the drive for

power also manifests itself in jealousy" (Peter Bonati, *Die Darstellung des Bösen im Werk Wilhelm Buschs*, Basler Studien zur deutschen Sprache und Literatur, no. 49 [Bern: Francke, 1973], p. 48). Although Bonati's comment is by no means incorrect, it is interesting that he does not pursue the question of why Mickefett's response was a scatological one. Throughout his book Bonati discusses aggression by children, adults, and animals in great detail, yet he never examines its frequently excremental nature. His avoidance of scatology appears to be shared by other Busch scholars.

4. Josef Ehrlich, *Wilhelm Busch der Pessimist: Sein Verhältnis zu Arthur Schopenhauer* (Bern: Francke, 1962), pp. 9, 11.

5. Ibid., p. 23.

6. Bonati, *Die Darstellung des Bösen*, p. 94.

7. In an illustration to *Max and Moritz*, Busch depicts three hens and a rooster who have been hanged as a result of the trickery of the two young knaves; just before the chickens succumb, the three hens lay eggs in unison, while the rooster provides an ironic imitation of their action by defecating (1:347). Dieter P. Lotze's commentary on this drawing is a classic case of the tendency of so many critics—and readers in general—to put on blinders when confronted with a blunt depiction of excrement: Lotze observes that "the fact that the rooster is included in the final production of eggs prevents any sympathetic reaction on the part of the reader." The critic fails to offer any explanation to his readers for the biological anomaly he has described, and through his possibly intentional obliqueness he sidesteps any discussion of Busch's sly wit (Dieter P. Lotze, *Wilhelm Busch*, Twayne's World Authors Series, no. 525 [Boston: Twayne, 1979], p. 47).

8. All biblical quotations are from the Authorized (King James) Version.

3. FRIEDRICH DÜRRENMATT AND SIEGFRIED LENZ

1. Elisabeth Brock-Sulzer, *Friedrich Dürrenmatt: Stationen seines Werkes*, 2nd ed. (Zurich: Verlag der Arche, 1964), pp. 43–44.

2. Friedrich Dürrenmatt, *Gesammelte Hörspiele* (Zurich: Verlag der Arche, 1970), p. 65.

3. Friedrich Dürrenmatt, *Komödien I* (Zurich: Verlag der Arche, 1957).

4. Friedrich Dürrenmatt, *Der Meteor* (Zurich: Verlag der Arche, 1966), p. 31.

5. Ibid., p. 35.

6. Brock-Sulzer, *Dürrenmatt*, p. 140. See also fig. 23, a self-explanatory drawing by Dürrenmatt entitled "Hercules and His Critics."

7. All page references to *Hercules and the Augean Stable* are from Friedrich Dürrenmatt, *Komödien II und frühe Stücke* (Zurich: Verlag der Arche, 1970).

8. This passage contains humorous allusions to Switzerland. The Swiss pride in their democracy, which they believe to be the freest society in the world, is satirized here. Furthermore, the fact that Elis is a manure-producing country is also strongly reminiscent of Switzerland, with its large dairy and cattle industry and the widespread use of natural fertilizer, which can be

smelled throughout large sections of the country. Elis's strong resemblances to Switzerland become especially clear in scene 12, in which Dürrenmatt gives the councilors of Elis hybrid names: Pentheus vom Säuliboden, Sisyphos von Milchiwil, and Kadmos von Käsingen.

9. Jones, *Papers*, p. 686.

10. Ibid., pp. 684, 683.

11. A German farmer named Ewald Dopper who has turned his farm into a tourist attraction for urbanites has composed an optimistic couplet: "Organic dung will be the sole base / Of the salvation of the human race" (Jürgen Kurth and Volker Krämer, "Der schlaue Bauer," *Stern*, 14 July 1983, p. 54).

12. All page references to Siegfried Lenz's stories are from Siegfried Lenz, *So zärtlich war Suleyken: Masurische Geschichten* (Hamburg: Hoffmann & Campe, 1955).

4. SCATOLOGY AND SELF-KNOWLEDGE

1. All page references to *A Man and his Dog* are from Thomas Mann, *"Death in Venice" and Seven Other Stories*, trans. H. T. Lowe-Porter (New York: Vintage Books, n.d.).

2. Thomas Mann, *Sämtliche Erzählungen* (Frankfurt am Main: Fischer, 1963), p. 425.

3. Ibid., p. 437.

4. Joachim Müller, "Thomas Manns Sinfonia Domestica," *Zeitschrift für deutsche Philologie* 83 (1964): 151.

5. Ibid., p. 154.

6. Frank X. Braun, "Thomas Mann's Canine Idyl," *Monatshefte* 49 (1957): 210–11.

7. *Herr und Hund*, prod. Bertelsmann, 1961.

8. Mann, *Sämtliche Erzählungen*, p. 491.

9. Ibid., p. 439.

5. "UNIDEAL NATURE"

1. Werner Hofmann, *Gustav Klimt* (Greenwich, Conn.: New York Graphic Society, n.d.), pp. 41–42.

2. Ibid., p. 16. For the original German, see Karl Kraus, *Beim Wort genommen* (Munich: Kösel, 1965), p. 341.

3. Martin Esslin, *Brecht: The Man and His Work* (Garden City, N.Y.: Doubleday, 1960), p. 170.

4. Max Spalter, *Brecht's Tradition* (Baltimore: Johns Hopkins University Press, 1967), p. 104.

5. All page references to *Woyzeck* are from Georg Büchner, *Woyzeck*, trans. Carl Richard Mueller, in *Masterpieces of the Modern German Theatre*, ed. Robert W. Corrigan (New York: Collier Books, 1967).

6. Spalter, *Brecht's Tradition*, p. 100.

7. Herbert Lindenberger, *Georg Büchner* (Carbondale: Southern Illinois University Press, 1964), pp. 93, 108.

8. Ronald Hauser, *Georg Büchner* (New York: Twayne, 1974), p. 118.

9. Henry J. Schmidt has found in the memoirs of Carl Vogt, who went to medical school with Büchner at the University of Giessen, another possible source for the figure of the Doctor: "While Büchner was in Giessen, the local prison was guarded by a detachment of soldiers who took part in experiments conducted by the scientist Liebig. Liebig weighed the amount of bread and sausage eaten by the soldiers and compared it with the weight and composition of their excrement. Büchner was probably aware of these experiments" (Henry J. Schmidt, *Satire, Caricature, and Perspectivism in the Works of Georg Büchner*, Stanford Studies in Germanics and Slavics, vol. 8, ed. Edgar Lohner, C. H. Van Schooneveld, and F. W. Strothmann [The Hague: Mouton, 1970], pp. 45–46).

10. Hauser, *Büchner*, p. 146.

11. Ibid., p. 120.

12. Spalter, *Brecht's Tradition*, p. 102.

13. Ibid., p. 161.

14. Ibid., p. 107; Hauser, *Büchner*, p. 124.

15. Spalter, *Brecht's Tradition*, pp. 105–6, 108.

16. Ibid., p. 161.

17. Unless otherwise noted, all page references to *Baal* are from Bertolt Brecht, *Baal*, trans. Eric Bentley and Martin Esslin, in *"Baal," "A Man's A Man," and "The Elephant Calf": Early Plays by Bertolt Brecht*, ed. Eric Bentley (New York: Grove Press, 1964).

18. Hauser, *Büchner*, p. 125.

19. Feuchtwanger adds, "Brecht used a coarser word" (Lion Feuchtwanger, "Bertolt Brecht," *Sinn und Form*, Zweites Sonderheft Bertolt Brecht, 9 [1957]: 106).

20. Esslin, *Brecht*, p. 116.

21. Bertolt Brecht, *Frühe Stücke* (Munich: Deutscher Taschenbuch Verlag, 1962), p. 36.

22. Charles R. Lyons, *Bertolt Brecht: The Despair and the Polemic*, Crosscurrents/Modern Critiques, ed. Harry T. Moore (Carbondale and Edwardsville: Southern Illinois University Press, 1968), p. 10.

23. Brecht, *Frühe Stücke*, p. 94.

24. Spalter, *Brecht's Tradition*, p. 160.

25. Herbert Luthy, "Of Poor Bert Brecht," *Encounter*, July 1956, pp. 36–37.

26. Lyons, *Brecht*, pp. 22–23, 24.

27. Walter Sokel, ed., *Anthology of German Expressionist Drama* (Garden City, N.Y.: Doubleday, 1963), p. xxviii.

28. John Fuegi, *The Essential Brecht*, University of Southern California Studies in Comparative Literature, vol. 4 (Los Angeles: Hennessey & Ingalls, 1972), pp. 13–14.

29. Erwin Piscator, *Das politische Theater* (1929; rpt. Reinbek bei Hamburg:

Rowohlt, 1963), p. 37. Richard Huelsenbeck, *En Avant Dada: Eine Geschichte des Dadaismus* (Hanover, Leipzig, Vienna, and Zurich: Steegemann, 1920), p. 35.

30. Huelsenbeck, *En Avant Dada*, p. 15.

31. Otto Dix, *Der Streichholzhändler I*, Staats-Galerie, Stuttgart; plate 21 in Fritz Löffler, *Otto Dix: Leben und Werk* (Dresden: VEB Verlag der Kunst, n.d.).

32. Esslin, *Brecht*, p. 171.

33. Grosz, *Pillars of Society*, Nationalgalerie, West Berlin; in *A Little Yes and a Big No*, opp. p. 272.

34. Grosz, "If the Workers Want to Stop Being Slaves, They Must Snatch the Knout from Their Masters"; fig. 50 in Beth Irwin Lewis, *George Grosz: Art and Politics in the Weimar Republic* (Madison: University of Wisconsin Press, 1971), p. 149.

35. Grosz, "Bellyache"; plate 65 in George Grosz, *Ecce Homo* (New York: Brussel & Brussel, 1965).

36. Grosz, "The Voice of the People Is the Voice of God"; fig. 44 in Lewis, *Grosz*, p. 140.

37. Richard Huelsenbeck, "Dada Lives!" (1936), in *The Dada Painters and Poets: An Anthology*, ed. Robert Motherwell (New York: Wittenborn, Schultz, 1951), p. 281.

38. Grosz, *A Little Yes and a Big No*, p. 120.

39. Lewis, *Grosz*, p. 21.

40. Hans Hess, *George Grosz* (New York: Macmillan, 1974), p. 11.

41. Lewis, *Grosz*, p. 57.

42. Ibid.

43. Ben Hecht, *Letters from Bohemia* (Garden City, N.Y.: Doubleday, 1964), pp. 140–41.

44. Grosz, *A Little Yes and a Big No*, pp. 146–47.

45. Grosz, illustration from *Rosarote Brille*; fig. 30 in Lewis, *Grosz*, p. 118.

46. Translated by Allan Carl Greenberg in his "Artists and the Weimar Republic: Dada and the Bauhaus, 1917–1925" (diss., University of Illinois, 1967), p. 80. Greenberg states that the original poster is in the private collection of Frau Clare Jung, East Berlin.

6. OF BATTLEFIELDS AND BOWELS

1. Lind, *Counting My Steps*, p. 22.

2. Erich Maria Remarque, *All Quiet on the Western Front*, trans. A. W. Wheen (Boston: Little, Brown, 1929).

3. All page references to *All Quiet on the Western Front* are from Erich Maria Remarque, *Im Westen nichts Neues* (Cologne: Kiepenheuer & Witsch, 1971).

4. Böll, *Werke: Romane und Erzählungen I, 1947–1951*, p. 386.

5. Unless otherwise noted, all page references to *And Where Were You, Adam?* are from Heinrich Böll, *Adam and the Train*, trans. Leila Vennewitz (New York: McGraw-Hill, 1974).

6. In the prologue to Wolfgang Borchert, *The Man Outside*, one finds a similar but nonscatological image conveying the finality of death. Here the belching undertaker, a grotesque symbol of surfeited death, says about dying: "A man is dead. So what? Nothing. Only a few circles in the water prove that he was ever there. And even they've soon subsided. And when they've disappeared, then the man's forgotten, vanished, without trace, as though he'd never existed. And that's all" (Wolfgang Borchert, *The Man Outside*, trans. David Porter [New York: New Directions, 1971], p. 83.) The image of a person's disappearing without a trace in a pit of liquid manure also appears in the Italian film *Seven Beauties*. Writer/director Lina Wertmuller includes among her characters an anarchist who finds that the only way to assert his individuality in a Nazi concentration camp is to break ranks, run to the latrine, and commit suicide by jumping into the cesspit (Lina Wertmuller, writer/director, *Seven Beauties*, with Giancarlo Giannini, Fernando Rey, and Shirley Stoler, Almi Libra Cinema 5, 1976).

7. Böll, *Werke: Romane und Erzählungen I, 1947–1951*, p. 310. In the English version, Leila Vennewitz translates this word as "rabble" (5), thus toning down Böll's original diction.

8. Fromm, "Die psychoanalytische Charakterologie," p. 262.

9. Could Bressen's loud, compulsive repetition of the words "champagne" or "champagne and a girl"—Böll tells us that he even called out these words when he was alone (21)—be an ironic representation of Gilles de la Tourette's disease? This syndrome, characterized by motor and verbal tics (including the compulsive utterance of obscenities), is know in German as *koordinierte Erinnerungskrämpfe* or *mimischer Krampf*. (See Eduard Ascher, "Motor Syndromes of Functional or Undetermined Origin: Tics, Cramps, Gilles de la Tourette's Disease, and Others," in *American Handbook of Psychiatry*, ed. Silvano Arieti [New York: Basic Books, 1959], 3:152. Bressen's recollections of his earlier life affect his frame of mind in the hospital, and the cramp he develops in his neck when he looks at a painting of a shepherd with his flock (17) is doubtless caused not only by physical discomfort—perhaps related in part to his years of nodding and bowing—but also by painful memories of his failure as a military leader; hence the neck disorder may be viewed as an *Erinnerungskrampf* (memory cramp), at least in metaphorical terms. Otto Fenichel has pointed out that victims of *mimischer Krampf* are usually narcissistic anal characters and that their tics may be masturbatory equivalents. (See Otto Fenichel, *The Psychoanalytic Theory of Neurosis* [New York: Norton, 1945], p. 320. Bressen's repetitive cries and neck cramps interestingly contrast with the intestinal cramps experienced by the markedly different but also mentally disturbed Greck. Whether or not Böll was aware of the existence of Gilles de la Tourette's disease when he wrote the passage depicting Bressen's hospitalization (we do know that Böll was acquainted with a syndrome characterized by the compulsive utterance of obscenities by the time he wrote *The Clown*—see chap. 7, herein), he in fact created a character whose behavior and personality call the disorder to mind.

10. Fromm, "Die psychoanalytische Charakterologie," p. 264.

11. According to Erich Fromm, such an extreme sense of duty is developed during the anal-erotic stage of a person's development: "Toilet training is closely connected to the problem of 'musts' and 'shoulds' or, more precisely, of what is impermissible, and clinical experience demonstrates that frequently an unusually deeply ingrained sense of duty goes back to this early period" ("Die psycholanalytische Charakterologie," p. 261).

12. Jones, *Papers*, p. 689.

13. Böll, *Werke: Romane und Erzählungen I, 1947–1951*, p. 351.

14. Ibid., p. 353. It is hoped that the reader will tolerate the translation of this sentence by these writers into American slang, which seems to capture the ironic meaning of Böll's "Er hatte eigentlich auf nichts Lust" somewhat more accurately than Vennewitz's "He really didn't want anything" (52).

15. Ibid., p. 354.

16. Ibid., p. 320.

17. Ibid., p. 324.

18. Ibid., p. 359.

19. Günter Grass , *Die Blechtrommel* (Neuwied am Rhein: Luchterhand, 1962), p. 113.

20. Böll, *The Clown*, trans. Leila Vennewitz (New York: McGraw-Hill, 1965), p. 17.

21. Böll, *Missing Persons and Other Essays*, trans. Leila Vennewitz (New York: McGraw-Hill, 1977), pp. 118, 131.

22. Böll, *The Clown*, p. 16.

23. Böll, "Eine deutsche Erinnerung," p. 516.

24. Böll, "Schreiben und Lesen," p. 259.

25. Böll, "Eine deutsche Erinnerung," p. 614.

26. Unless otherwise indicated, all page references to "Soul of Wood" are from Jakov Lind, *"Soul of Wood" and Other Stories*, trans. Ralph Manheim (New York: Grove Press, 1964).

27. H. David Kirk, *Shared Fate: A Theory of Adoption and Mental Health* (New York: Free Press; London: Collier-Macmillan, 1964), pp. 44–45.

28. It is interesting that Ralph Manheim's English translation chooses a sexual corruption of Mückenpelz's name, whereas in the original German Wimper had insulted the professor by distorting his name in a way suggestive of filth: *Mückenschwein* (Jakov Lind, *Eine Seele aus Holz* [Munich and Zurich: Knaur, 1964], p. 57).

29. Gershon Legman, *Rationale of the Dirty Joke: An Analysis of Sexual Humor*, 2nd ser. (New York: Breaking Point, 1975), pp. 373, 382–92.

30. Lind, *Eine Seele aus Holz*, p. 65.

31. Wohlbrecht's speech is a literary reprise of a type of verse that has appeared for more than a century in the folklore of German-speaking countries. Dundes quotes three versions of this genre (*Chicken Coop Ladder*, pp. 284–86).

32. Cat excrement and a stifling atmosphere also combine to lend a sense of foreboding in the nightmare of Beckmann in *The Man Outside*: the ghosts

of dead soldiers "rise up out of their mass graves and their bloody groaning stinks to the white moon. That's what makes the nights what they are. As piercing as cat's dirt. . . . Then the nights are such that we can't breathe" (Borchert, *The Man Outside*, pp. 100–1).

33. Lind, *Eine Seele aus Holz*, p. 78.

34. Ibid., p. 81.

35. Quoted in Lewis, *Grosz*, p. 234, from a letter from Grosz to Wieland Herzfelde, the original typescript of which is in the George Grosz Estate, Princeton, N.J.

36. Lewis, *Grosz*, p. 210.

37. Terrence Des Pres, *The Survivor: An Anatomy of Life in the Death Camps* (New York: Oxford University Press, 1976), pp. 175–77.

38. Peter Weiss, *Dramen 2* (Frankfurt am Main: Suhrkamp, 1968), p. 465. (This statement, which was not included in the Swan and Grosbard translation mentioned below [n. 39], was translated by Dieter and Jacqueline Rollfinke.)

39. Peter Weiss, *The Investigation*, trans. Jon Swan and Ulu Grosbard (New York: Atheneum, 1975). Unless otherwise indicated, all page references to *The Investigation* are from this edition.

40. Des Pres, *Survivor*, p. 66.

41. Ibid., pp. 67–68.

42. Richard L. Rubenstein, *After Auschwitz: Radical Theology and Contemporary Judaism* (Indianapolis, New York, and Kansas City: Bobbs-Merrill, 1966), p. 32.

43. Ibid., pp. 32–33.

44. Weiss, *Dramen 2*, p. 77.

45. Rubenstein, *After Auschwitz*, pp. 36–37, 38.

46. Lind, *Counting My Steps*, p. 97.

47. English and Pearson, *Emotional Problems*, p. 64.

48. Rubenstein, *After Auschwitz*, p. 38.

49. Böll, "Schreiben und Lesen," p. 261.

50. Jones, *Papers*, p. 558.

51. Des Pres, *Survivor*, pp. 59, 60.

52. Manfred Durzak, *Dürrenmatt, Frisch, Weiss: Deutsches Drama der Gegenwart zwischen Kritik und Utopie*, 2nd ed. (Stuttgart: Philipp Reclam jun., 1973), p. 293.

53. Des Pres, *Survivor*, pp. 61–62.

54. Gilbert, *Psychology of Dictatorship*, pp. 272–73.

55. Ibid., p. 232.

56. Ibid., pp. 289, 278–79.

57. Ibid., pp. 275, 276.

58. Ibid., p. 280.

59. Joachim C. Fest, *The Face of the Third Reich: Portraits of the Nazi Leadership*, trans. Michael Bullock (New York: Pantheon Books, 1970), pp. 282, 285, 286.

60. Robert Jay Lifton, "What Made This Man? Mengele," *New York Times Magazine*, 21 July 1985, p. 24.

61. Grosz, *A Little Yes and a Big No*, p. 78.

62. Grosz, *Ein kleines Ja und ein großes Nein: Sein Leben von ihm selbst erzählt* (Reinbek bei Hamburg: Rowohlt Taschenbuch Verlag, 1974), p. 67. The autobiography was published in English first but is a translation (and, according to Grosz's son Peter, an edited version) of the original German text. See Lewis, *Grosz*, pp. 281–82.

63. Grosz, *A Little Yes and a Big No*, p. 82. Grosz's assertion that Mueller was representative of a type of person who really existed in Germany, a type that had not been wiped out by the Nazi defeat, is given credence by the evidence presented in *The Investigation* that the cleanliness fixations of the Nazi war criminals lingered after the war was over. The attribution of extraordinary skills of sanitization or purification to military leaders persisted at least to some extent as late as 1973, when an advertisement for a German all-purpose cleaner called Der General declared, "This floor is more than clean. It is 'General-ly sanitized.'" The martial emphasis of the ad is underlined by the medal- and braid-bedecked uniform worn by the housewife, the bands of stars setting off the ad's heading and adorning the solution's label, and the product's slogan, "Conquers every type of dirt" (*Frau im Spiegel*, 5 July 1973, p. 69). The advertising and packaging of Der General stand in strong contrast to those for a virtually identical American product, Mr. Clean. Although the appearance of the so-called Mr. Clean bears a marked resemblance to that of General (and later President) Dwight D. Eisenhower, the American war hero has been stripped of his uniform and rank by the ad agency's artists and is depicted as a genie in a plain white T-shirt who cleans one's floor by magic rather than military maneuvers. Traditionally, the American product, as exemplified by its name, ads, and jingles, has projected a positive tone in promoting the desirability of becoming clean; Der General stresses the more negative goal of obliterating dirt. In terms of the artistic design of the two labels, it might be noted that Mr. Clean is depicted with a softly contoured, agreeable-looking human face, whereas we never see the General himself but see only his military decorations, angular stars. This formality and dehumanization is highly reminiscent of that of First Lieutenant Greck, who looked first at his soldiers' medals and then at their faces.

64. Hess, *Grosz*, p. 22.

65. Paul Fussell, "The Fiction of Fact," Lecture 3 in the "Perspectives in Military History" Seminar Series, U.S. Army War College, Carlisle, Pa.: 20 Oct. 1983. Fussel also deals with the phenomenon of ironies of war that "haunt the memory" in the section "Irony and Memory," pp. 29–35 in *The Great War and Modern Memory* (New York and London: Oxford University Press, 1975).

66. Ernest Jones finds a psychological explanation for this seeming anomaly. He observes that the military insistence on strict discipline and adherence to orders in wartime (Jones does not specifically mention the observance of hygienic measures, although they logically could be included) is a psychologi-

cal mechanism to counteract the breaking of taboos of polite peacetime society. Those who give vent to impulses that would be held in check under normal circumstances attempt to offset their indulgent behavior by observing systematized rituals. Jones, *Papers*, p. 585.

67. Böll, "Schreiben und Lesen," p. 259.

68. Fest, *Face of the Third Reich*, p. 276.

7. "AS BEAUTIFUL AS SNOW"

1. Böll, *The Clown*, p. 25.

2. Ibid., p. 26.

3. Ibid., p. 63.

4. Böll, *Werke: Essayistische Schriften und Reden II*, pp. 34, 71.

5. Ibid., p. 89.

6. Reinhard Baumgart, review of *Gruppenbild mit Dame*, *Der Spiegel*, 2 Aug. 1971, p. 104.

7. Manfred Durzak, *Der deutsche Roman der Gegenwart*, 2nd rev. ed. (Stuttgart, Berlin, Cologne, and Mainz: Kohlhammer, 1973), p. 107. Durzak's view that there is a chasm between Hölderlin's poetry and excremental motifs apparently was not shared by Günter Eich, who rhymes "Hölderlin" with "urine" in the third stanza of "Latrine." Not only the stench of his immediate surroundings but also the countryside, the clouds, and poetry permeate the consciousness of the author as he sits in the latrine: "I hear, in muddled echoes, / Verses by Hölderlin. / Clouds pure as the driven snow are / Mirrored in my urine" (Günter Eich, *Abgelegene Gehöfte: Gedichte* [Frankfurt am Main: Suhrkamp, 1968], p. 41).

8. All page references to *Group Portrait with Lady* are from Heinrich Böll, *Group Portrait with Lady*, trans. Leila Vennewitz (New York: Avon Books, 1973).

9. Victor Lange, "Erzählen als moralisches Geschäft," in *Die subversive Madonna: Ein Schlüssel zum Werk Heinrich Bölls*, ed. Renate Matthaei (Cologne: Kiepenheuer & Witsch, 1975), pp. 110–11.

10. Böll, *Werke: Essayistische Schriften und Reden II*, pp. 216, 226.

11. Thomas Merton, *Mystics and Zen Masters* (New York: Dell, 1961), p. 250.

12. Des Pres, *Survivor*, pp. 166, 207.

13. Ibid., pp. 166, 208.

14. Durzak, *Der deutsche Roman der Gegenwart*, pp. 105–6.

15. Böll, "Schreiben und Lesen," pp. 258–59.

16. Bruno Bettelheim, *The Uses of Enchantment: The Meaning and Importance of Fairy Tales* (New York: Knopf, 1976), p. 214.

17. Böll's metaphor is strikingly similar to George Grosz's view of the Germans as somewhat constipated (see chapter 5, herein).

18. Böll, *Werke: Essayistische Schriften und Reden II*, p. 223.

19. Leni may have a predecessor in German folklore in the person of Aschenputtel (Cinderella); both are part of a tradition that considers the loveliest, most noble princess or heroine to be the one who is familar with, and/or not

uncomfortable in the presence of filth. A modern journalistic example of this concept is the lead photo feature in the 18 October 1973 issue of *Frau im Spiegel*, which shows then Crown Princess Beatrix of the Netherlands gazing down with a smile at some horse droppings during a visit to the city of Utrecht. (It is in keeping with the German interest in scatology that this particular moment in the princess' visit was the one deemed worthy of prominent coverage; magazines select for their lead photo features only those topics that are considered to have wide reader appeal.) In tone and diction, the feature's caption is reminiscent of the depiction of overly fastidious, orderly characters by some German authors; in fact, the word used to describe the hoped-for condition of the city's streets, *blitzblank*, is the same adjective that was used by Remarque to describe the soon-to-be-showered Himmelstoß. Although the Utrecht dignitaries glare with horror at the unexpected mess, Crown Princess Beatrix seems to share Leni's amiable matter-of-factness regarding natural functions: "'Doesn't it in fact bring good luck if one steps in it?' she asked." German tradition suggests that it is precisely this sort of attitude that helps to make her a princess or Fortune's favorite ("Das Bild zum Freuen," *Frau im Spiegel*, 18 Oct. 1973, p. 7).

20. Böll goes a step farther in *Fürsorgliche Belagerung* (*The Safety Net*) by using the bathroom as the setting for the sexual encounter that begins the affair between Hubert Hendler, who at the time of the union has just been pelted with mud, and Sabine Fischer (Heinrich Böll, *Fürsorgliche Belagerung* [Cologne: Kiepenheuer & Witsch, 1979], p. 94).

21. R. H. Blyth, *Haiku* (Tokyo: Hokuseido Press, 1952), 3:194–96.

22. This unappetizing scatological food additive did not make its literary debut in Böll's 1971 novel. Almost half a millenium earlier, in Sebastian Brant's *Ship of Fools*, one finds amid a listing of the deceptive practices of unscrupulous merchants the following affront to the consumer: "They mix mouse droppings in with the peppercorns" (Sebastian Brant, *Das Narrenschiff*, ed. Manfred Lemmer, 2nd ed., expanded [Tübingen: Max Niemeyer, 1968], p. 271).

23. Böll, "Drei Tage im März: Gespräch mit Christian Linder vom 11.-13. 3. 1975," in *Werke: Interviews I*, p. 412.

24. Böll, "Schreiben und Lesen," pp. 261–62.

25. Böll, *Missing Persons and Other Essays*, p. 42.

26. Böll, "Schreiben und Lesen," p. 261.

27. A similarly complex intertwining of Böll's motifs may be found in the case of Rahel's exile in the broom closet. If we look at this setting from one point of view, it seems appropriate that the nuns would choose such a spot as the hiding place for a woman whom they considered to be "halfway between toilet attendant and cleaning woman." In their eyes, Rahel's scatological interests were "dirty," and thus it was fitting to punish her, as an angry parent might lock a naughty little girl in her room, by imprisonment in a closet full of cleaning utensils. Furthermore, when the nuns rationalized this chastisement by viewing it as a noble rescue mission, they "sanitized" their motives and cleansed themselves of guilt. From the perspective of author Böll, however,

Rahel represents "good dirt," a wholesome attitude toward the scatological. Leni's remark that the German poets "never flinched from cleaning out a john" is also applicable to her mentor Rahel. For this reason, too, it is particularly fitting (but in a more ironic way than the nuns would have dreamed) that Rahel should end her days among cleaning implements. Once again Böll has made his point that human beings often try to make survival difficult for the person who, by not being afraid to get dirty, *truly* cleanses society. As the author himself stated in a 1969 book review, "It has always seemed to me axiomatic that those we call nest-foulers are those who are seeking to clean up their own nests" (Böll, *Missing Persons and Other Essays*, p. 147).

28. Böll, *Ansichten eines Clowns*, in *Werke: Romane und Erzählungen IV, 1961–1970*, p. 86.

29. Böll, *The Clown*, pp. 163–64.

30. Böll, "Schreiben und Lesen," p. 262.

8. THE EXCREMENTAL WHEEL OF FORTUNE

1. Jakov Lind, *Eine bessere Welt* (Berlin: Wagenbach, 1966), p. 110. All page references to *A Better World* are from this edition.

2. *Stern*, 20 May 1976, p. 157.

3. All page and volume references to the poems of Gottfried Benn are from Gottfried Benn, *Gesammelte Werke in acht Bänden* (Wiesbaden: Limes, 1960).

4. In a most curious example of the all too common evasiveness of critics when faced with excrement in literature, Christoph Eykman selectively quotes in succession the two most scatological lines in "Room of the Women in Labor"—"Excrement, too, comes from the pushing!" and "Urine and feces anoint its skin" as proof of the fact that the poem "connects the aspects of devouring and coupling in the description of a birth." Although fully one third of the words in these two lines have excremental denotations or connotations, Eykman seems determined to put distance between Benn's repellent diction and his own interpretation; the critic's insistence on finding the significance of the lines in the copulation and the eating that took place nine months and perhaps nine hours, respectively, before the actual event so graphically described by Benn constitutes a strangely remote, indirect approach to scatological imagery (Christoph Eykman, *Die Funktion des Hässlichen in der Lyrik Georg Heyms, Georg Trakls, und Gottfried Benns: Zur Krise der Wirklichkeitserfahrung im deutschen Expressionismus* [Bonn: Bouvier, 1965], p. 144).

5. All page references to the poems of Kästner are from vol. 1 of Erich Kästner, *Gesammelte Schriften für Erwachsene* (Zurich: Atrium, 1969).

6. All page references to *Methusalem* are from Iwan Goll, *Methusalem; or, The Eternal Bourgeois*, trans J. M. Ritchie, in *Seven Expressionist Plays*, German Expressionist Drama Series, ed. J. M. Ritchie (London: Calder & Boyars, 1968).

7. Agreeing that the left-wing element does not triumph over the bourgeoisie in *Methusalem*, J. M. Ritchie states in his introduction to *Seven Expressionist*

Plays that, when the drama has concluded, "the image that probably remains in the memory is not one of a shattered enemy, but of Methusalem contentedly farting in the face of the audience" (p. 18).

8. Emil Otttinger, "Zur mehrdimensionalen Erklärung von Straftaten Jugendlicher am Beispiel der Novelle 'Katz und Maus' von Günter Grass," *Monatsschrift für Kriminologie und Strafrechtsreform*, May/June 1962; reprinted in Gert Loschütz, ed., *Von Buch zu Buch: Günter Grass in der Kritik* (Neuwied: Luchterhand, 1968), p. 39.

9. All page references to *Cat and Mouse* are from Günter Grass, *Cat and Mouse*, trans. Ralph Manheim (New York: Harcourt Brace & World, 1963).

10. Ottinger, "Zur mehrdimensionalen Erklärung," p. 41.

11. Johanna F. Behrendt, "Auf der Suche nach dem Adamsapfel: Der Erzähler Pilenz in Günter Grass' Novelle *Katz und Maus*," *Germanisch-romanische Monatsschrift* 19 (July 1969): 316–17.

12. Erhard M. Friedrichsmeyer, "Aspects of Myth, Parody, and Obscenity in Grass' *Die Blechtrommel* and *Katz und Maus*," *Germanic Review* 40, no. 3 (May 1965): 248–49.

13. Ibid., p. 248.

14. Robert H. Spaethling, "Günter Grass: *Cat and Mouse*," *Monatshefte* 62, no. 2 (summer 1970): 148.

15. Loschütz, *Von Buch zu Buch*, p. 51.

16. All page references to *The Flounder* are from Günter Grass, *The Flounder*, trans. Ralph Manheim (New York: Harcourt Brace Jovanovich, 1978).

17. Abraham, *Selected Papers*, p. 376.

18. English and Pearson, *Emotional Problems*, p. 46.

19. F. W. Murnau, dir., *Der letzte Mann*, with Emil Jannings, Union-Ufa, 1924. An examination of scatology in the German film could constitute a volume in itself. German films containing scatological elements include, to name a few, *Der zerbrochene Krug, Wir Wunderkinder, Wilder Reiter G.m.b.H., Stroszek,* and the television film of *Herr und Hund. Der letzte Mann* was singled out for inclusion in this study because of its status as an internationally recognized classic of the German cinema and because the restroom and societal values assigned to the functions performed there assume such great importance in the film. Although this study has concerned itself primarily with scatological elements in literature and, to a lesser degree, in art, it does not seem inappropriate to conclude with an examination of this highly successful attempt to render a theme with literary precedents in a relatively new visual medium.

20. Siegfried Kracauer, *From Caligari to Hitler: A Psychological History of the German Film* (London: Dobson, 1947), p. 100.

21. Fussell, *The Great War and Modern Memory*, p. 51.

22. Ernst Barlach, "The Far-sighted Members of the Commission Report," Deutsche Akademie der Künste, Berlin; plate 71 in Werner Hofmann, *Caricature from Leonardo to Picasso* (London: Calder, 1957), p. 131.

23. Illustration courtesy of the Museum of Modern Art/Film Stills Archive, 11 West 53rd Street, New York.

24. Karl Freund, "A Film Artist," in Paul Rotha, *The Film Till Now: A Survey of World Cinema*, rev. ed. (New York: Funk & Wagnalls, 1949), p. 716.

25. A fictional character who goes down the drain more literally than does the porter is Gregor Samsa in Franz Kafka's *Die Verwandlung* (*The Metamorphosis*). Transformed to a specimen of vermin and exiled by his family to his room, Gregor dies; his body, which resembles a dehydrated piece of dung, is discarded unceremoniously by the Samsas' cleaning woman (Franz Kafka, *Das Urteil und andere Erzählungen* [Frankfurt am Main: Fischer Bücherei, 1952]).

26. Kracauer, *Caligari to Hitler*, p. 100.

27. Des Pres, *Survivor*, pp. 65–66.

28. Horney, *Neurotic Personality*, p. 94.

29. Des Pres, *Survivor*, p. 71.

30. Ibid., p. 183.

31. George Huaco, *The Sociology of Film Art* (New York and London: Basic Books, 1965), pp. 55–56.

32. Brown, *Life Against Death*, p. 257. It may be recalled that the leitmotivs of money, food, and excrement combined with that of sex to form the thematic cornerstones of Goll's *Methusalem* and the artistic works of George Grosz. The excrement–aliment motif also appears in a café scene in Günter Grass's *Local Anaesthetic* (*örtlich betäubt*), in which "opulent stately ladies" in furs gluttonously devour desserts; their actions "infer a corresponding process: simultaneous and continuous bowel movements; for this obsessive abundance of apple strudel, almond crescents, cream kisses, and cheesecake could only be counterbalanced by a contrary image, by steaming excrement" (Günter Grass, *Local Anaesthetic*, trans. Ralph Manheim [New York: Harcourt Brace & World, 1970], pp. 184–86). The scatological trinity of money, food, and excrement may be found, too, in Heinrich Gruyten's letter describing manure disposal regulations; the authorities suggest that the soldiers either sell the horse manure for money or exchange it for fodder—calling to mind images of the young men as "cannon fodder," valued as little by the army as manure (Böll, *Group Portrait with Lady*, p. 321).

9. CONCLUSION

1. Rotha, *The Film Till Now*, p. 100. Thomas Wiseman, *Cinema* (New York: Barnes, 1965), p. 28

2. Kracauer, *Caligari to Hitler*, p. 102.

3. Paul Fussell (*The Great War and Modern Memory*, pp. 333–34) has taken note of the connections among "perverse sexual desire, memories of war, and human excrement" in such modern American works as Thomas Pynchon's *Gravity's Rainbow* and Norman Mailer's *American Dream* (the perversions referred to are coprophagy and sodomy). Sometimes what is *not* present in a body of literature is as significant as its actual contents. Coprophagy as a sexual practice and sodomy (the acts themselves, not symbolic suggestions) have

not appeared in any of the literary works the writers of this study have examined, with the exception of Günter Grass's novel *The Flounder*. Not having read everything that has ever been written in the German language, we would not be so foolhardy as to state that these motifs have *never* appeared in German literature prior to Grass's inclusion of them. Furthermore, as taboos fall, there is certainly a possibility that these acts will become more prevalent in "respectable" German literary works in the near future. It is, however, probably safe to state that coprophagy for sexual purposes and sodomy have not constituted a significant part of the scatological imagery used by major German writers, in war literature or other works up until the present. German writers tend to use scatology with nonsexual connotations, and when excrement does appear in connection with sex or amorous adventures, as in the cases of Lind's Wacholder or Busch's Hieronymus Jobs, it serves as a despoiler of romantic illusions rather than as an integral part of the sexual act.

4. Franz Maria Feldhaus, *Ka-Pi-Fu und andere verschämte Dinge* (Berlin-Friedenau, 1921), pp. 22–23.

5. As was indicated earlier, Böll was strongly influenced by "Aschenputtel," the Brothers Grimm's version of the Cinderella story, when he wrote *Group Portrait with Lady*. Bruno Bettelheim has pointed out in his discussion of this fairy tale the basically clean nature of ashes, which have been used in many societies as a cleansing agent. Modern society has lost sight of this view and is "so accustomed to thinking of living as a lowly servant among the ashes of the hearth as an extremely degraded situation that we have lost any recognition that, in a different view, it may be experienced as a very desirable, even exalted position. In ancient times, to be the guardian of the hearth—the duty of the Vestal Virgins—was one of the most prestigious ranks, if not the most exalted, available to a female. . . . To be a Vestal Virgin meant . . . to be absolutely pure. Thus, innocence, purity, and being guardian of the hearth go together in ancient connotations" (Bettelheim, *Uses of Enchantment*, pp. 254–55).

6. Rosebury, *Life on Man*, p. 123.

7. Ernst Barlach, *Das dichterische Werk* (Munich: Piper, 1956), 1:79–80.

8. Böll, *Missing Persons and Other Essays*, p. 111.

9. Ibid., pp. 112, 113, 114.

10. Böll, *The Clown*, p. 233.

11. Paul Fussell remarks, "Compared with the actual sights and smells of the front, the word *shit* is practically genteel" (Fussell, *The Great War and Modern Memory*, p. 331).

12. Ibid., p. 191.

13. The modern tendency toward more frequent use of obscenities, scatological and otherwise, has been explained by psychiatrist Eduard Ascher of the Johns Hopkins School of Medicine: "It is related to the great upsurge in what is considered to be a free expression of emotion in which you don't have to eliminate words because they are forbidden. . . . it's tied to the new movement which relates honesty to freedom of expression" (quoted in Richard N. Westcott, "#!¢*&+(*!@#," *Johns Hopkins Magazine* 21, no. 4 [October 1970]:26).

Bibliography

Abraham, Karl. *Selected Papers of Karl Abraham*. Translated by Douglas Bryan and Alix Strachey. New York: Basic Books, 1954.

Amory, Cleveland. Review of "Lotsa Luck." *TV Guide*, 13 October 1973, p. 56.

Ascher, Eduard. "Motor Syndromes of Functional or Undetermined Origin: Tics, Cramps, Gilles de la Tourette's Disease, and Others." In *American Handbook of Psychiatry*, ed. Silvano Arieti, 3:148–57. New York: Basic Books, 1959.

Azrin, Nathan H., and Richard M. Foxx. *Toilet Training in Less Than a Day*. New York: Simon & Schuster, 1974.

Banta, Martha. "American Apocalypses: Excrement and Ennui." *Studies in the Literary Imagination* 7, no. 1 (1974): 1–30.

Barlach, Ernst. *Das dichterische Werk*. Vol. 1. Munich: Piper, 1956.

———. "The Far-sighted Members of the Commission Report." Deutsche Akademie der Künste, Berlin. Plate 71 in *Caricature from Leonardo to Picasso*, by Werner Hofmann. London: Calder, 1957.

Baumgart, Reinhard. Review of *Gruppenbild mit Dame*. *Der Spiegel*, 2 August 1971, p. 104.

Behrendt, Johanna F. "Auf der Suche nach dem Adamsapfel: Der Erzähler Pilenz in Günter Grass' Novelle *Katz und Maus*." *Germanisch-romanische Monatsschrift* 19 (July 1969): 313–26.

Benn, Gottfried. *Gesammelte Werke in acht Bänden*. Wiesbaden: Limes, 1960.

Bettelheim, Bruno. *The Uses of Enchantment: The Meaning and Importance of Fairy Tales*. New York: Knopf, 1976.

"Das Bild zum Freuen." *Frau im Spiegel*, 18 October 1973, p. 7.

Blyth, R. H. *Haiku*. Vol. 3. Tokyo: Hokuseido Press, 1952.

Böll, Heinrich. *Adam and The Train*. Translated by Leila Vennewitz. New York: McGraw-Hill, 1974.

———. *The Clown*. Translated by Leila Vennewitz. New York: McGraw-Hill, 1965.

———. *Fürsorgliche Belagerung*. Cologne: Kiepenheuer & Witsch, 1979.

———. *Group Portrait with Lady*. Translated by Leila Vennewitz. New York: Avon Books, 1973.

———. *Missing Persons and Other Essays*. Translated by Leila Vennewitz. New York: McGraw-Hill, 1977.

————. *Werke: Essayistische Schriften und Reden I, II; Interviews I; Romane und Erzählungen I, 1947–1951; Romane und Erzählungen IV, 1961–1970.* Edited by Bernd Balzer. Cologne: Kiepenheuer & Witsch, [1978].

Bonati, Peter. *Die Darstellung des Bösen im Werk Wilhelm Buschs.* Basler Studien zur deutschen Sprache und Literatur, no. 49. Bern: Francke, 1973.

Borchert, Wolfgang. *The Man Outside.* Translated by David Porter. New York: New Directions, 1971.

Bourke, Capt. John G. *Scatalogic Rites of all Nations: a Dissertation upon the Employment of Excrementitious Remedial Agents in Religion, Therapeutics, Divination, Witchcraft, Love-Philters, etc. in all Parts of the Globe.* New York: American Anthropological Society, 1934.

Brant, Sebastian. *Das Narrenschiff.* Edited by Manfred Lemmer. 2nd ed., expanded. Tübingen: Max Niemeyer, 1968.

Braun, Frank X. "Thomas Mann's Canine Idyl." *Monatshefte* 49 (1957): 207–11.

Brazelton, T. Berry. *Toddlers and Parents: A Declaration of Independence.* New York: Dell (Delacorte Press), 1974.

Brecht, Bertolt. *Baal.* Translated by Eric Bentley and Martin Esslin. In *"Baal," "A Man's A Man," and "The Elephant Calf": Early plays by Bertolt Brecht,* ed. Eric Bentley, pp. 17–97. New York: Grove Press, 1964.

————. *Baal.* In *Frühe Stücke,* pp. 15–110. Munich: Deutscher Taschenbuch Verlag, 1962.

Brock-Sulzer, Elisabeth. *Friedrich Dürrenmatt: Stationen seines Werkes.* 2nd ed. Zurich: Verlag der Arche, 1964.

Brown, Norman O. *Life Against Death: The Psychoanalytical Meaning of History.* Middletown, Conn.: Wesleyan University Press, 1959.

Büchner, Georg. *Woyzeck.* Translated by Carl Richard Mueller. In *Masterpieces of the Modern German Theater,* ed. Robert W. Corrigan, pp. 37–66. New York: Collier Books, 1967.

Busch, Wilhelm. *Werke: Historisch-kritische Gesamtausgabe.* Edited by Friedrich Bohne. 4 vols. Hamburg: Standard-Verlag, 1959.

Clark, John R. "Bowl Games: Satire in the Toilet." *Modern Language Studies* 4, no. 2 (1974): 43–58.

Craig, Gordon A. *The Germans.* New York: New American Library (Meridian Books), 1983.

————. *Germany: 1866–1945.* New York: Oxford University Press, 1978.

Des Pres, Terrence. *The Survivor: An Anatomy of Life in the Death Camps.* New York: Oxford University Press, 1976.

"Deutsch wie es nicht im Wörterbuch steht." Advertising brochure for *Illustriertes Lexikon der deutschen Umgangssprache.* Stuttgart: Ernst Klett, 1983.

Dix, Otto. *Der Streichholzhändler I.* Staats-Galerie, Stuttgart. Plate 29 in *Otto Dix: Leben und Werk,* by Fritz Löffler. Dresden: VEB Verlag der Kunst, n.d.

Dundes, Alan. *Life Is Like a Chicken Coop Ladder: A Portrait of German Culture Through Folklore.* New York: Columbia University Press, 1984.

Dürrenmatt, Friedrich. *Gesammelte Hörspiele.* Zurich: Verlag der Arche, 1970.

————. "Herkules und seine Kritiker." In *Friedrich Dürrenmatt: Stationen seines*

Werkes, by Elisabeth Brock-Sulzer. 2nd ed. Zurich: Verlag der Arche, 1964.

————. *Komödien I.* Zurich: Verlag der Arche, 1957.

————. *Komödien II und Frühe Stücke.* Zurich: Verlag der Arche, 1970.

————. *Der Meteor.* Zurich: Verlag der Arche, 1966.

Durzak, Manfred. *Der deutsche Roman der Gegenwart.* 2nd rev. ed. Stuttgart, Berlin, Cologne, and Mainz: Kohlhammer, 1973.

————. *Dürrenmatt, Frisch, Weiss: Deutsches Drama der Gegenwart zwischen Kritik und Utopie.* 2nd ed. Stuttgart: Philipp Reclam jun., 1973.

Ehrlich, Josef. *Wilhelm Busch der Pessimist: Sein Verhältnis zu Arthur Schopenhauer.* Bern: Francke, 1962.

Eich, Günter. *Abgelegene Gehöfte: Gedichte.* Frankfurt am Main: Suhrkamp, 1968.

Englisch, Paul. *Das skatologische Element in Literatur, Kunst, und Volksleben.* Stuttgart: Julius Püttmann, 1928.

English, O. Spurgeon, and Gerald H. J. Pearson. *Emotional Problems of Living: Avoiding the Neurotic Pattern.* New York: Norton, 1945.

Enzensberger, Christian. *Smut: An Anatomy of Dirt.* Translated by Sandra Morris. London: Calder & Boyars, 1972.

Esslin, Martin. *Brecht: The Man and His Work.* Garden City, N.Y.: Doubleday, 1960.

Eykman, Christoph. *Die Funktion des Hässlichen in der Lyrik Georg Heyms, Georg Trakls, und Gottfried Benns: Zur Krise der Wirklichkeitserfahrung im deutschen Expressionismus.* Bonn: Bouvier, 1965.

Farb, Peter. *Word Play: What Happens When People Talk.* New York: Knopf, 1974.

Fayard, Judy. Review of "Lotsa Luck." *Time,* 29 October, 1973, p. 125.

Feldhaus, Franz Maria. *Ka-Pi-Fu und andere verschämte Dinge.* Berlin-Friedenau, 1921.

Fenichel, Otto. *The Psychoanalytic Theory of Neurosis.* New York: Norton, 1945.

Fest, Joachim C. *The Face of the Third Reich: Portraits of the Nazi Leadership.* Translated by Michael Bullock. New York: Pantheon Books, 1970.

Feuchtwanger, Lion. "Bertolt Brecht." *Sinn und Form,* Zweites Sonderheft Bertolt Brecht, 9 (1957): 103–8.

Fisher, Seymour, and Roger P. Greenberg. *The Scientific Credibility of Freud's Theories and Therapy.* New York: Basic Books, 1977.

Frau im Spiegel, 6 March 1980, p. 119. Also various issues 1973.

Freiburger Zeitung, 3 October 1977, p. 15.

Freud, Sigmund. "Character and Anal Eroticism." In *The Standard Edition of the Complete Psychological Works of Sigmund Freud,* trans. under the general editorship of James Strachey, 9: 167–75. 1959; rpt. London: Hogarth Press and the Institute of Psycho-Analysis, 1962.

Freund, Karl. "A Film Artist." In *The Film Till Now: A Survey of World Cinema,* by Paul Rotha, pp. 716–17. Rev. ed. New York: Funk & Wagnalls, 1949.

Friedrichsmeyer, Erhard M. "Aspects of Myth, Parody, and Obscenity in Grass' *Die Blechtrommel* and *Katz und Maus.*" *Germanic Review* 40, no. 3 (May 1965): 240–50.

Fromm, Erich. "Die psychoanalytische Charakterologie und ihre Bedeutung für die Sozialpsychologie." *Zeitschrift für Sozialforschung* 1, no. 3 (1932): 253–77.

Fuegi, John. *The Essential Brecht*. University of Southern California Studies in Comparative Literature, vol. 4. Los Angeles: Hennessey & Ingalls, 1972.

Fussell, Paul. "The Fiction of Fact." Lecture 3 in the "Perspectives in Military History" Seminar Series, U.S. Army War College, Carlisle, Pa., 20 October 1983.

———. *The Great War and Modern Memory*. New York and London: Oxford University Press, 1975.

Gilbert, G. M. *The Psychology of Dictatorship*. New York: Ronald Press, 1950.

Goethe, Johann Wolfgang. *Gedenkausgabe der Werke, Briefe und Gespräche*. Vol. 5. Edited by Ernst Beutler. Zurich: Artemis, 1950.

———. *Sämtliche Werke*. Vol. 8. Munich: Deutscher Taschenbuch Verlag, 1962.

Goll, Iwan. *Methusalem; or, The Eternal Bourgeois*. Translated by J. M. Ritchie. In *Seven Expressionist Plays*, German Expressionist Drama Series, ed. J. M. Ritchie, pp. 79–112. London: Calder & Boyars, 1968.

Grabbe, Christian Dietrich. *Werke und Briefe: Historisch-kritische Gesamtausgabe in sechs Bänden*. Vol. 1. Edited by Alfred Bergmann. Emsdetten: Lechte, 1960.

Grass, Günter. *Die Blechtrommel*. Neuwied am Rhein: Luchterhand, 1962.

———. *Cat and Mouse*. Translated by Ralph Manheim. New York: Harcourt Brace & World, 1963.

———. *The Flounder*. Translated by Ralph Manheim. New York: Harcourt Brace Jovanovich, 1978.

———. *Local Anaesthetic*. Translated by Ralph Manheim. New York: Harcourt Brace & World, 1970.

Grosz, George. "Bellyache." Plate 65 in *Ecce Homo*, by George Grosz. New York: Brussel & Brussel, 1965.

———. Dada Plakat. Translated by Allan Carl Greenberg. In "Artists and the Weimar Republic: Dada and the Bauhaus, 1917–1925," by Allan Carl Greenberg. Diss., University of Illinois, 1967.

———. *Ein kleines Ja und ein großes Nein: Sein Leben von ihm selbst erzählt*. Reinbek bei Hamburg: Rowohlt Taschenbuch Verlag, 1974.

———. "If the Workers Want to Stop Being Slaves, They Must Snatch the Knout from Their Masters." Fig. 50 in *George Grosz: Art and Politics in the Weimar Republic*, by Beth Irwin Lewis. Madison: University of Wisconsin Press, 1971.

———. *A Little Yes and a Big No: The Autobiography of George Grosz*. Translated by Lola S. Dorin. New York: Dial Press, 1946.

———. *Pillars of Society*. Nationalgalerie, West Berlin. Illustration opp. p. 272 in *A Little Yes and a Big No*.

———. "The Voice of the People Is the Voice of God." Fig. 44 in *George Grosz: Art and Politics in the Weimar Republic*, by Beth Irwin Lewis.

Hauser, Ronald. *Georg Büchner*. New York: Twayne, 1974.

Hecht, Ben. *Letters from Bohemia*. Garden City, N.Y.: Doubleday, 1964.

Hermand, Jost. *Stänker und Weismacher: Zur Dialektik eines Affekts.* Texte Metzler, no. 18. Stuttgart: Metzler, 1971.

Herr und Hund. Produced by Bertelsmann. 1961.

Hess, Hans. *George Grosz.* New York: Macmillan, 1974.

Hofmann, Werner. *Caricature from Leonardo to Picasso.* London: Calder, 1957.

————. *Gustav Klimt.* Greenwich, Conn.: New York Graphic Society, n.d.

Horney, Karen. *The Neurotic Personality of Our Time.* New York: Norton, 1937.

Huaco, George. *The Sociology of Film Art.* New York and London: Basic Books, 1965.

Huelsenbeck, Richard. "Dada Lives!" 1936. In *The Dada Painters and Poets: An Anthology,* ed. Robert Motherwell, pp. 277–81. New York: Wittenborn, Schultz, 1951.

————. *En Avant Dada: Eine Geschichte des Dadaismus.* Hanover, Leipzig, Vienna, and Zurich: Steegemann, 1920.

Jones, Ernest. *Papers on Psycho-Analysis.* 3rd ed. London: Baillière, Tindall, & Cox, 1923.

Jurreit, Marielouise. "Alles über Scheiße." *twen,* December 1969, pp. 118–23, 140.

Kafka, Franz. *Das Urteil und andere Erzählungen.* Frankfurt am Main: Fischer Bücherei, 1952.

Kant, Immanuel. *Anthropology from a Pragmatic Point of View.* Translated by Mary J. Gregor. The Hague: Nijhoff, 1974.

————. *Education.* Translated by Annette Churton. Ann Arbor: University of Michigan Press, 1960.

————. *Kants Werke: Akademie-Textausgabe.* Vol. 9. 1907; rpt. Berlin: Walter de Gruyter, 1968.

Kästner, Erich. *Gesammelte Schriften für Erwachsene.* Vol. 1. Zurich: Atrium, 1969.

Kirk, H. David. *Shared Fate: A Theory of Adoption and Mental Health.* New York: Free Press; London: Collier-Macmillan, 1964.

Kracauer, Siegfried. *From Caligari to Hitler: A Psychological History of the German Film.* London: Dobson, 1947.

Kraus, Karl. *Beim Wort genommen.* Munich: Kösel, 1965.

Kurth, Jürgen, and Volker Krämer. "Der schlaue Bauer." *Stern,* 14 July 1983, pp. 51–54.

Lange, Victor. "Erzählen als moralisches Geschäft." In *Die subversive Madonna: Ein Schlüssel zum Werk Heinrich Bölls,* ed. Renate Matthaei, pp. 100–22. Cologne: Kiepenheuer & Witsch, 1975.

Lee, Jae Num. *Swift and Scatological Satire.* Albuquerque: University of New Mexico Press, 1971.

Legman, Gershon. *Rationale of the Dirty Joke: An Analysis of Sexual Humor.* 1st ser. Castle Books, 1968.

————. *Rationale of the Dirty Joke: An Analysis of Sexual Humor.* 2nd ser. New York: Breaking Point, 1975.

Lenz, Siegfried. *So zärtlich war Suleyken: Masurische Geschichten.* Hamburg: Hoffmann & Campe, 1955.

Leonhardt, Rudolf Walter. *This Germany: The Story Since the Third Reich.* Translated and adapted by Catherine Hutter. Greenwich, Conn.: New York Graphic Society, n.d.

Lewis, Beth Irwin. *George Grosz: Art and Politics in the Weimar Republic.* Madison: University of Wisconsin Press, 1971.

Lifton, Robert Jay. "What Made This Man? Mengele." *New York Times Magazine,* 21 July 1985, pp. 16–25.

Lind, Jakov. *Eine bessere Welt.* Berlin: Wagenbach, 1966.

———. *Counting My Steps: An Autobiography.* London: Macmillan, 1969.

———. *Eine Seele aus Holz.* Munich and Zurich: Knaur, 1964.

———. *"Soul of Wood" and Other Stories.* Translated by Ralph Manheim. New York: Grove Press, 1964.

Lindenberger, Herbert. *Georg Büchner.* Carbondale: Southern Illinois University Press, 1964.

Löffler, Fritz. *Otto Dix: Leben und Werk.* Dresden: VEB Verlag der Kunst, n.d.

Loschütz, Gert, ed. *Von Buch zu Buch: Günter Grass in der Kritik.* Neuwied: Luchterhand, 1968.

Lotze, Dieter P. *Wilhelm Busch.* Twayne's World Authors Series, no. 525. Boston: Twayne, 1979.

Ludwig, Emil. "The German Mind." *Atlantic Monthly,* February 1938, pp. 255–63.

Luther, Martin. *Sämmtliche Schriften.* Vol. 22. St. Louis: Lutherischer Concordia Verlag, 1887.

Luthy, Herbert. "Of Poor Bert Brecht." *Encounter,* July 1956, pp. 33–53.

Lyons, Charles R. *Bertolt Brecht: The Despair and the Polemic.* Crosscurrents/ Modern Critiques, ed. Harry T. Moore. Carbondale and Edwardsville: Southern Illinois University Press, 1968.

Mann, Thomas. "Germany and the Germans." *Yale Review* 35, no. 2 (December 1945):223–41.

———. *A Man and his Dog.* In *"Death in Venice" and Seven Other Stories,* translated by H. T. Lowe-Porter, pp. 217–91. New York: Vintage Books, n.d.

McKenzie, John G. *Nervous Disorders and Religion: A Study of Souls in the Making.* London: Allen & Unwin, 1951. Originally the Tate Lectures, delivered at Manchester College, Oxford, 1947.

Merton, Thomas. *Mystics and Zen Masters.* New York: Dell, 1961.

Müller, Joachim. "Thomas Manns Sinfonia Domestica." *Zeitschrift für deutsche Philologie* 83 (1964):142–70.

Müller-Schwefe, Hans-Rudolf. *Sprachgrenzen: Das sogenannte Obszöne, Blasphemische, und Revolutionäre bei Günter Grass und Heinrich Böll.* Munich: Pfeiffer, 1978.

Murnau, F. W., dir. *Der letzte Mann,* with Emil Jannings. Union-Ufa, 1924.

Ottinger, Emil. "Zur mehrdimensionalen Erklärung von Straftaten Jugendlicher am Beispiel der Novelle 'Katz und Maus' von Günter Grass." *Monatsschrift für Kriminologie und Strafrechtsreform,* May/June 1962. Reprinted in *Von Buch zu Buch: Günter Grass in der Kritik,* ed. Gert Loschütz, pp. 38–48. Neuwied: Luchterhand, 1968.

Pelikan, Jaroslav. "The Enduring Relevance of Martin Luther 500 Years After His Birth." *New York Times Magazine*, 18 September 1983, pp. 43–45, 99–100, 102–4.

Piscator, Erwin. *Das politische Theater*. 1929; rpt. Reinbek bei Hamburg: Rowohlt, 1963.

Remarque, Erich Maria. *All Quiet on the Western Front*. Greenwich, Conn.: Fawcett, 1966.

———. *Im Westen nichts Neues*. Cologne: Kiepenheuer & Witsch, 1971.

Riess, Curt. *Theaterdämmerung oder Das Klo auf der Bühne*. Hamburg: Hoffmann & Campe, 1970.

Ritchie, J. M., and H. F. Garten, trans. *Seven Expressionist Plays*. German Expressionist Drama Series, ed. J. M. Ritchie. London: Calder & Boyars, 1968.

Rodnick, David. *Postwar Germans: An Anthropologist's Account*. New Haven: Yale University Press, 1948.

Rosebury, Theodor. *Life on Man*. New York: Viking Press, 1969.

Rubenstein, Richard L. *After Auschwitz: Radical Theology and Contemporary Judaism*. Indianapolis, New York, and Kansas City: Bobbs-Merrill, 1966.

Ruhleder, Karl H. "A Pattern of Messianic Thought in Günter Grass' *Cat and Mouse*." *German Quarterly* 39 (1966): 599–612.

Rühmkorf, Peter. *Über das Volksvermögen: Exkurse in den literarischen Untergrund*. Reinbek bei Hamburg: Rowohlt, 1967.

Schmidt, Henry J. *Satire, Caricature, and Perspectivism in the Works of Georg Büchner*. Stanford Studies in Germanics and Slavics, vol. 8, ed. Edgar Lohner, C. H. Van Schooneveld, and F. W. Strothmann. The Hague: Mouton, 1970.

Schwab-Felisch, Hans. "Der Böll der frühen Jahre." In *In Sachen Böll: Ansichten und Einsichten*, ed. Marcel Reich-Ranicki, pp. 163–71. 3rd ed. Munich: Deutscher Taschenbuch Verlag, 1973.

Sokel, Walter, ed. *Anthology of German Expressionist Drama*. Garden City, N.Y.: Doubleday, 1963.

Spaethling, Robert H. "Günter Grass: *Cat and Mouse*." *Monatshefte* 62, no. 2 (summer 1970): 141–53.

Spalter, Max. *Brecht's Tradition*. Baltimore: Johns Hopkins University Press, 1967.

Der Spiegel, 23 February 1970, p. 193.

Spock, Benjamin. *Baby and Child Care*. New York: Pocket Books, 1976.

Stern, 7 March 1974, p. 128; 20 May 1976, p. 157; 22 September 1977, pp. 150–51; 29 September 1977, pp. 104–5; 19 July 1979, p. 69.

Suzuki, D. T., Erich Fromm, and Richard De Martino. *Zen Buddhism and Psychoanalysis*. New York: Grove Press, 1960.

"Underground: Jahr des Schweins." *Der Spiegel*, 9 June 1969, pp. 141–43, 145–46, 148, 150–51, 153–55.

Vormweg, Heinrich. "Apokalypse mit Vogelscheuchen." *Deutsche Zeitung*, 31 August 1963, as quoted in *Von Buch zu Buch: Günter Grass in der Kritik*, ed. Gert Loschütz, pp. 70–75. Neuwied: Luchterhand, 1968.

Watts, Alan. *Psychotherapy East and West.* New York: Random House (Vintage Books), 1975.

Weiss, Peter. *Dramen 2.* Frankfurt am Main: Suhrkamp, 1968.

———. *The Investigation.* Translated by Jon Swan and Ulu Grosbard. New York: Atheneum, 1975.

Wertmuller, Lina, writer/director. *Seven Beauties,* with Giancarlo Giannini, Fernando Rey, and Shirley Stoler. Almi Libra Cinema 5, 1976.

West, Michael. "Scatology and Eschatology: The Heroic Dimensions of Thoreau's Wordplay." *PMLA* 89 (1974): 1043–64.

Westcott, Richard N. "#!¢*&+(*!@#." *Johns Hopkins Magazine* 21, no. 4 (October 1970): 26–27.

Wiseman, Thomas. *Cinema.* New York: Barnes, 1965.

Wölfflin, Heinrich. *The Sense of Form in Art.* Translated by Alice Muehsam and Norma Shatan. New York: Chelsea, 1958.

Zimmer, Dieter E. "Die Flüche des Präsidenten." *Die Zeit,* 28 June 1974, pp. 9–10.

Index

Page numbers in italics refer to illustrations